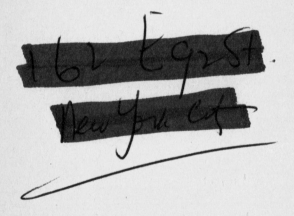

Primer of Intellectual Freedom

If all mankind minus one were of one opinion, and only one person were of the contrary opinion, mankind would be no more justified in silencing that one person, than he, if he had the power, would be justified in silencing mankind.

JOHN STUART MILL

Primer of Intellectual Freedom

Edited by

HOWARD MUMFORD JONES

HARVARD UNIVERSITY PRESS
Cambridge, Massachusetts

1949

LONDON · GEOFFREY CUMBERLEGE
OXFORD UNIVERSITY PRESS

For

CAROL AND RAY
IN HOPE OF A MORE RATIONAL WORLD

Contents

Introduction

"Congress," so runs the First Amendment to the Constitution, "shall make no law respecting an establishment of religion, or prohibiting the free exercise thereof; or abridging the freedom of speech, or of the press, or the right of the people peacefully to assemble, and to petition the government for a redress of grievances."

But what *is* the freedom of speech and of the press? In the twentieth century these are the fighting phrases around which civic and educational controversies revolve. Two crucial issues are almost constantly before the public: the rights of minority parties, particularly the Communist Party; and academic freedom, or the theory that the teacher shall, by virtue of his profession, lose no ordinary civic rights and shall retain the special professional right (somewhat resembling that guaranteed to members of Congress) not to be questioned by outside persons who do not like what he "teaches" and who want to get rid of him.

This book is a collection of significant pronouncements running from the year of its publication back to 1605 when Bacon issued *The Advancement of Learning*, the first formal claim of the research worker to labor in freedom toward professional ends. These pronouncements are in the nature of a casebook, even if the cases are all on one side. They show how for three centuries and a half distinguished minds have met innumerable threats to intellectual freedom. The selections have been edited and condensed for ease of reading and for clarity. In their light the reader is asked to make up his mind as to proper policy in such matters as, let us say, the right of the House Committee on un-American Activities to act as it does, the toleration to be extended to Communists, the privilege of college presidents and governing boards to fire teachers whose views they do not like, and the legislative duty to put down opinions held by the majority to be "subversive." In this sense the book is a primer of intellectual liberty.

II

The Bill of Rights appears as the first ten amendments to the Constitution. It — or they — are repeated in many state constitutions. They are enforced by many statutes explicit in language. Freedom of research in the Baconian tradition has obviously brought us many rewards we would not have had if conservative, reactionary, or traditionalist minds had limited the activities of thinkers. By and large, we are as a nation used to public discussion. Despite these facts, the theory of intellectual toleration is still imperfectly understood. Perhaps this is true because so much of the discussion has been confined to university and college circles that the people at large have not grasped what is at stake.

It is assumed by many, for example, that "freedom" is freedom to tell the truth. We don't want to listen to a lot of lies, do we? The only thing to do with liars is to stop their lying, isn't it, before they persuade a lot of half-baked people to believe them?

This principle would be excellent if truth and the expression of truth were always in a one-to-one relationship like the proposition that a triangle has three sides. If anybody asserts the contrary, you can refer him to any triangle and so end the controversy. But "truth" is not always thus simply to be reached. Is it true, for example, that every particle of matter in the universe attracts every other particle inversely in proportion to the square of the distance between them? Yes, in a Newtonian universe; no, in a Ptolemaic one; perhaps, in the universe of the future. Is it true that Abraham Lincoln deliberately encouraged the Confederates to attack Fort Sumter in order thus to unify Northern emotion? Yes, if you are of the revisionist school of historians; perhaps, if you feel all the evidence is not yet in; no, if you are of an older orthodoxy. Is compulsory vaccination a lawful use of the police powers of the state? Yes, if you are a medical graduate; perhaps, if you are a vegetarian; no, if you are a Christian Scientist. Is the "classical" political economy of Mill, Ricardo, McCulloch, and their contemporaries "true"? Yes, in nineteenth-century British industrial society; perhaps, if you refer to other countries; yes and no, or no, if you are a disciple of Henry George, or of Marx, or of Thomas Aquinas. How "true" is Henry George? Marx? Thomas Aquinas? The answer will vary according to whether you are a Roman Catholic, a Communist, a Single-Taxer, a Protestant, a Keynesian economist, or a Republican in a certain age bracket.

A second misunderstanding arises from the assumption that education is a commodity to be bought by its customers. We pay for the schools, don't we? We tax ourselves to give our young people every advantage, don't we? Why should we pay the salaries of a bunch of reds (or crackpots, or impractical dreamers, or damyankees, or foreigners, etc., etc.) to come in here and ruin the minds of our children? I guess if we pay the bills, we're entitled to say what shall and what shall not be taught and who shall teach it.

This argument has great weight, inasmuch as in the light of it the American people have created the great public school systems, the state teachers colleges, and the state-supported colleges and universities which are central to the American system of things. Law or public opinion prevents, or would prevent if anybody tried it, the "teaching" of atheism, polygamy, free love, and a variety of other theories in the schools, even though atheism is intellectually defensible, polygamy was once practiced in Utah and appears blamelessly in the Old Testament, and radical modifications of our present marriage practice have been urged by persons like Judge Ben B. Lindsay. Unfortunately the capacity of the public to determine what is to be "taught" is not always clear.

For example, a western state legislature, exasperated by the pertinacity of mathematicians, once passed a law that *pi*, or the relation of the diameter to the circumference of the circle, should thereafter in the schools of the state be reckoned $3\frac{1}{7}$. The facts of nature and of mathematical reasoning obviously overrule legislative wisdom here, and most of us are inclined to smile. But we do not smile quite so broadly when another legislature directs that the "theory of evolution," branded as atheistical and immoral, shall forever disappear from state-supported institutions under penalty of fine and imprisonment. What is meant by "teaching" the "theory of evolution"? Almost all astronomical, geological, biological, botanical, anthropological, and historical reasoning (to name only familiar fields) today rests upon some sort of evolutionary hypothesis, so that, if the statute were literally carried out, the commonwealth would remain in darkness. And how does the legislature know that the "theory of evolution" is atheistical and immoral? And when another statute forbids the "teaching" of "atheistical communism" in still another commonwealth, the problem becomes even more complex. Is the historian to ignore the life of Marx, the Russian Revolution, and the conduct of Soviet diplomacy in the twentieth century? Is the economist not to explain what is meant by the dictatorship of the proletariat? Is the philosopher never to point to *Das Kapital* as one of the crucial intellectual documents of the modern world? Ignorance is not innocence; and you cannot protect your children against ideas when ideas are abroad. They will have to make up their minds just as you, in your generation, had to make up yours.

A third difficulty appears in the word "teach." If somebody teaches you mathematics, you learn it, don't you? To be taught is to learn, isn't it? So, then, if a Communist teaches economics, you learn to be a Communist, don't you, and if an evolutionist teaches you about monkeys, you learn to doubt the Bible, don't you?

Two fallacies are fused in this attitude One is to assume that the teacher you don't like is the only teacher that is going to be effective. At the University of Washington the faculty numbers about 700; investigation revealed that six members of the faculty were, or had been, members of the Communist Party. Three were dismissed. Surely this is no compliment to the 697 other teachers at the University of Washington. Surely this is to assume that the theory you don't like is so dazzling, so fascinating, so compelling that all other theories (like all other teachers) have no influence whatsoever. Was this true in your own experience? Did one teacher shape your whole life? Or do you not now, looking backward, see yourself as the product of various personalities and conflicting points of view?

The second fallacy is the confusion between the verb "to teach" and the verb "to indoctrinate." Some things are indisputable, like the order of letters in the alphabet and the fact that two and two forever make four, and these are to be learned, no matter what ticket the teacher votes. But most information is a matter of more or less. Was Napoleon a benefactor or a tyrant? Is Goethe's *Faust* a masterpiece, or a dull poem, over the heads of modern readers? Is a hot-air furnace "better" than a hot-water one, and how do you tell? Should the airlines be compelled to install radar equipment? Various views, various denials, various affirmations can be given; and "teaching" them is explanation, not dogma. It means, fundamentally, that the answer to questions like these seems to be such-and-such in the opinion of well-informed persons, but that there is opportunity for doubt. Teaching is not indoctrination. To analyze a theory is not to accept it, or to say that it is right, or to turn the teacher into a master and the students into intellectual slaves. As anybody in the teaching business by and by learns, young America is pretty canny; and so far as one can learn, no single teacher has ever succeeded in indoctrinating a single class wholeheartedly with dogma, provided that the school in question was freely permitted to present varying points of view.

III

The problem swings into active political agitation when the word "Communism" is uttered. Shall a Communist be allowed to teach American youth? Prominent educators, including distinguished university presidents, have said that Communists shall not be allowed to teach by virtue of the fact that they belong to a party owing allegiance to a foreign power, are engaged in secretly trying to capture the United States government, and are so indoctrinated with an absolute theory of history, philosophy, economics, science, and other branches of learning as to close the mind to intellectual inquiry. Prominent educators, including distinguished university professors, have said that to set up categories of citizenship is to deny democratic equality, that to set up "Communism" as a test is to open the door to the grossest abuses, that it is not the business of educational institutions or their governing boards to establish political orthodoxy, and that to deny a sincere Communist opportunity to expound views held by millions of human beings is as wrong as to deny a sincere democrat the same right. They place their trust in the competition of ideas and believe that in such a competition Communism is bound to lose. Otherwise, they argue, why do the Communists prevent competition in ideas?

Shall Roman Catholics be allowed to teach American youth? The question may come as a shock to the very persons who deny Communists the right to teach. Nevertheless, the oldest lecture foundation at the oldest American college had as one of its specific purposes the duty of exposing the errors of the Church of Rome, an assignment that has been allowed gracefully to lapse. So convinced were hundreds of thousands of Americans a century ago that Roman Catholics owed their primary allegiance to a foreign power, engaged in secret activities looking towards the capture of the United States government, and were so indoctrinated by an absolute theory of history, philosophy, and the rest, as to close the mind, that they created a political party (the Know Nothings) determined to reduce Roman Catholics to a perpetual condition of second-class citizenship by denying them, if they could, the right to hold positions of trust in the government, the army, the navy, and, so far as possible, education.

Shall members of the Masonic order be allowed to teach? The question seems fantastic. Nevertheless, a little over a century and a quarter ago, another political party arose, determined to crush Masonry on the ground that it owed allegiance to a foreign power, that it engaged in secret activities looking towards the capture of the government (had not the Masons landed several presidents in the White House?), and that it so indoctrinated its members with an absolute theory, etc., etc., etc., as to close the mind to new ideas. This in turn followed upon the belief of an earlier generation that, during the era of the French Revolution, a vast international order, known as the Society of the Illuminati, for which Masonry was probably a "front," owed allegiance to a foreign power (France), engaged in secret activities looking towards the capture of the government (Jefferson was suspect), and was so indoctrinated — this time with atheism and materialism — as to close the mind, etc. etc.

Freedom of inquiry, toleration of unpopular notions, faith in the long-run ability of the American people to reject zany ideas and to adopt workable ones — these involve a perpetual struggle. Intellectual liberty has always been a battle and a march. Persecution is the first law of society because it is always easier to suppress criticism than to meet it. Persecution is the direct, logical, and primitive expression of the herd. We take the first step away from the herd when we try to protect society against its own urge to destroy, by throwing the protection of law and custom around the malcontent, the lonely thinker, the passionate few, the minority group. When we do this, we make as great an advance in human culture as was made when mankind discovered the wheel.

Unlike mechanical invention, however, intellectual liberty is not automatically self-evident. Now that we have the wheel, we are not likely to revert to the stoneboat. But society is continually under the pressure of numbers to revert to the herd.

Intellectual liberty is never an absolute, it is always a matter of more or less. On the whole it is an individual matter, a matter of persons and not of arbitrary classifications of citizenship, a matter of ideas considered pragmatically and not of ideologies. As the *New Yorker* said of the University of Washington case, "We believe that teachers should be fired not in blocks of three for political wrongness, but in blocks of one for unfitness." Start classifications, and you will end by refusing to hire vegetarians on the ground that they have prejudiced views in biology. In the American system, whatever the radio, the newspaper, and the correspondent may say, voters tend to size up men rather than platforms, with the result that we are safely governed by a perpetual coalition government, call it Democratic or Republican. So long as this tradition continues, it is difficult to believe that Communists or atheists, or Catholics, or Jews, or Jehovah's Witnesses, or persons who believe the earth is flat, or people who hate Truman, or any other conceivable category of Americans have to be put down by law. The pragmatic test with us is the conflict of ideas out of which truth and policy are born.

This book is dedicated to making clearer the philosophy of that conflict.

One final word. Never, said the late Raymond Clapper, overestimate the information of the American people. But, he added thoughtfully, never underestimate their intelligence.

HOWARD MUMFORD JONES

Peacham, Vermont
July 4, 1949

Primer of
Intellectual
Freedom

1949

JAMES RHYNE KILLIAN

Statement in the Case of Professor Dirk Struik

In New York, speaking as a witness in the trial of several members of the Communist Party for conspiracy against the government, one Philbrick testified that Professor Dirk Struik of the Massachusetts Institute of Technology had lectured on the subject of revolution through the world, more recently on the revolutionary movement in Indonesia. He further asserted that alleged Communists lectured to the same groups. This was on April 8, 1949. Earlier still, an article in the Saturday Evening Post *of March 12, 1949, described the Jefferson School of Social Science (of which Professor Struik is a trustee) as a nest of "reds" or something similar. Newspapers thereupon twisted this material into the assertion that Professor Struik had been, was, or is, a Communist, and some agitation was thereby created to dismiss him from the Institute. The statement by President James Rhyne Killian, who had just assumed the headship of the Institute, was occasioned by these events.*

MASSACHUSETTS INSTITUTE OF TECHNOLOGY

Office of the President

RECENT REPORTS IN THE PUBLIC PRESS regarding the activities of Dirk J. Struik, Professor of Mathematics at M.I.T., call for a statement of the Institute's attitude toward Communism and toward freedom of inquiry.

The Institute is unequivocally opposed to Communism; it is also sternly opposed to the Communistic method of dictating to scholars the opinions they must have and the doctrines they must teach. M.I.T. seeks first a faculty and staff of thoroughly competent scholars and teachers of high integrity. Assuming this competence and integrity, it believes that its faculty, as long as its members abide by the law, and maintain the dignity and responsibilities of their position, must be free to inquire, to challenge, and to doubt in their search for what is true and good. They must be free to examine controversial matters, to reach conclusions of their own, to criticize and be criticized. Only through such unqualified freedom of thought and investigation can an educational institution, especially one dealing with science, perform its function of seeking truth.

The Institute's attitude toward the charges which have been made against Professor Struik must be viewed against this background and in the light of these considerations. Professor Struik is an American citizen. As required in Massachusetts, he has taken the "teacher's oath" to support the constitutions of the United States and of the Commonwealth. He has only by implication been charged with illegal actions, and he staunchly denies that he has at any time committed acts that are improper for a loyal American citizen. The Institute has secured a transcript of Mr. Philbrick's testimony in New York and finds no statement in it charging Professor Struik with an unlawful act. He has also discharged competently and faithfully his duties as a professor of mathematics. Careful investigation by the Institute has revealed no evidence which would indicate that he has sought to indoctrinate at the Institute his beliefs in regard to Marxism or improperly to influence students or colleagues.

The Institute believes that Professor Struik, who denies that he has committed any crime, should be considered innocent of any criminal action unless he is proved guilty. The Institute feels that if criminal charges are to be brought against Professor Struik, they should be brought by the government and handled in orderly fashion by the courts. An educational institution has no competence to carry on a trial to determine whether a law has been broken.

Should a member of our staff be indicted for advocating the violent overthrow of the American government or other criminal acts, or if the evidence of such actions were incontrovertible, immediate action would be taken which would protect the Institute and at the same time preserve his rights. If this staff member should be convicted of this charge, he would be discharged.

The Institute also wishes to make it clear that it believes that the teacher, as a teacher, must be free of doctrinaire control originating outside of his own mind. He must be free to be critical and objective in his own way, and above all he must work in the clear daylight without hidden allegiances or obligations which require him to distort his research or teaching in accord with dictates from without. If a teacher were found to be subject to improper outside control in his teaching, the Institute would regard him as incompetent.

The Institute believes that one of the greatest dangers of the present cold war and of the present fear of Communism is the danger that they will cause America to relinquish or distort or weaken basic civil rights. This may be a greater danger than the occasional impact or influence of a Communist.

No American college or university has a more impressive record than

M.I.T. of devotion to our national welfare or of wholehearted support of the ideals of American democracy. It has been the training ground for thousands of alumni who serve and strengthen our system of free enterprise and who vigorously uphold the principles of our free society. Its faculty serves the community, the state, and the nation in a spirit of complete dedication to the public service. I need only cite the Institute's war record and the major contributions it made through research and training to the national cause.

I believe it is equally true that it would be hard to find an educational institution in which the students are so unanimously devoted to American ideals. They are too critical and independent to be easy marks for any special pleaders. The overwhelming majority of our students are so thoroughly imbued with their democratic heritage and with their responsibilities and privileges as American citizens that there is no danger of their being corrupted.

The Institute proposes to deal with all charges of Communism or other ideologies in the light of these considerations and convictions.

1949

ROBERT MAYNARD HUTCHINS

Statement to the Subversive Activities Commission of the Illinois State Legislature

In 1948–1949 it was alleged by members of the Illinois legislature that teachers at the University of Chicago and at Roosevelt College in Chicago were engaged in "subversive activities," by which seemed to be meant that a significant number of professors at these institutions were either members of the Communist Party, followers of the Communist party line, or (more vaguely) "radical," "un-American," or the like. A commission popularly known as the Broyles Commission was granted $75,000 to "investigate" these colleges. Summoned before this commission in April 1949, Chancellor Robert Maynard Hutchins delivered the formal statement which follows. This statement, here reprinted by Mr. Hutchins's permission, was published in the June 1949 issue of Tower Topics, *the quarterly alumni bulletin of the University of Chicago.*

MY NAME IS ROBERT M. HUTCHINS. I have been the chief executive officer of the University of Chicago for twenty years.

The subpoena I have received summons me to testify concerning subversive activities at the University of Chicago. This is a leading question: the answer is assumed in the question. I cannot testify concerning subversive activities at the University of Chicago, because there are none.

The Trustees of the University of Chicago are:

Here Chancellor Hutchins read the names and business connections of the 34 Trustees.

These gentlemen are responsible for the conduct of the University of Chicago. Legally they *are* the University of Chicago. They, and particularly those who reside in Chicago, spend countless hours familiarizing themselves with what is going on at the University. It will not be charged that they are engaged in subversive activities. It can hardly be supposed that they would sanction such activities.

The faculty of the University is, as everybody knows, one of the most distinguished in the world. The faculty numbers 1,000. None of its members is engaged in subversive activities. The principal reason why the University has such a distinguished faculty is that the University guarantees its professors absolute and complete academic freedom.

Nobody has ever ventured to say that any member of the faculty of the University of Chicago is a Communist.

It has sometimes been said that some members of the faculty belong to some so-called "Communist-front" organizations. The University of Chicago does not believe in the un-American doctrine of guilt by association.

The fact that some Communists belong to, believe in, or even dominate some of the organizations to which some of our professors belong does not show that those professors are engaged in subversive activities. All that such facts would show would be that these professors believed in some of the objects of the organizations. It is entirely possible to belong to organizations combating fascism and racial discrimination, for example, without desiring to subvert the government of the United States, even though some other members of these organizations may desire to subvert the government of the United States.

The University has many thousands of students. None of them, so far as I know, is engaged in subversive activities. One or two students are alleged to have said publicly that they are Communists. I am not aware that they have advocated the overthrow of the government by violence. If they have, they have broken the law of this state, and the proper officials should have instituted proceedings against them.

As is well known, there is a Communist Club among the students of the University. Eleven students belong to it. The Club has not sought to subvert the government of this state. Its members claim that they are interested in studying communism, and some of them, perhaps all of them, may be sympathetic toward communism. But the study of communism is not a subversive activity. I am not sympathetic toward communism; but I do not see how the sympathetic feelings of ten or a dozen students at the University of Chicago can be a danger to the state.

The policy of the University is to admit law-abiding students who have the qualifications to do the University's work. It would not be in the public interest to exclude students of Communistic leanings. If we did, how would they ever learn better?

The policy of the University is to permit students to band together for any lawful purpose in terms of their common interests. This is conformable to the spirit of the Constitution of the United States, which guarantees free speech and the right of the people peaceably to assemble. There are 130 student clubs of one kind or another on the campus.

Fourteen years ago a legislative committee attempted to find evidence of subversive activities at the University. You know that no evidence was found. There have been no changes since that would justify this investigation. Since the last investigation the University has been intrusted by the government of the United States with the most momentous military secret in history. The first chain reaction took place on the campus of the University. The University today manages for the government its principal laboratory of atomic reasearch. In addition, the University is engaged in many other secret research projects on behalf of the defense establishment. The government maintains a security officer on the campus. Because of the secret projects I have referred to, federal agents constantly visit the campus. It is unlikely that if there were subversive activities there they would not have reported them.

An investigator for this commission spent days on the campus a year ago. Neither the Legislature nor the University has been informed that he discovered any subversive activities at the University. I can only conclude that he found none.

The resolution calling for this investigation originated in the House, of which the chairman of this commission is not a member. The reason given was that some hundreds of young people, about 20 per cent of whom were students at the University of Chicago, demonstrated in an impolite manner against certain bills pending in the Legislature.

The penalty does not seem to fit the crime. Rudeness and redness are not the same. I recognize that it is provoking to the Legislature to be impolitely treated when it is conscientiously performing its duties. But even if I admitted that students of the University of Chicago were as impolite as they are alleged to have been, I could not admit that impoliteness was even presumptive evidence of subversive activity or that the fact that students were impolite showed that they had been taught to be impolite or subversive by the faculty of the University of Chicago.

The bills against which these students demonstrated were not so obviously perfect as to suggest that anybody who demonstrated against them was subversive or engaged in subversive activities. Three out of four newspapers in Chicago are opposed to these bills.

These students exercised their right as American citizens to protest against pending legislation of which they disapproved. They were entirely right to disapprove of this pending legislation. The Broyles bills are unnecessary, since any dangers against which they are designed to protect us are already covered by laws now on the statute-books. They are, in my opinion as a former professor of law, unconstitutional. And, worst of all, they are un-American, since they aim at thought control. They aim at the suppression of ideas.

It is now fashionable to call anybody with whom you disagree a Communist or a fellow-traveler. So Branch Rickey darkly hinted the other day that the attempt to eliminate the reserve clause in baseball contracts was the work of Communists.

One who criticizes the foreign policy of the United States, or the draft, or the Atlantic Pact, or who believes that our military establishment is too expensive can be called a fellow-traveler, for the Russians are of the same opinion. One who thinks that there are too many slums and too much lynching in America can be called a fellow-traveler, for the Russians say the same. One who opposes racial discrimination or the Ku Klux Klan can be called a fellow-traveler, for the Russians claim that they ought to be opposed. Anybody who wants any change of any kind in this country can be called a fellow-traveler, because the Russians want change in this country, too.

The Constitution of the United States guarantees freedom of speech and the right of the people peaceably to assemble. The American way has been to encourage thought and discussion. We have never been afraid of thought and discussion. The whole educational system, and not merely the University of Chicago, is a reflection of the American faith in thought and discussion as the path to peaceful change and improvement.

The danger to our institutions is not from the tiny minority who do not believe in them. It is from those who would mistakenly repress the free spirit upon which those institutions are built. The miasma of thought control that is now spreading over the country is the greatest menace to the United States since Hitler.

There are two ways of fighting subversive ideas. One is the policy of repression. This policy is contrary to the letter and spirit of the Constitution of this country. It cannot be justly enforced, because it is impossible to tell precisely what people are thinking; they have to be judged by their acts. It has been generally thought that the widest possible latitude should be given to freedom of speech and publication, on the ground that the expression of differing points of view, some of which are bound to be unpopular, is the way to progress in the state. Hyde Park Corner in London, where anybody may say anything, has long been a symbol of the confidence of the Anglo-Saxon world in the ability of democratic institutions to withstand criticism, and even to nourish itself upon it. There are numerous laws already on the books which provide for the punishment of subversive acts.

The policy of repression of ideas cannot work and never has worked. The alternative to it is the long, difficult road of education. To this the American people have been committed. It requires patience and tolerance, even in the face of intense provocation. It requires faith in the principles and practices of democracy, faith that when the citizen understands all forms of government he will prefer democracy and that he will be a better citizen if he is convinced than he would be if he were coerced.

The Legislature and the University of Chicago are both opposed to communism. The task of the Legislature is not merely to protect the people by passing laws that prevent the minority from overthrowing the state. It is to eliminate those social and economic evils and those political injustices which are the sources of discontent and disaffection. The members of the faculty of the University have many times assisted the Legislature in its efforts to discover and remedy these evils and injustices, and they are ready at all times to assist it.

The task of the University is to enlighten the community, to provide citizens who know the reasons for their faith and who will be a bulwark to our democracy because they have achieved conviction through study and thought. The University does not claim that it is perfect or that it always succeeds. It asserts, however, that the policy of education is better than the policy of repression and that it is earnestly dedicated to making the policy of education produce the results that the American people have believed it can produce. All the University asks of the Legislature, and all it has ever asked of it, is a sympathetic understanding of this task.

1949

GRENVILLE CLARK
JAMES BRYANT CONANT

Freedom at Harvard

On April 26, 1949, Frank B. Ober, a Maryland lawyer, wrote the President of Harvard University a letter declaring that so long as his Alma Mater (Mr. Ober is a graduate of the Harvard Law School) continued to condone the presence upon the faculty of professors who used the "prestige" of the university "in a manner hostile to our own country," he could not subscribe to the Harvard Law School Fund. He objected to the participation by John Ciardi, Assistant Professor of English, in a rally of the Progressive Party in Maryland directed against anti-Communist legislation in the Maryland legislature sponsored by Mr. Ober; and he objected to the so-called "Peace Meeting" in New York City under the chairmanship of Harlow Shapley, Professor of Astronomy. President Conant acknowledged the letter and asked Grenville Clark, a senior member of the "Corporation" (i.e., the President and Fellows of Harvard College) to answer Mr. Ober. Mr. Clark's letter, dated May 27, 1949, was printed in the Harvard Alumni Bulletin *for June 25, 1949. The first section of the letter is an attempt at "a fair summary and interpretation" of Mr. Ober's complaint and recommendations. Mr. Clark then goes on to the larger issues involved. The second, third, and fourth portions of his reply are here reprinted by permission of the editors of the* Bulletin.

II. I REPEAT THAT THE THINGS YOU ASK FOR will not and cannot be done at Harvard — at least as long as Harvard retains its basic principles and holds by its tradition. And if the day ever came that such things were done at the physical place on which the Harvard buildings stand or anywhere by the Harvard authorities, it would not be "Harvard" doing them; it would be an institution of an entirely different sort, with wholly different ideas and purposes.

The fundamental reason is that for Harvard to take the course you recommend would be to repudiate the very essence of what Harvard stands for — the search for truth by a free and uncoerced body of students and teachers. And it would be to make a mockery of a long tradition of Harvard freedom for both its students and its faculties.

As to the history of that tradition, while it is much more than eighty years old, it is sufficient, I think, to go back to President Charles W. Eliot's inaugural address in 1869 and follow down from there.

Mr. Eliot then said: "A university must be indigenous; it must be rich; but, above all, it must be free. The winnowing breeze of freeedom must blow through all its chambers . . . This University aspires to serve the nation by training men to intellectual honesty and independence of mind. The Corporation demands of all its teachers that they be grave, reverent, and high-minded; but it leaves them, like their pupils, free."

The tradition so expressed was well understood and applied under President Eliot. It was then carried on and emphasized during the more controversial term of President A. Lawrence Lowell from 1909 to 1933.

In his report for 1916–17 (from which Mr. Conant sent you an extract) Mr. Lowell took notice that the war had "brought to the front" questions of academic freedom, especially "liberty of speech on the part of the professor." He then went on to make so discriminating an analysis of the subject that in the opinion of many, including myself, the writing of those few pages was the most lasting public service of his long career.

As applied to the "extracurricular" activities that you stress, the essence of the report is that "beyond his chosen field and outside of his classroom" the professor "speaks only as a citizen"; that his professorship gives him no rights that he did not possess before; but, on the other hand, it is unwise to restrict those rights because "the objections to restraint upon what professors may say as citizens seem to me far greater than the harm done by leaving them free." Mr. Lowell declared that by accepting a chair under restrictive conditions, the professor "would cease to be a free citizen" and that "such a policy would tend seriously to discourage some of the best men from taking up the scholar's life." "It is not," he emphasized, "a question of academic freedom, but of personal liberty from constraint..." Beyond that, he made a point very applicable to what you propose, i.e., that: "If a university or college censors what its professors may say, if it restrains them from uttering something that it does not approve, it thereby assumes responsibility for that which it permits them to say . . . There is no middle ground." And, therefore, he concluded, the University, assuming the sincerity of the professor's utterances on public matters, should take "no responsibility whatever" but should leave "them to be dealt with like other citizens by the public authorities according to the laws of the land."

I have tried to state only the essence of Mr. Lowell's thought as applied to your letter. Doubtless you are familiar with his report and I can only commend a restudy of its closely reasoned pages. The point is that this report, which became famous, stands today as part of the Harvard tradition of freedom of expression, and as a definite guide for Harvard policy.

Coming now to President Conant's term, we find the same basic thought expressed with equal clarity and force. In his address at the Harvard Tercentenary Celebration in 1936, he said:

"We must have a spirit of tolerance which allows the expression of all opinions however heretical they may appear . . . Unfortunately there are ominous signs that a new form of bigotry may arise. This is most serious, for we cannot develop the unifying educational forces we so sorely need unless all matters may be openly discussed . . . On this point there can be no compromise; we are either afraid of heresy or we are not."

These declarations of three Harvard presidents are, as you observe, all of a piece. They embody a consistent doctrine that can, I think, be summed up as follows:

(*1*) *Harvard believes in the "free trade in ideas" of Justice Holmes — a graduate of 1861 — which is no more than saying that she believes in the principles of Milton's Areopagitica (1644), of Jefferson's First Inaugural (1801), and of Mill's "Essay on Liberty" (1859). She thinks that repression is not wise or workable under our system, that wide latitude for conflicting views affords the best chance for good government, and that in suppression usually lies the greater peril. Harvard is not afraid of freedom, and believes adherence to this principle to be fundamental for our universities and for the integrity of our institutions.*

(*2*) *She believes that the members of the faculties, in their capacity as citizens, have the same rights to express themselves as other citizens, and that those rights should not be restricted by the University by trying to keep a "watch" on professors or otherwise.*

(*3*) *She believes that wide limits for free expression by professors are in the interest of her students as well as the teachers. The teachers have rights as citizens to speak and write as men of independence; the students also have their rights to be taught by men of independent mind.*

(*4*) *Harvard, like any great privately supported university, badly needs money; but Harvard will accept no gift on the condition, express or implied, that it shall compromise its tradition of freedom.*

These beliefs are not a matter of lip service. They have been applied in practice at Harvard for a long time. Thus there certainly prevailed at Harvard during the forty years of Mr. Eliot's term, an atmosphere highly favorable to free expression by both students and teachers. I know that when I was at Cambridge, 1899–1906, one felt it in the very air that neither the students nor professors were under constraint. The absence of restriction on free expression by faculty and students at that time, and during the early years of Mr. Lowell's term, was implicit rather than something needing constant assertion; but it was none the less real.

In later years of the Lowell administration, however, in what has been called the period of "uneasy fears" — much like the present — during and after the first World War, cases arose which provided an acid test for the Harvard doctrine.

The two best-known incidents were those of Professor Zechariah Chafee, Jr., and of Harold J. Laski. They are related in Professor Yeomans' recent life of Mr. Lowell.

In the former case, Professor Chafee wrote an article condemning the conduct of the trial judge in the famous Abrams sedition case. This was in 1920 at the height of the post-war alarm about sedition and Bolshevism. It was the period of Attorney General Palmer's "raids," and of the expulsion of duly elected Socialist members from the New York Legislature, in the face of powerful opposition led by Charles E. Hughes. Some Harvard men in New York accused Professor Chafee of inaccuracies in his article and, without specifying exactly what should be done, asked the Overseers to take notice of his conduct. The Overseers' Committee to Visit the Law School took up the matter and there occurred what was known as "The Trial at the Harvard Club.." Mr. Lowell appeared and in effect acted as counsel for Professor Chafee. He took an unequivocal position in defense of the professor's right to espouse an unpopular cause, and the net result was a dismissal or dropping of the complaint. That case remains a landmark in Harvard's course.

In the Laski case, Mr. Laski, then a young lecturer at Harvard, spoke up for the side of the police strikers in Boston in 1919. Feeling on that issue was terrific; emotion ran high against anyone taking the strikers' side and there were insistent demands for the dismissal of Mr. Laski. Nevertheless, Mr. Lowell stood firmly for Mr. Laski's right to speak his mind; there was no dismissal and that set another great precedent.

Since then there have been various other incidents in which the principle has been vindicated. Perhaps the very latest was the permission given a month ago to the Harvard Law School Forum to have Mr. Laski (now, thirty years later, Professor Laski of the University of London) speak in Sanders Theater. Because of the Cambridge School Board's objections to Mr. Laski, the Forum had been denied the use of a public school auditorium where its meetings had customarily been held. The Forum then asked for the use of Sanders Theater and, in accordance with established practice on student meetings, the request was granted.

It is, I think, unnecessary to go into more detail. For it is well-established and known that Harvard has a long-declared and, on the whole, well-adhered-to tradition favoring a wide degree of freedom for teacher and student and, therefore, as you must perceive, a tradition utterly at variance with what you recommend.

Mr. Conant mentioned the "significance" as well as the "history" of the tradition.

To my mind, its fundamental significance lies in the thought that the principles back of it are essential to the American Idea — to the workability of our free institutions, and to enabling Americans to live satisfactory lives.

The professor's right to speak his mind and to espouse unpopular causes should not be regarded as something separate and apart from the maintenance of our civil rights in general. I think what is usually called academic freedom is simply part and parcel of American freedom — merely a segment of the whole front.

I believe, however, that it is an especially vital segment because it concerns the students quite as much as the professors. If the professors are censored, constrained, or harassed, it affects not only themselves; it affects also those whom they teach — the future voters and leaders upon whose integrity and independence of mind will depend the institutions by which we live and breathe a free air. For if the professors have always to conform and avoid unpopular views whether in class or out, what kind of men will they be? And where will our young men and women go to hear and weigh new ideas, to consider both sides and acquire balance and integrity?

In *The Wild Flag* the essayist E. B. White has defined democracy in a way closely touching this point. "Democracy," he said, "is the recurrent suspicion that more than half of the people are right more than half of the time." This is about it, is it not — the very basis of our system? But how can we possibly expect most of the people to be right most of the time if they are taught by men and women of a sort who are constrained to work under conditions where they may lose their jobs if, pursuant to conviction, they attend meetings that some, or even the majority of the moment, do not approve?

In that inaugural address of Mr. Eliot's, it is also said: "In the modern world the intelligence of public opinion is the one indispensable condition of social progress." And further: "The student should be made acquainted with all sides of these [philosophical and political] controversies, with the salient points of each system . . . The notion that education consists in the authoritative inculcation of what the teacher deems true may be logical and appropriate in a convent, or a seminary for priests, but it is intolerable in universities and public schools, from primary to professional."

But how can we fulfill the "indispensable condition" of intelligent opinion; and how can we have non-dogmatic and excellent instruction for our leaders if their teachers are coerced or harassed?

It is impossible; and since I believe that the very existence of our free institutions depends on the independence and integrity of our teachers, the main significance for me of the Harvard tradition is that it powerfully helps to sustain those institutions.

No doubt there are other more specialized significances. No doubt the Harvard tradition has significance because, if abandoned, it would make many good people, members of our faculties, very unhappy. No doubt it is significant because its abandonment would force others — administrators and Governing Boards — either to resign or, against conscience, to engage in work bitterly hateful to them. These things are true and important. But it is enough for me that the tradition is in harmony with and necessary to the maintenance of the free institutions of America, and to the values that make life in our country most worth while.

III. I CANNOT HELP wondering whether you have thought through the implications of what you propose.

Since you wish to discipline professors for taking active part in meetings such as those at which Professors Ciardi and Shapley spoke, would it not be fair to pass in advance on the kind of meetings professors could safely attend? Would this not call for a University licensing board? And would not such a board have an obnoxious and virtually impossible task?

The very cases you mention illustrate this. The Maryland meeting was called by the Maryland branch of the official Progressive Party (the Wallace party) which is a legal organization for whose ticket over a million citizens voted in 1948. The New York meeting was to advocate peace and was sponsored by many reputable citizens whose motives were above question.

If the University should undertake to decide whether or not a professor, in his capacity as a citizen, could take part in these or other meetings, what Mr. Lowell referred to would necessarily occur. If attendance at the meeting were disapproved, the professor would be deprived, under penalty of discipline, of a right enjoyed by other citizens; while if approved, the University would assume the responsibility for endorsing the meeting.

Moreover, I think you will agree that there would be little sense in censoring attendance at meetings and leaving free from censorship speeches on the radio or writings in the press, magazines, pamphlets, and books. Would not your proposals call for a censorship of all these? . . .

Beyond that, however, how could an effective "closer watch" on "extra-curricular activities" be maintained unless the watch extended to conversations and correspondence? And how could that be done without a system of student and other informers — the classic and necessary method of watching for "subversive" utterances?

You may not have realized the full implications of what you ask. But if you will stop to consider what would necessarily be involved if your point of view were accepted, you must agree, I think, that these things are precisely what would be required.

What I have just said applies to the professors. But how about the students? Would it be sensible to have the teachers censored and watched while the students remain at liberty freely to speak and write and to attend such meetings as they choose, subject only to the laws of the land? On your philosophy are you not driven on to restrict, censor, and discipline the students also?

What sort of a place would Harvard be if it went down this road? It would, I think, not require six months to destroy the morale of both our teachers and students, and thereby our usefulness to the country. I think one need do no more than state the necessary implications of what you ask to demonstrate that nothing could be more alien to the principle of free expression that Harvard stands for.

IV. I WANT to add a comment on your decision not to subscribe to the Law School Fund. As Mr. Conant wrote you, it has happened before that subscriptions have been withheld because of objections to the acts or opinions of professors or because of disapproval of University policy. This is natural and normal, I think; and it is certainly the right of anyone not to aid an institution with which he is as out of harmony as you now seem to be with Harvard. But it is also true, I am sure you will agree, that Harvard cannot be influenced at all to depart from her basic tradition of freedom by any fear that gifts will be withheld.

An interesting test case on this point came up during the first World War. It related to Professor Hugo Münsterberg, who was a German and very pro-German, and is described in Professor Yeomans' biography of President Lowell. It appears that the press reported that a certain Harvard man had, in Professor Yeomans' words, "threatened to annul a bequest to the University of $10,000,000 unless Münsterberg was immediately deprived of his professorship." Thereupon Professor Münsterberg wrote to the Harvard Corporation offering to resign if the graduate would immediately remit $5,000,000 to the Corporation. The Professor's letter was returned and the Corporation issued, as Professor Yeomans puts it, "one of its rare public pronouncements," as follows: "It is now officially stated that, at the instance of the authorities, Professor Münsterberg's resignation has been withdrawn, and that the University cannot tolerate any suggestion that it would be willing to accept money to abridge free speech, to remove a professor or to accept his resignation."

I think it will always be Harvard policy not to be influenced in any way "to abridge free speech" by the withholding of any subscription. And if $5,000,000 or any sum were offered tomorrow as the price of the removal of Professor Ciardi or Professor Shapley, or of instituting the "closer watch" that you recommend, nothing is more certain than that the Corporation would again reply that it "cannot tolerate" the suggestion.

On this money matter, the practical question has always interested me as to whether Harvard's adherence to this principle has in fact been to her financial detriment. Certainly one can point to some specific cases, besides your own, where gifts have not been made because the possible donors thought Harvard should have disciplined professors or students for their supposed "sedition" or "radicalism." I well remember how much was said on that score during the early days of the New Deal as relating to the activities, actual or supposed, of Professor Felix Frankfurter. So I do not doubt that some gifts have been withheld for reasons of this sort. On the other hand, less is heard, usually nothing at all, of those others who instead of being repelled by the steadiness of Harvard's adherence to free expression, find in it the true glory of Harvard and a principal reason for supporting her finances.

Thus I am quite sure that there are many Harvard men and others who, if they read your letter and were told that Harvard must firmly decline to follow your views, would find in that very refusal a strong reason for adding to their gifts. I think that many such would say: "If Harvard is again under pressure to depart from its tradition but is holding to it as solidly as ever, that is the place on which I want to put my money, because if we want to preserve the essence of the American Idea we must encourage those who adhere consistently to uncoerced teaching."

So I just don't know, and no one can know, whether, *on balance*, Harvard gains or loses money by its policy in this regard. But, although it cannot be proved, I have a shrewd suspicion that, while Harvard may for a few years, in times of emotion like the present, lose some gifts and bequests by its adherence to free expression, it loses no money at all over a generation by holding to this principle.

In any case, while that is an intriguing question, it is not the real one. For whether the policy gains money or loses it, Harvard, in order to *be* Harvard, has to hew to the line. That is what Mr. Eliot meant, I am sure, when he said, in 1869, that while a university "must be rich" it must "above all" be free. That choice is as clear today as 80 years ago.

I am under no illusion that this letter, or any similar argument, is likely to affect your attitude in this matter, at least for some time. For my observation in the corresponding period after the first World War was that in a period of alarm, proposals to restrict free expression rest on strong feelings which for the time being override sound judgment. That was certainly true of the above mentioned successful effort to oust the Socialist Assemblymen in New York, and the unsuccessful effort to discipline Professor Chafee. Several years later, I think that some of those who promoted those efforts came to see that they had been impairing the very values which, no doubt sincerely, they purported to preserve. But during the period of stress, they found it hard even to comprehend the other side.

I hope, though, that I may have convinced you that there is another side, and that there is a deep-rooted tradition at Harvard utterly opposed to your view — a tradition that must and will be upheld as long as Harvard remains true to herself.*

President Conant has several times stated his theory of the principle of intellectual toleration; and inasmuch as the reply to Mr. Ober was instigated by Mr. Conant, the following extract is given from Mr. Conant's Education in a Divided World (*Cambridge, 1948*), *chapter ix, "The University."*

One condition is essential: freedom of discussion, unmolested inquiry. As in the early days of this century, we must have a spirit of tolerance which allows the expression of a great variety of opinions. On this point there can be no compromise even in days of an armed truce. But we should be completely unrealistic if we failed to recognize the difficulties which arise from the ideological conflict which according to the premise of this book will be with us for years to come. Excited citizens are going to be increasingly alarmed about alleged "communist infiltration" into our schools and colleges. Reactionaries are going to use the tensions inherent in our armed truce as an excuse for attacking a wide group of radical ideas and even some which are in the middle of the road.

How are we to answer the thoughtful and troubled citizen who wonders if our universities are being used as centers for fifth column activities? By emphasizing again the central position in this country of tolerance of diver-

---

* In a subsequent letter to Mr. Ober, dated June 11, 1949, Mr. Clark reiterates the essence of the Harvard position as follows: ". . . There will be no harassment of professors for engaging in open and legal meetings. There will be no apparatus of inquiry and 'closer watch.' The harm done by the effort necessary to discover even a single clandestine Party Member would outweigh any possible benefit. To go beyond that by searching for 'reasonable grounds' concerning 'loyalty,' would still more disrupt Harvard or any free university."

sity of opinion and by expressing confidence that *our* philosophy is superior
to all alien importations. After all, this is but one version of the far wider
problem which we encounter at the outset: how are we to win the ideological conflict if it continues on a non-shooting basis? Clearly not by destroy-
ing our basic ideas but by strengthening them; clearly not by retreating in
fear from the Communist doctrine but by going out vigorously to meet it.
Studying a philosophy does not mean endorsing it, much less proclaiming
it. We study cancer in order to learn how to defeat it. We must study the
Soviet philosophy in our universities for exactly the same reason. No one
must be afraid to tackle that explosive subject before a class. If an avowed
supporter of the Marx-Lenin-Stalin line can be found, force him into the open
and tear his arguments to pieces with counter-arguments. Some of the success of the Communist propaganda in this country before the war was due
to the fact that it was like pornographic literature purveyed through an
academic black market, so to speak. For a certain type of youth this under-
cover kind of knowledge has a special attraction. And doctrines that are
not combated in the classroom but treated merely with silence or contempt
may be appealing to the immature.

The first requirement for maintaining a healthy attitude in our universities in these days, therefore, is to get the discussion of modern Marxism
out into the open. The second is to recognize that we are not at peace but
in a period of an armed truce. That means that the activities which go
with war, such as vigorous secret intelligence, sabotage, and even planned
disruption of the basic philosophy of a nation may well proceed. We must
be on our guard. We must be realistic about the activities of agents of foreign powers, but at the same time be courageous in our support of the basis
of our own creed, the maximum of individual freedom. We should be certain that any steps we take to counteract the work of foreign agents within
our borders do not damage irreparably the very fabric we seek to save. The
government, of course, must see to it that those who are employed in positions of responsibility and trust are persons of intelligence, discretion, and
unswerving loyalty to the national interest. But in disqualifying others we
should proceed with the greatest caution. Certain men and women who
temperamentally are unsuited for employment by a Federal agency none
the less can serve the nation in other ways. They may be entitled to our full
respect as citizens though we may disagree with their opinions. For example, a person whose religious beliefs make him a conscientious objector is
automatically disqualified from employment by the nation in matters per-
taining to the use of force or preparation for the use of force. On the other
hand, such a man may be an intellectual and moral leader of the greatest
importance for the welfare of our society.

These obvious considerations have bearing on the problems of staffing a university. Universities, however they may be financed or controlled, are neither government bureaus nor private corporations; the professors are not hired employees. The criteria for joining a community of scholars are in some ways unique. They are not to be confused with the requirements of a Federal bureau. For example, I can imagine a naïve scientist or a philosopher with strong loyalties to the advancement of civilization and the unity of the world who would be a questionable asset to a government department charged with negotiations with other nations; the same man because of his professional competence might be extremely valuable to a university. Such conclusions are obvious to anyone who takes the trouble to think carefully about the degrees of prudence and sophistication met with in human beings. Such considerations will be self-evident to all who analyze the complex problem of loyalty.

The third condition necessary for maintaining free inquiry within our universities is to ask the scholars themselves to declare their own basic social philosophy. We must then be prepared in our universities to be sure that we have a variety of views represented and that in the classroom our teachers be careful scholars rather than propagandists. But the unpopular view must be protected for we would be quite naïve to imagine that there are no reactionaries who would like to drive all liberals from the halls of learning.

Those who worry about radicalism in our schools and colleges are often either reactionaries who themselves do not bear allegiance to the traditional American principles or defeatists who despair of the success of our own philosophy in an open competition. The first group are consciously or unconsciously aiming at a transformation of this society, perhaps initially not as revolutionary or violent as that which the Soviet agents envisage, but one eventually equally divergent from our historic goals. The others are unduly timid about the outcome of a battle of *ideas*; they lack confidence in our own intellectual armament. (I mean literally the battle of ideas, not espionage or sabotage by secret agents.) They often fail to recognize that diversity of opinion within the framework of loyalty to our free society is not only basic to a university but to the entire nation. For in a democracy with our traditions only those reasoned convictions which emerge from diversity of opinion can lead to that unity and national solidarity so essential for the welfare of our country — essential not only for our own security but even more a requisite for intelligent action toward the end we all desire, namely, the conversion of the present armed truce into a firm and lasting peace.

Like all other democratic institutions based on the principles of toleration, individual freedom, and the efficacy of rational methods, the universities are certain to meet with many difficulties as they seek to preserve their integrity during this period of warring ideologies. But we would do well to remember this is not the first time that communities of scholars have been disturbed by doctrinal quarrels so deep-seated as to be in the nature of smoldering wars. The history of Oxford and Cambridge during the Civil Wars of the seventeenth century is interesting reading on this point. At that time the "true friends of learning" rallied to the support of those ancient institutions and protected them against the excesses of both sides. Today, likewise, the friends of learning must recognize the dangers which might threaten the universities if tempers rise as the armed truce lengthens. They must seek to increase the number of citizens who understand the true nature of universities, the vital importance of the tradition of free inquiry, the significance of life tenure for the older members of each faculty, the fact that violent differences of opinion are essential for education. They must be realistic about the fanatic followers of the Soviet philosophy who seek to infiltrate, control, and disrupt democratic organizations including student clubs. But they must also recognize the threat that comes from those reactionaries who are ready if a wave of hysteria should mount to purge the institutions of all doctrines contrary to their views. In short, our citadels of learning must be guarded by devoted laymen in all walks of life who realize the relation between education and American democracy. So protected, the universities need not worry unduly about infiltration of Marxist subversive elements or intimidation from without. They will remain secure fortresses of our liberties.

1949

WILBUR J. BENDER

Freedom in the College: A Policy

On the evening of Monday, February 21, 1949, in the Harvard Yard, Gerhart Eisler, then professor-elect at the University of Leipzig and at the time under sentence of fine and imprisonment for refusing to answer questions about the Communist Party before the House Committee on un-American Activities, addressed an open meeting of the John Reed Club, composed of undergraduates and others. He spoke on "The Marxist Theory of Social Change." His audience overflowed the largest lecture room in Emerson Hall. Almost simultaneously over the radio Fulton Lewis, Jr., denounced this lecture as "subversive activity" and urged that Harvard authorities be deluged with letters and telegrams of protest. About three hundred letters and telegrams were received. The controversy over the propriety of allowing a left-wing organization of students to listen to a speaker under sentence of fine and imprisonment drew from Wilbur J. Bender, Dean of Harvard College, the following statement of belief. It is reprinted from the Harvard Alumni Bulletin *for March 12, 1949, by permission of the editors.*

THE WORLD IS FULL OF DANGEROUS IDEAS, and we are both naive and stupid if we believe that the way to prepare intelligent young men to face the world is to try to protect them from such ideas while they are in college. Four years spent in an insulated nursery will produce gullible innocents, not tough-minded realists who know what they believe because they have faced the enemies of their beliefs. We are not afraid of the enemies of democracy who are willing to express their ideas in the forum. We have confidence in the maturity and intelligence of Harvard students. We have confidence in the strength of our free and dynamic American democracy. There is no danger from an open communist which is half as great as the danger from those who would destroy freedom in the name of freedom. These decadent descendants of Jefferson and Lincoln reveal their lack of faith in American ideals and in Americans. If Harvard students can be corrupted by an Eisler, Harvard College had better shut down as an educational institution.

I know of no faster way of producing communists than by making martyrs out of the handful of communists we now have. Forbidding them to speak would be not only treason to the ancient traditions of Harvard and America:

It would be proof that we have something to hide, that we have lost faith in our principles and in our way of life. It would be accepting communist practices in the name of Americanism. Whatever may have happened elsewhere, Harvard still believes in freedom and the American way.

Our policy for student organizations is simple. Any recognized student organizations can hold a meeting in a Harvard building, if they can find a room available, and listen to any speaker they can persuade to come. The fact that a man speaks at Harvard does not mean that Harvard in any way endorses his views or even that the organization involved does. If the Dean's Office were to attempt to decide who would be allowed to speak to a Harvard organization, whose views were safe and whose weren't, the views of those permitted to speak would then carry Harvard's official endorsement. Furthermore, it would be impossible in practice to agree on what speakers threatened to corrupt our youth. Some people would bar President Truman, others Senator Taft. Still others would bar anti-vivisectionists or opponents of birth control or World Federalists or Christian Scientists or Monsignor Sheen or Colonel McCormick. The answer is not suppression of "dangerous" ideas as in Russia or Japan or Hitler's Germany, but more vigorous statement of American ideas, and faith — which would be well-founded — in the ability of our students to distinguish between good and evil.

Harvard College is dedicated to the task of producing mature and independent educated men. I devoutly hope that the time will never come when we are faced with the sorry spectacle of a great University and a great country trembling timorously in fear of the words of a communist or of a demagogic commentator.

1947

HENRY STEELE COMMAGER

Who is Loyal to America?

The direct occasion of this article is evident from its opening paragraphs. It appeared in Harper's Magazine *for September, 1947, and is reprinted by permission of the author.*

ON MAY 6 A RUSSIAN-BORN GIRL, Mrs. Shura Lewis, gave a talk to the students of the Western High School of Washington, D. C. She talked about Russia — its school system, its public health program, the position of women, of the aged, of the workers, the farmers, and the professional classes — and compared, superficially and uncritically, some American and Russian social institutions. The most careful examination of the speech — happily reprinted for us in the *Congressional Record* — does not disclose a single disparagement of anything American unless it is a quasi-humorous reference to the cost of having a baby and of dental treatment in this country. Mrs. Lewis said nothing that had not been said a thousand times, in speeches, in newspapers, magazines, and books. She said nothing that any normal person could find objectionable.

Her speech, however, created a sensation. A few students walked out on it. Others improvised placards proclaiming their devotion to Americanism. Indignant mothers telephoned their protests. Newspapers took a strong stand against the outrage. Congress, rarely concerned for the political or economic welfare of the citizens of the capital city, reacted sharply when its intellectual welfare was at stake. Congressmen Rankin and Dirksen thundered and lightened; the District of Columbia Committee went into a huddle; there were demands for housecleaning in the whole school system, which was obviously shot through and through with Communism.

All this might be ignored, for we have learned not to expect either intelligence or understanding of Americanism from this element in our Congress. More ominous was the reaction of the educators entrusted with the high responsibility of guiding and guarding the intellectual welfare of our boys and girls. Did they stand up for intellectual freedom? Did they insist that high-school children had the right and the duty to learn about other countries? Did they protest that students were to be trusted to use intelligence and common sense? Did they affirm that the Americanism of their students was staunch enough to resist propaganda? Did they perform even the elementary task, expected of educators above all, of analyzing the much-criticized speech?

Not at all. The District Superintendent of Schools, Dr. Hobart Corning, hastened to agree with the animadversions of Representatives Rankin and Dirksen. The whole thing was, he confessed, "a very unfortunate occurrence," and had "shocked the whole school system." What Mrs. Lewis said, he added gratuitously, was "repugnant to all who are working with youth in the Washington schools," and "the entire affair contrary to the philosophy of education under which we operate." Mr. Danowsky, the hapless principal of the Western High School, was "the most shocked and regretful of all." The District of Columbia Committee would be happy to know that though he was innocent in the matter, he had been properly reprimanded!

It is the reaction of the educators that makes this episode more than a tempest in a teapot. We expect hysteria from Mr. Rankin and some newspapers; we are shocked when we see educators, timid before criticism and confused about first principles, betray their trust. And we wonder what can be that "philosophy of education" which believes that young people can be trained to the duties of citizenship by wrapping their minds in cotton-wool.

Merely by talking about Russia Mrs. Lewis was thought to be attacking Americanism. It is indicative of the seriousness of the situation that during the same week the House found it necesary to take time out from the discussion of the labor bill, the tax bill, the International Trade Organization, and the world famine, to meet assaults upon Americanism from a new quarter. This time it was the artists who were undermining the American system, and members of the House spent some hours passing around reproductions of the paintings which the State Department had sent abroad as part of its program for advertising American culture. We need not pause over the exquisite humor which congressmen displayed in their comments on modern art: weary statesmen must have their fun. But we may profitably remark the major criticism which was directed against this unfortunate collection of paintings. What was wrong with these paintings, it shortly appeared, was that they were un-American. "No American drew those crazy pictures," said Mr. Rankin. Perhaps he was right. The copious files of the Committee on un-American Activities were levied upon to prove that of the forty-five artists represented "no less than twenty were definitely New Deal in various shades of Communism." The damning facts are specified for each of the pernicious twenty; we can content ourselves with the first of them, Ben-Zion. What is the evidence here? "Ben-Zion was one of the signers of a letter sent to President Roosevelt by the United American

Artists which urged help to the USSR and Britain after Hitler attacked Russia." He was in short a fellow-traveler of Churchill and Roosevelt.

The same day that Mr. Dirksen was denouncing the Washington school authorities for allowing students to hear about Russia ("In Russia equal right is granted to each nationality. There is no discrimination. Nobody says, you are a Negro, you are a Jew.") Representative Williams of Mississippi rose to denounce the *Survey-Graphic* magazine and to add further to our understanding of Americanism. The *Survey-Graphic*, he said, "contained 129 pages of outrageously vile and nauseating anti-Southern, anti-Christian, un-American, and pro-Communist tripe, ostensibly directed toward the elimination of the custom of racial segregation in the South." It was written by "meddling un-American purveyors of hate and indecency."

All in all, a busy week for the House. Yet those who make a practice of reading their *Record* will agree that it was a typical week. For increasingly Congress is concerned with the eradication of disloyalty and the defense of Americanism, and scarcely a day passes that some congressman does not treat us to exhortations and admonitions, impassioned appeals and eloquent declamations, similar to those inspired by Mrs. Lewis, Mr. Ben-Zion, and the editors of the *Survey-Graphic*. And scarcely a day passes that the outlines of the new loyalty and the new Americanism are not etched more sharply in public policy.

And this is what is significant — the emergence of new patterns of Americanism and of loyalty, patterns radically different from those which have long been traditional. It is not only the Congress that is busy designing the new patterns. They are outlined in President Truman's recent disloyalty order; in similar orders formulated by the New York City Council and by state and local authorities throughout the country; in the programs of the D.A.R., the American Legion, and similar patriotic organizations; in the editorials of the Hearst and the McCormick-Patterson papers; and in an elaborate series of advertisements sponsored by large corporations and business organizations. In the making is a revival of the red hysteria of the early 1920's, one of the shabbiest chapters in the history of American democracy; and more than a revival, for the new crusade is designed not merely to frustrate Communism but to formulate a positive definition of Americanism, and a positive concept of loyalty.

What is the new loyalty? It is, above all, conformity. It is the uncritical and unquestioning acceptance of America as it is — the political institutions, the social relationships, the economic practices. It rejects inquiry into the race question or socialized medicine, or public housing, or into the wisdom or validity of our foreign policy. It regards as particularly heinous any challenge to what is called "the system of private enterprise," identifying that system with Americanism. It abandons evolution, repudiates the once popular concept of progress, and regards America as a finished product, perfect and complete.

It is, it must be added, easily satisfied. For it wants not intellectual conviction nor spiritual conquest, but mere outward conformity. In matters of loyalty it takes the word for the deed, the gesture for the principle. It is content with the flag salute, and does not pause to consider the warning of our Supreme Court that "a person gets from a symbol the meaning he puts into it, and what is one man's comfort and inspiration is another's jest and scorn." It is satisfied with membership in respectable organizations and, as it assumes that every member of a liberal organization is a Communist, concludes that every member of a conservative one is a true American. It has not yet learned that not everyone who saith Lord, Lord, shall enter into the kingdom of Heaven. It is designed neither to discover real disloyalty not to foster true loyalty.

II

What is wrong with this new concept of loyalty? What, fundamentally, is wrong with the pusillanimous retreat of the Washington educators, the barbarous antics of Washington legislators, the hysterical outbursts of the D.A.R., the gross and vulgar appeals of business corporations? It is not merely that these things are offensive. It is rather that they are wrong — morally, socially, and politically.

The concept of loyalty as conformity is a false one. It is narrow and restrictive, denies freedom of thought and of conscience, and is irremediably stained by private and selfish considerations. "Enlightened loyalty," wrote Josiah Royce, who made loyalty the very core of his philosophy,

> means harm to no man's loyalty. It is at war only with disloyalty, and its warfare, unless necessity constrains, is only a spiritual warfare. It does not foster class hatreds; it knows of nothing reasonable about race prejudices; and it regards all races of men as one in their need of loyalty. It ignores mutual misunderstandings. It loves its own wherever upon earth its own, namely loyalty itself, is to be found.

Justice, charity, wisdom, spirituality, he added, were all definable in terms of loyalty, and we may properly ask which of these qualities our contemporary champions of loyalty display.

Above all, loyalty must be to something larger than oneself, untainted by private purposes or selfish ends. But what are we to say of the attempts by the NAM and by individual corporations to identify loyalty with the system of private enterprise? Is it not as if officeholders should attempt to identify loyalty with their own party, their own political careers? Do not those corporations which pay for full-page advertisements associating Americanism with the competitive system expect, ultimately, to profit from that association? Do not those organizations that deplore, in the name of patriotism, the extension of government operation of hydro-electric power expect to profit from their campaign?

Certainly it is a gross perversion not only of the concept of loyalty but of the concept of Americanism to identify it with a particular economic system. This precise question, interestingly enough, came before the Supreme Court in the Schneiderman case not so long ago — and it was Wendell Willkie who was counsel for Schneiderman. Said the Court:

> *Throughout our history many sincere people whose attachment to the general Constitutional scheme cannot be doubted have, for various and even divergent reasons, urged differing degrees of governmental ownership and control of natural resources, basic means of production, and banks and the media of exchange, either with or without compensation. And something once regarded as a species of private property was abolished without compensating the owners when the institution of slavery was forbidden. Can it be said that the author of the Emancipation Proclamation and the supporters of the Thirteenth Amendment were not attached to the Constitution?*

There is, it should be added, a further danger in the willful identification of Americanism with a particular body of economic practices. Many learned economists predict for the near future an economic crash similar to that of 1929. If Americanism is equated with competitive capitalism, what happens to it if competitive capitalism comes a cropper? If loyalty and private enterprise are inextricably associated, what is to preserve loyalty if private enterprise fails? Those who associate Americanism with a particular program of economic practices have a grave responsibility, for if their program should fail, they expose Americanism itself to disrepute.

The effort to equate loyalty with conformity is misguided because it assumes that there is a fixed content to loyalty and that this can be determined and defined. But loyalty is a principle, and eludes definition except in its own terms. It is devotion to the best interests of the commonwealth, and may require hostility to the particular policies which the government pursues, the particular practices which the economy undertakes, the particular institutions which society maintains. "If there is any fixed star in our Constitutional constellation," said the Supreme Court in the Barnette case, "it is that no official, high or petty, can prescribe what shall be orthodox in politics, nationalism, religion, or other matters of opinion, or force citizens to confess by word or act their faith therein. If there are any circumstances which permit an exception they do not now occur to us."

True loyalty may require, in fact, what appears to the naïve to be disloyalty. It may require hostility to certain provisions of the Constitution itself, and historians have not concluded that those who subscribed to the "Higher Law" were lacking in patriotism. We should not forget that our tradition is one of protest and revolt, and it is stultifying to celebrate the rebels of the past — Jefferson and Paine, Emerson and Thoreau — while we silence the rebels of the present. "We are a rebellious nation," said Theodore Parker, known in his day as the Great American Preacher, and went on:

> Our whole history is treason; our blood was attainted before we were born; our creeds are infidelity to the mother church; our constitution, treason to our fatherland. What of that? Though all the governors in the world bid us commit treason against man, and set the example, let us never submit.

Those who would impose upon us a new concept of loyalty not only assume that this is possible, but have the presumption to believe that they are competent to write the definition. We are reminded of Whitman's defiance of the "never-ending audacity of elected persons." Who are those who would set the standards of loyalty? They are Rankins and Bilbos, officials of the D.A.R. and the Legion and the NAM, Hearst and McCormicks. May we not say of Rankin's harangues on loyalty what Emerson said of Webster at the time of the Seventh of March speech: "The word honor in the mouth of Mr. Webster is like the word love in the mouth of a whore."

What do men know of loyalty who make a mockery of the Declaration of Independence and the Bill of Rights, whose energies are dedicated to stirring up race and class hatreds, who would straitjacket the American spirit? What indeed do they know of America — the America of Sam Adams and Tom Paine, of Jackson's defiance of the Court and Lincoln's celebration of labor, of Thoreau's essay on Civil Disobedience and Emerson's championship of John Brown, of the America of the Fourierists and the Come-Outers, of cranks and fanatics, of socialists and anarchists? Who among American heroes could meet their tests, who would be cleared by their committees? Not Washington, who was a rebel. Not Jefferson, who wrote that all men are created equal and whose motto was "rebellion to tyrants is obedience to God." Not Garrison, who publicly burned the Constitution; or Wendell Phillips, who spoke for the underprivileged everywhere and counted himself a philosophical anarchist; not Seward of the Higher Law or Sumner of racial equality. Not Lincoln, who admonished us to have malice toward none, charity for all; or Wilson, who warned that our flag was "a flag of liberty of opinion as well as of political liberty"; or Justice Holmes, who said that our Constitution is an experiment and that while that experiment is being made "we should be eternally vigilant against attempts to check the expression of opinions that we loath and believe to be fraught with death."

III

There are further and more practical objections against the imposition of fixed concepts of loyalty or tests of disloyalty. The effort is itself a confession of fear, a declaration of insolvency. Those who are sure of themselves do not need reassurance, and those who have confidence in the strength and the virtue of America do not need to fear either criticism or competition. The effort is bound to miscarry. It will not apprehend those who are really disloyal, it will not even frighten them; it will affect only those who can be labeled "radical." It is sobering to recall that through the Japanese relocation program, carried through at such incalculable cost in misery and tragedy, was justified to us on the ground that the Japanese were potentially disloyal, the record does not disclose a single case of Japanese disloyalty or sabotage during the whole war. The warning sounded by the Supreme Court in the Barnett flag-salute case is a timely one:

> *Ultimate futility of such attempts to compel obedience is the lesson of every such effort from the Roman drive to stamp out Christianity as a disturber of pagan unity, the Inquisition as a means to religious and dynastic unity, the Siberian exiles as a means to Russian unity, down to the fast-failing efforts of our present totalitarian enemies. Those who begin coercive elimination of dissent soon find themselves exterminating dissenters. Compulsory unification of opinion achieves only the unanimity of the graveyard.*

Nor are we left to idle conjecture in this matter; we have had experience enough. Let us limit ourselves to a single example, one that is wonderfully relevant. Back in 1943 the House un-American Activities Committee, deeply disturbed by alleged disloyalty among government employees, wrote a definition of subversive activities and proceeded to apply it. The definition was admirable, and no one could challenge its logic or its symmetry:

> *Subversive activity derives from conduct intentionally destructive of or inimical to the Government of the United States — that which seeks to undermine its institutions, or to distort its functions, or to impede its projects, or to lessen its efforts, the ultimate end being to overturn it all.*

Surely anyone guilty of activities so defined deserved not only dismissal but punishment. But how was the test applied? It was applied to two distinguished scholars, Robert Morss Lovett and Goodwin Watson, and to one able young historian, William E. Dodd, Jr., son of our former Ambassador to Germany. Of almost three million persons employed by the government, these were the three whose subversive activities were deemed the most pernicious, and the House cut them off the payroll. The sequel is familiar. The Senate concurred only to save a wartime appropriation; the President signed the bill under protest for the same reason. The Supreme Court declared the whole business a "bill of attainder" and therefore unconstitutional. Who was it, in the end, who engaged in "subversive activities"—Lovett, Dodd, and Watson, or the Congress which flagrantly violated Article One of the Constitution?

Finally, disloyalty tests are not only futile in application, they are pernicious in their consequences. They distract attention from activities that are really disloyal, and silence criticism inspired by true loyalty. That there are disloyal elements in America will not be denied, but there is no reason to suppose that any of the tests now formulated will ever be applied to tthem. It is relevant to remember that when Rankin was asked why his Committee did not investigate the Ku Klux Klan he replied that the Klan was not un-American, it was American!

Who are those who are really disloyal? Those who inflame racial hatreds, who sow religious and class dissensions. Those who subvert the Constitution by violating the freedom of the ballot box. Those who make a mockery of majority rule by the use of the filibuster. Those who impair democracy by denying equal educational facilities. Those who frustrate justice by lynch law or by making a farce of jury trials. Those who deny freedom of speech and of the press and of assembly. Those who press for special favors against the interest of the commonwealth. Those who regard public office as a source of private gain. Those who would exalt the military over the civil. Those who for selfish and private purposes stir up national antagonisms and expose the world to the ruin of war.

Will the House Committee on un-American Activities interfere with the activities of these? Will Mr. Truman's disloyalty proclamation reach these? Will the current campaigns for Americanism convert these? If past experience is any guide, they will not. What they will do, if they are successful, is to silence criticism, stamp out dissent—or drive it underground. But if our democracy is to flourish it must have criticism, if our government is to function it must have dissent. Only totalitarian governments insist upon conformity and they—as we know—do so at their peril. Without criticism abuses will go unrebuked; without dissent our dynamic system will become static. The American people have a stake in the maintenance of the most thorough-going inquisition into American institutions. They have a stake in nonconformity, for they know that the American genius is nonconformist. They have a stake in experimentation of the most radical character, for they know that only those who prove all things can hold fast that which is good.

IV

It is easier to say what loyalty is not than to say what it is. It is not conformity. It is not passive acquiescence in the status quo. It is not preference for everything American over everything foreign. It is not an ostrich-like ignorance of other countries and other institutions. It is not the indulgence in ceremony — a flag salute, an oath of allegiance, a fervid verbal declaration. It is not a particular creed, a particular version of history, a particular body of economic practices, a particular philosophy.

It is a tradition, an ideal, and a principle. It is a willingness to subordinate every private advantage for the larger good. It is an appreciation of the rich and diverse contributions that can come from the most varied sources. It is allegiance to the traditions that have guided our greatest statesmen and inspired our most eloquent poets — the traditions of freedom, equality, democracy, tolerance, the tradition of the higher law, of experimentation, co-operation, and pluralism. It is a realization that America was born of revolt, flourished on dissent, became great through experimentation.

Independence was an act of revolution; republicanism was something new under the sun; the federal system was a vast experimental laboratory. Physically Americans were pioneers; in the realm of social and economic institutions, too, their tradition has been one of pioneering. From the beginning, intellectual and spiritual diversity have been as characteristic of America as racial and linguistic. The most distinctively American philosophies have been transcendentalism—which is the philosophy of the Higher Law — and pragmatism — which is the philosophy of experimentation and pluralism. These two principles are the very core of Americanism: the principle of the Higher Law, or of obedience to the dictates of conscience rather than of statutes, and the principle of pragmatism, or the rejection of a single good and of the notion of a finished universe. From the beginning Americans have known that there were new worlds to conquer, new truths to be discovered. Every effort to confine Americanism to a single pattern, to constrain it to a single formula, is disloyalty to everything that is valid in Americanism.

1918 — 1929
OLIVER WENDELL HOLMES
Dissenting Opinions

(1)

The Naturalization Act of 1906 required applicants for United States citizenship to swear to support and defend the constitution and the laws against all enemies. Mrs. Rosika Schwimmer, a pacifist, offered to swear allegiance to the United States but would not promise to take up arms if called upon to do so. Her case went to the Supreme Court, where a majority of the judges held that objectors to military force were as detrimental to the safety of the republic as those who merely refused to bear arms. Justices Brandeis and Holmes dissented, Mr. Justice Holmes writing the minority opinion, here reprinted from 279 U.S. 653.

THE APPLICANT SEEMS TO BE A WOMAN OF SUPERIOR CHARACTER AND IN-TELLIGENCE, obviously more than ordinarily desirable as a citizen of the United States. It is agreed that she is qualified for citizenship except so far as the views set forth in a statement of facts "may show that the applicant is not attached to the principles of the Constitution of the United States and well disposed to the good order and happiness of the same, and except in so far as the same may show that she cannot take the oath of allegiance without a mental reservation." The views referred to are an extreme opinion in favor of pacificism and a statement that she would not bear arms to defend the Constitution. So far as the adequacy of her oath is concerned I hardly can see how it is affected by the statement, inasmuch as she is a woman over fifty years of age, and would not be allowed to bear arms if she wanted to. And as to the opinion, the whole examination of the applicant shows that she holds none of the now-dreaded creeds but thoroughly believes in organized government and prefers that of the United States to any other in the world. Surely it cannot show lack of attachment to the principles of the Constitution that she thinks it can be improved. I suppose that most intelligent people think that it might be. Her particular improvement looking to the abolition of war seems to me not materially different in its bearing on this case from a wish to establish cabinet government as in England, or a single house, or one term of seven years for the President. To touch a more burning question, only a judge mad with partisanship would exclude because the applicant thought that the Eighteenth Amendment should be repealed.

Of course the fear is that if a war came the applicant would exert activities such as were dealt with in *Schenck* v. *United States*, 249 U.S. 47. But that seems to me unfounded. Her position and motives are wholly different from those of Schenck. She is an optimist and states in strong and, I do not doubt, sincere words her belief that war will disappear and that the impending destiny of mankind is to unite in peaceful leagues. I do not share that optimism nor do I think that a philosophic view of the world would regard war as absurd. But most people who have known it regard it with horror, as a last resort, and even if not yet ready for cosmopolitan efforts, would welcome any practicable combinations that would increase the power on the side of peace. The notion that the applicant's optimistic anticipations would make her a worse citizen is sufficiently answered by her examination, which seems to me a better argument for her admission than any I can offer. Some of her answers might excite popular prejudice, but if there is any principle of the Constitution that more imperatively calls for attachment than any other it is the principle of free thought — not free thought for those who agree with us but freedom for the thought that we hate. I think that we should adhere to that principle with regard to admission into, as well as to life within, this country. And recurring to the opinion that bars this applicant's way, I would suggest that the Quakers have done their share to make the country what it is, that many citizens agree with the applicant's belief, and that I had not supposed hitherto that we regretted our inability to expel them because they believe more than some of us do in the teachings of the Sermon on the Mount.

(2)

Because he had written a pamphlet entitled The Left Wing Manifesto, *published by the Socialist Party in New York City, Benjamin Gitlow was found guilty of violating a New York statute prohibiting the advocacy of "criminal anarchy," or the theory that force or violence should be exercised to overthrow government. The case went to the Supreme Court, where in 1924 a majority of the judges upheld the conviction on the ground that the necessary "revolutionary spark" appeared in such a sentence as: "The Communist International calls the proletariat of the world to the final struggle." Justice Brandeis and Holmes dissented. Mr. Justice Holmes wrote the minority opinion, reprinted from 268 U.S. 673.*

Mr. Justice Brandeis and I are of the opinion that this judgment should be reversed. The general principle of free speech, it seems to me, must be taken to be included in the Fourteenth Amendment, in view of the scope that has been given to the word "liberty" as there used, although perhaps it may be accepted with a somewhat larger latitude of interpretation than is allowed to Congress by the sweeping language that governs or ought to govern the laws of the United States. If I am right, then I think that the criterion sanctioned by the full Court in *Schenck* v. *United States*, 249 U.S. 47, 52 applies, "The question in every case is whether the words used are used in such circumstances and are of such a nature as to create a clear and present danger that will bring about the substantive evils that [the State] has a right to prevent." It is true that in my opinion this criterion was departed from in *Abrams* v. *United States*, 250 U.S. 616, but the convictions that I expressed in that case are too deep for it to be possible for me as yet to believe that it and *Schaefer* v. *United States*, 251 U.S. 466, have settled the law. If what I think the correct test is applied, it is manifest that there was no present danger of an attempt to overthrow the Government by force on the part of the admittedly small minority who shared the defendant's views. It is said that this manifesto is more than a theory, that it was an incitement. Every idea is an incitement. It offers itself for belief and if believed it is acted on unless some other belief outweighs it or some failure of energy stifles the movement at its birth. The only difference between the expression of an opinion and an incitement in the narrower sense is the speaker's enthusiasm for the result. Eloquence may set fire to reason. But whatever may be thought of the redundant discourse before us it had no chance of starting a present conflagration. If in the long run the beliefs expressed in proletarian dictatorship are destined to be accepted by the dominant forces of the community, the only meaning of free speech is that they should be given their chance and have their way.

If the publication of this document had been laid as an attempt to induce an uprising against government at once and not at some indefinite time in the future, it would have presented a different question. The object would have been one with which the law might deal, subject to the doubt whether there was any danger that the publication could produce any result, or in other words, whether it was not futile and too remote from possible consequences. But the indictment alleges the publication and nothing more.

(3)

Four men and one woman were sentenced to prison in 1918 because they had printed two leaflets protesting against American intervention in Russia after the Revolution of 1917. Their circulars were secretly printed and distributed, some being scattered from a roof top in New York City. Ferreted out by agents of the Department of Justice, the five, all Russian-born, were found guilty in the lower courts; and when their case was appealed to the Supreme Court, a majority held that the leaflets in question were practical incentives to bring about a change of government by force and violence. Justices Brandeis and Holmes dissented. The opinion of Mr. Justice Holmes is here reprinted from 250 U.S. 624 f.

This indictment is founded wholly upon the publication of two leaflets which I shall describe in a moment. The first count charges a conspiracy pending the war with Germany to publish abusive language about the form of government of the United States, laying the preparation and publishing of the first leaflet as overt acts. The second count charges a conspiracy pending the war to publish language intended to bring the form of government into contempt, laying the preparation and publishing of the two leaflets as overt acts. The third count alleges a conspiracy to encourage resistance to the United States in the same war and to attempt to effectuate the purpose by publishing the same leaflets. The fourth count lays a conspiracy to incite curtailment of production of things necessary to the prosecution of the war and to attempt to accomplish it by publishing the second leaflet to which I have referred.

The first of these leaflets says that the President's cowardly silence about the intervention in Russia reveals the hypocrisy of the plutocratic gang in Washington. It intimates that "German militarism combined with Allied capitalism to crush the Russian revolution," goes on that the tyrants of the world fight each other until they see a common enemy — working-class enlightenment — when they combine to crush it; and that now militarism and capitalism combined, though not openly, to crush the Russian revolution. It says that there is only one enemy of the workers of the world and that is capitalism; that it is a crime for workers of America, etc., to fight the workers' republic of Russia, and ends "Awake! Awake, you workers of the world!" Signed "Revolutionists." A note adds, "It is absurd to call us pro-German. We hate and despise German militarism more than do you hypo-critical tyrants. We have more reasons for denouncing German militarism than has the coward of the White House."

The other leaflet, headed "Workers — Wake Up," with abusive language says that America together with the Allies will march for Russia to help the Czecho-Slovaks in their struggle against the Bolsheviki, and that this time the hypocrites shall not fool the Russian emigrants and friends of Russia in America. It tells the Russian emigrants that they now must spit in the face of false military propaganda by which their sympathy and help to the prosecution of the war have been called forth and says that with the money they have lent or are going to lend "they will make bullets not only for the Germans but also for the Workers' Soviets of Russia," and further, "Workers in the ammunition factories, you are producing bullets, bayonets, cannon, to murder not only the Germans but also your dearest, best, who are in Russia fighting for freedom." It then appeals to the same Russian emigrants at some length not to consent to the "inquisitionary expedition to Russia," and says that the destruction of the Russian revolution is "the politics of the march on Russia." The leaflet winds up by saying "Workers, our reply to this barbaric intervention has to be a general strike!" and after a few words on the spirit of revolution, exhortations not to be afraid, and some usual tall talk, ends, "Woe unto those who will be in the way of progress. Let solidarity live! The Rebels."

No argument seems to me necessary to show that these pronunciamentos in no way attack the form of government of the United States, or that they do not support either of the first two counts. What little I have to say about the third count may be postponed until I have considered the fourth. With regard to that it seems too plain to be denied that the suggestion to workers in ammunition factories that they are producing bullets to murder their dearest, and the further advocacy of a general strike, both in the second leaflet, do urge curtailment of production of things necessary to the prosecution of the war within the meaning of the Act of May 16, 1918 . . . amending §3 of the earlier Act of 1917. But to make the conduct criminal that statute requires that it should be "with intent by such curtailment to cripple or hinder the United States in the prosecution of the war." It seems to me that no such intent is proved.

I am aware of course that the word intent as vaguely used in ordinary legal discussion means no more than knowledge at the time of the act that the consequences said to be intended will ensue. Even less than that will satisfy the general principle of civil and criminal liability. A man may have to pay damages, may be sent to prison, at common law might be hanged, if at the time of his act he knew facts from which common experience showed that the consequences would follow, whether he individually could foresee them or not. But, when words are used exactly, a deed is not done with intent to produce a consequence unless that consequence is the aim of the deed. It may be obvious, and obvious to the actor, that the consequence will follow, and he may be liable for it even if he forgets it, but he does not do the act with intent to produce it unless the aim to produce it is the proximate motive of the specific act, although there may be some deeper motive behind.

It seems to me that this statute must be taken to use its words in a strict and accurate sense. They would be absurd in any other. A patriot might think that we were wasting money on aeroplanes, or making more cannon of a certain kind than we needed, and might advocate curtailment with success, yet even if it turned out that the curtailment hindered and was thought by other minds to have been obviously likely to hinder the United States in the prosecution of the war, no one would hold such conduct a crime. I admit that my illustration does not answer all that might be said but it is enough to show what I think and to let me pass to a more important aspect of the case. I refer to the First Amendment to the Constitution that Congress shall make no law abridging the freedom of speech.

I never have seen any reason to doubt that the questions of law that alone were before this Court in the cases of *Schenck*, *Frohwerk* and *Debs*, were rightly decided. I do not doubt for a moment that by the same reasoning that would justify punishing persuasion to murder, the United States constitutionally may punish speech that produces or is intended to produce a clear and imminent danger that it will bring about forthwith certain substantive evils that the United States constitutionally may seek to prevent. The power undoubtedly is greater in time of war than in time of peace because war opens dangers that do not exist at other times.

But as against dangers peculiar to war, as against others, the principle of the right to free speech is always the same. It is only the present danger of immediate evil or an intent to bring it about that warrants Congress in setting a limit to the expression of opinion where private rights are not concerned. Congress certainly cannot forbid all effort to change the mind of the country. Now nobody can suppose that the surreptitious publishing of a silly leaflet by an unknown man, without more, would present any immediate danger that its opinions would hinder the success of the Government arms or have any appreciable tendency to do so. Publishing these opinions for the very purpose of obstructing, however, might indicate a greater danger and at any rate would have the quality of an attempt. So I assume that the second leaflet, if published for the purpose alleged in the fourth count, might be punishable. But it seems pretty clear to me that nothing less than that would bring these papers within the scope of this law. An actual intent in the sense that I have explained is necessary to constitute an attempt, where a further act of the same individual is required to complete the substantive crime, for reasons given in *Swift and Co*. v. *United States*, 196 U.S. 375, 396. It is necessary where the success of the attempt depends upon others, because if that intent is not present the actor's aim may be accomplished without bringing about the evils sought to be checked. An intent to prevent interference with the revolution in Russia might have been satisfied without any hindrance to carrying on the war in which we were engaged.

I do not see how anyone can find the intent required by the statute in any of the defendants' words. The second leaflet is the only one that affords even a foundation for the charge, and there, without invoking the hatred of German militarism expressed in the former one, it is evident from the beginning to the end that the only object of the paper is to help Russia and stop American intervention there against the popular government — not to impede the United States in the war that it was carrying on. To say that two phrases taken literally might import a suggestion of conduct that would have interference with the war as an indirect and probably undesired effect seems to me by no means enough to show an attempt to produce that effect.

I return for a moment to the third count. That charges an intent to provoke resistance to the United States in its war with Germany. Taking the clause in the statute that deals with that in connection with the other elaborate provisions of the Act, I think that resistance to the United States means some forcible act of opposition to some proceeding of the United States in pursuance of the war. I think the intent must be the specific intent that I have described and for the reasons that I have given. I think that no such intent was proved or existed in fact. I also think that there is no hint at resistance to the United States as I construe the phrase.

In this case sentences of twenty years' imprisonment have been imposed for the publishing of two leaflets that I believe the defendants had as much right to publish as the Government has to publish the Constitution of the United States now vainly invoked by them. Even if I am technically wrong and enough can be squeezed from these poor and puny anonymities to turn the color of legal litmus paper — I will add, even if what I think the necessary intent were shown — the most nominal punishment seems to me all that possibly could be inflicted, unless the defendants are to be made to suffer not for what the indictment alleges but for the creed that they avow — a creed that I believe to be the creed of ignorance and immaturity when honestly held, as I see no reason to believe that it was held here, but which, although made the subject of examination at the trial, no one has a right even to consider in dealing with the charges before the Court.

Persecution for the expression of opinions seems to me perfectly logical. If you have no doubt of your premises or your power and want a certain result with all your heart you naturally express your wishes in law and sweep away all opposition. To allow opposition by speech seems to indicate that you think speech impotent, as when a man says that he has squared the circle, or that you do not care wholeheartedly for the result, or that you doubt either your power or your premises. But when men have realized that time has upset many fighting faiths, they may come to believe even more than they believe the very foundations of their own conduct that the ultimate good desired is better reached by free trade in ideas — that the best test of truth is the power of the thought to get itself accepted in the competition of the market, and that truth is the only ground upon which their wishes safely can be carried out. That, at any rate, is the theory of our Constitution. It is an experiment, as all life is an experiment. Every year if not every day we have to wager our salvation upon some prophecy based upon imperfect knowledge. While that experiment is part of our system I think that we should be eternally vigilant against attempts to check the expression of opinions that we loathe and believe to be fraught with death, unless they so imminently threaten immediate interference with the lawful and pressing purposes of the law that an immediate check is required to save the country. I wholly disagree with the argument of the Government that the First Amendment left the common law as to seditious libel in force. History seems to me against the notion. I had conceived that the United States through many years had shown its repentance for the Sedition Act of 1798 by repaying fines that it imposed. Only the emergency that makes it immediately dangerous to leave the correction of evil counsels to time warrants making any exception to the sweeping command, "Congress shall make no law . . . abridging the freedom of speech." Of course I am speaking only of expressions of opinion and exhortations, which were all that were uttered here, but I regret that I cannot put into more impressive words my belief that in their conviction upon this indictment the defendants were deprived of their rights under the Constitution of the United States.

1919

ZECHARIAH CHAFEE, JR.

Freedom of Speech in the Constitution

During and after World War I federal legislation like the Espionage Act and state legislation like the notorious "Lusk laws" in New York again raised the issue of freedom of speech. Men were imprisoned, indicted, tried, convicted, deported, or threatened with deportation for opposing the war, supporting a minority party, opposing the sale of Liberty Bonds, "interfering with the draft," or advocating "radicalism." Socialist members of the New York legislature were denied their seats. In the Harvard Law Review *for June 1919 Zechariah Chafee, Jr., now Langdell Professor of Law in that university, published a famous essay entitled "Freedom of Speech in War Time." The substance of this essay, modernized, forms much of the first chapters of Professor Chafee's book,* Free Speech in the United States (*Cambridge, 1941*). *Omitting the citation of cases and other technical matter and a few minor phrases, his text is here reprinted by his permision from the latest issue of his book.*

NEVER IN THE HISTORY OF OUR COUNTRY since the Alien and Sedition Laws of 1798, has the meaning of free speech been the subject of such sharp controversy as during the years since 1917. Over nineteen hundred prosecutions and other judicial proceedings during the war, involving speeches, newspaper articles, pamphlets, and books, were followed after the armistice by a widespread legislative consideration of bills punishing the advocacy of extreme radicalism. It is becoming increasingly important to determine the true limits of freedom of expression, so that speakers and writers may know how much they can properly say, and governments may be sure how much they can lawfully and wisely suppress.

This book is an inquiry into the proper limitations upon freedom of speech, and is in no way an argument that any one should be allowed to say whatever he wants anywhere and at any time. We can all agree from the very start that there must be some point where the government may step in, and my main purpose is to make clear from many different angles just where I believe that point to lie. We ought also to agree that a man may believe that certain persons have a right to speak or other constitutional rights without at all identifying himself with the position and views of such persons. In a country were John Adams defended the British soldiers involved in the Boston Massacre and Alexander Hamilton represented British Loyalists and General Grant insisted upon amnesty for Robert E. Lee, it is surprising how between 1917 and 1920 it was impossible for any one to uphold the rights of a minority without subjecting himself to the accusation that he shared their opinions. If he urged milder treatment of conscientious objectors, he was a pacifist. If he held that the treaty with Germany should not violate the terms of the armistice, he was a pro-German. This popular argument reached its climax when an opponent of the disqualified Socialist assembly informed the world that he had always suspected Charles Evans Hughes of being disloyal.

I am not an atheist, but I would not roast one at the stake as in the sixteenth century, or even exclude him from the witness stand as in the nineteenth. Neither am I a pacifist or an anarchist or a Socialist or a Bolshevik. I have no sympathy myself with the views of most of the men who have been imprisoned since the war began for speaking out. My only interest is to find whether or not the treatment which they have received accords with freedom of speech. That principle may be invoked just as eagerly in future years by conservatives. Whatever political or economic opinion falls within the scope of the First Amendment ought to be safeguarded from governmental interference by every man who has sworn to uphold the Constitution of the United States, no matter how much he disagrees with those who are entitled to its protection or how lofty the patriotism of those who would whittle away the Bill of Rights into insignificance.

A friend of Lovejoy, the Abolitionist printer killed in the Alton riots, said at the time:

> *We are more especially called upon to maintain the principles of free discussion in case of unpopular sentiments or persons, as in no other case will any effort to maintain them be needed.*

The free speech clauses of the American constitutions are not merely expressions of political faith without binding legal force. Their history shows that they limit legislative action as much as any other part of the Bills of Rights. The United States Constitution as originally drafted contained no guaranty of religious or intellectual liberty, except that it forbade any religious test oath and gave immunity to members of Congress for anything said in debates. Pinckney, of South Carolina, had sought to insert a free speech clause, grouping liberty of the press with trial by jury and habeas corpus as "essentials in free governments." His suggestion was rejected by a slight majority as unnecessary, in that the power of Congress did not extend to the press, a natural belief before Hamilton and Marshall had developed the doctrine of incidental and implied powers. Hamilton himself defended the omission on the ground that liberty of the press was indefinable and depended only on public opinion and the general spirit of the people and government for its security, little thinking that he himself would frame a definition now embodied in the constitutions of half the states. The citizens of the states were not satisfied, and the absence of the guaranty of freedom of speech was repeatedly condemned in the state conventions and in outside discussion. Virginia, New York, and Rhode Island embodied a declaration of this right in their ratifications of the federal Constitution. Virginia expressly demanded an amendment and Maryland drafted one in its convention, basing it on a very significant reason, to be mentioned shortly. At the first session of Congress a Bill of Rights, including the present First Amendment, was proposed for adoption by the states, and became part of the Constitution December 15, 1791. Massachusetts, Virginia, and Pennsylvania already had similar provisions, and such a clause was eventually inserted in the constitutions of all other states. Thus the guaranty of freedom of speech was almost a condition of the entry of four original states into the Union, and is now declared by every state to be as much a part of its fundamental law as trial by jury or compensation for property taken by eminent domain. Such a widely recognized right must mean something, and have behind it the obligation of the courts to refuse to enforce any legislation which violates freedom of speech.

We shall not, however, confine ourselves to the question whether a given form of federal or state action against pacifist and similar utterances is void under the constitutions. It is often assumed that, so long as a statute is held valid under the Bill of Rights, that document ceases to be of any importance in the matter, and may be henceforth disregarded. On the contrary, a provision like the First Amendment to the federal Constitution,

> *Congress shall make no law respecting an establishment of religion, or prohibiting the free exercise thereof; or abridging the freedom of speech, or of the press; or the right of the people peaceably to assemble, and to petition the Government for a redress of grievances*

is much more than an order to Congress not to cross the boundary which marks the extreme limits of lawful suppression. It is also an exhortation and a guide for the action of Congress inside that boundary. It is a declaration of national policy in favor of the public discussion of all public questions. Such a declaration should make Congress reluctant and careful in the enactment of all restrictions upon utterance, even though the courts will not refuse to enforce them as unconstitutional. It should influence the judges in their construction of valid speech statutes, and the prosecuting attorneys who control their enforcement. The Bill of Rights in a European constitution is a declaration of policies and nothing more, for the courts cannot disregard the legislative will though it violates the Constitution. Our Bills of Rights perform a double function. They fix a certain point to halt the government abruptly with a "Thus far and no farther"; but long before that point is reached they urge upon every official of the three branches of the state a constant regard for certain declared fundamental policies of American life.

Our main task, therefore, is to ascertain the nature and scope of the policy which finds expression in the First Amendment to the United States Constitution and the similar clauses of all the state constitutions. We can then determine the place of that policy in the conduct of war, and particularly the war with Germany. The free speech controversy during the war chiefly gathered about the federal Espionage Act . . . This statute, which imposes a maximum of twenty years' imprisonment and a $10,000 fine on several kinds of spoken or written opposition to the war, was enacted and vigorously enforced under a Constitution which provides: "Congress shall make no law . . . abridging the freedom of speech, or of the press."

Clearly, the problem of the limits of freedom of speech in war time is no academic question. On the one side, thoughtful men and journals were asking how scores of citizens could be imprisoned under this Constitution only for their open disapproval of the war as irreligious, unwise, or unjust. On the other, federal and state officials pointed to the great activities of German agents in our midst and to the unprecedented extension of the business of war over the whole nation, so that, in the familiar remark of Ludendorff, wars are no longer won by armies in the field, but by the *morale* of the whole people. The widespread Liberty Bond campaigns, and the shipyards, munition factories, government offices, training camps, in all parts of the country, were felt to make the entire United States a theater of war, in which attacks upon our cause were as dangerous and unjustified as if made among the soldiers in the rear trenches. The government regarded it as inconceivable that the Constitution should cripple its efforts to maintain public safety. Abstaining from countercharges of disloyalty and tyranny, let us recognize the issue as a conflict between two vital principles, and endeavor to find the basis of reconciliation between order and freedom.

At the outset, we can reject two extreme views in the controversy. First, there is the view that the Bill of Rights is a peace-time document and consequently freedom of speech may be ignored in war. This view has been officially repudiated. At the opposite pole is the belief of many agitators that the First Amendment renders unconstitutional any Act of Congress without exception "abridging the freedom of speech, or of the press," that all speech is free, and only action can be restrained and punished. This view is equally untenable. The provisions of the Bill of Rights cannot be applied with absolute literalness, but are subject to exceptions. For instance, the prohibition of involuntary servitude in the Thirteenth Amendment does not prevent military conscription, or the enforcement of a "work or fight" statute. The difficulty, of course, is to define the principle on which the implied exceptions are based, and an effort to that end will be made subsequently.

Since it is plain that the true solution lies between these two extreme views, and that even in war time freedom of speech exists subject to a problematical limit, it is necessary to determine where the line runs between utterances which are protected by the Constitution from governmental control and those which are not. Many attempts at a legal definition of that line have been made, but two mutually inconsistent theories have been especially successful in winning judicial acceptance, and frequently appear in the Espionage Act cases.

One theory construes the First Amendment as enacting Blackstone's statement that "the liberty of the press . . . consists in laying no *previous* restraints upon publications and not in freedom from censure for criminal matter when published." The line where legitimate suppression begins is fixed chronologically at the time of publication. The government cannot interfere by a censorship or injunction *before* the words are spoken or printed, but can punish them as much as it pleases *after* publication, no matter how harmless or essential to the public welfare the discussion may be. This Blackstonian definition is sometimes urged as a reason why civil libels should not be enjoined, so that on this theory liberty of the press means opportunity for blackmailers and no protection for political criticism. Of course, if the First Amendment does not prevent prosecution and punishment of utterances, no serious question could arise about the constitutionality of the Espionage Act.

This Blackstonian theory dies hard, but it ought to be knocked on the head once for all. In the first place, Blackstone was not interpreting a constitution, but trying to state the English law of his time, which had no censorship and did have extensive libel prosecutions. Whether or not he stated that law correctly, an entirely different view of the liberty of the press was soon afterwards enacted in Fox's Libel Act . . . so that Blackstone's view does not even correspond to the English law of the last hundred and twenty-five years. Furthermore, Blackstone is notoriously unfitted to be an authority on the liberties of American colonists, since he upheld the right of Parliament to tax them, and was pronounced by one of his own colleagues to have been "we all know, an anti-republican lawyer."

Not only is the Blackstonian interpretation of our free speech clauses inconsistent with eighteenth-century history, soon to be considered, but it is contrary to modern decisions, thoroughly artificial, and wholly out of accord with a common-sense view of the relations of state and citizen. In some respects this theory goes altogether too far in restricting state action. The total prohibition of previous restraint would not allow the government to prevent a newspaper from publishing the sailing dates of transports or the number of troops in a sector. It would forbid the removal of an indecent poster from a billboard. Censorship of moving pictures before exhibition has been held valid under a free speech clause. And whatever else may be thought of the decision under the Espionage Act with the unfortunate title *United States* v. *The Spirit of '76*, it was clearly previous restraint for a federal court to direct the seizure of a film which depicted the Wyoming Massacre and Paul Revere's Ride, because it was "calculated reasonably so to excite or inflame the passions of our people or some of them as that they will be deterred from giving that full measure of co-operation, sympathy, assistance, and sacrifice which is due to Great Britain, as an ally of ours," and "to make us a little bit slack in our loyalty to Great Britain in this great catastrophe."

On the other hand, it is hardly necessary to argue that the Blackstonian definition gives very inadequate protection to the freedom of expression. A death penalty for writing about socialism would be as effective suppression as a censorship. The government which holds twenty years in prison before a speaker and calls him free to talk resembles the peasant described by Galsworthy:

> *The other day in Russia an Englishman came on a street-meeting shortly after the first revolution had begun. An extremist was addressing the gathering and telling them that they were fools to go on fighting, that they ought to refuse and go home, and so forth. The crowd grew angry, and some soldiers were for making a rush at him; but the chairman, a big burly peasant, stopped them with these words: "Brothers, you know that our country is now a country of free speech. We must listen to this man, we must let him say anything he will. But, brothers, when he's finished, we'll bash his head in!"*

Cooley's comment on Blackstone is unanswerable:

> *. . . The mere exemption from previous restraints cannot be all that is secured by the constitutional provisions, inasmuch as of words to be uttered orally there can be no previous censorship, and the liberty of the press might be rendered a mockery and a delusion, and the phrase*

itself a byword, if, while every man was at liberty to publish what he pleased, the public authorities might nevertheless punish him for harmless publications, . . . Their purpose [of the free-speech clauses] has evidently been to protect parties in the free publication of matters of public concern, to secure their right to a free discussion of public events and public measures, and to enable every citizen at any time to bring the government and any person in authority to the bar of public opinion by any just criticism upon their conduct in the exercise of the authority which the people have conferred upon them. . . . The evils to be prevented were not the censorship of the press merely, but any action of the government by means of which it might prevent such free and general discussion of public matters as seems absolutely essential to prepare the people for an intelligent exercise of their rights as citizens.

If we turn from principles to precedents, we find several decisions which declare the constitutional guaranty of free speech to be violated by statutes and other governmental action which imposed no previous restraint, but penalized publications after they were made. And most of the decisions in which a particular statute punishing for talking or writing is sustained do not rest upon the Blackstonian interpretation of liberty of speech, but upon another theory, now to be considered. Therefore, the severe punishments imposed by the Espionage Act might conceivably violate the First Amendment, although they do not interfere with utterances before publication.

A second interpretation of the freedom of speech clauses limits them to the protection of the use of utterance and not of its "abuse." It draws the line between "liberty" and "license." Chief Justice White rejected:

the contention that the freedom of the press is the freedom to do wrong with impunity and implies the right to frustrate and defeat the discharge of those governmental duties upon the performance of which the freedom of all, including that of the press, depends. . . . However complete is the right of the press to state public things and discuss them, that right, as every other right, enjoyed in human society, is subject to the restraints which separate right from wrong-doing.

A statement of the same view in another peace case was made by Judge Hamersley of Connecticut:

Every citizen has an equal right to use his mental endowments, as well as his property, in any harmless occupation or manner; but he has no right to use them so as to injure his fellow-citizens or to endanger the vital interests of society. Immunity in the mischievous use is as inconsistent with civil liberty as prohibition of the harmless use. . . .

The liberty protected is not the right to perpetrate acts of licentiousness, or any act inconsistent with the peace or safety of the State. Freedom of speech and press does not include the abuse of the power of tongue or pen, any more than freedom of other action includes an injurious use of one's occupation, business, or property.

The decisions in the war were full of similar language, of which a few specimens will suffice:

In this country it is one of our foundation stones of liberty that we may freely discuss anything we please, provided that that discussion is in conformity with law, or at least not in violation of it.

No American worthy of the name believes in anything else than free speech; but free speech means, not license, not counseling disobedience of the law. Free speech means that frank, free, full, and orderly expression which every man or woman in the land, citizen or alien, may engage in, in lawful and orderly fashion.

No one is permitted under the constitutional guaranties to commit a wrong or violate the law.

Just the same sort of distinction was made by Lord Kenyon during the French revolution:

The liberty of the press is dear to England. The licentiousness of the press is odious to England. The liberty of it can never be so well protected as by beating down the licentiousness.

This exasperated Sir James Fitzjames Stephen into the comment, "Hobbes is nearly the only writer who seems to me capable of using the word 'liberty' without talking nonsense."

A slightly more satisfactory view was adopted by Cooley, that the clauses guard against repressive measures by the several departments of government, but not against utterances which are a public offense, or which injure the reputation of individuals.

We understand liberty of speech and of the press to imply not only liberty to publish, but complete immunity from legal censure and punishment for the publication, so long as it is not harmful in its character, when tested by such standards as the law affords.

To a judge obliged to decide whether honest and able opposition to the continuation of a war is punishable, these generalizations furnish as much help as a woman forced, like Isabella in *Measure for Measure*, to choose between her brother's death and loss of honor, might obtain from the pious maxim, "Do right." What is abuse? What is license? What standards does the law afford? To argue that the federal Constitution does not prevent punishment for criminal utterances begs the whole question, for utterances within its protection are not crimes. If it only safeguarded lawful speech, Congress could escape its operation at any time by making any class of speech unlawful. Suppose, for example, that Congress declared any criticism of the particular administration in office to be a felony, punishable by ten years' imprisonment. Clearly, the Constitution must limit the power of Congress to create crimes. But how far does that limitation go?

Shall we say that the constitutional guaranties must be interpreted in the light of the contemporary common law; and that Congress and the state legislatures may punish as they please any speech that was criminal or tortious before 1791? We can all agree that the free speech clauses do not wipe out the common law as to obscenity, profanity, and defamation of individuals. But how about the common law of sedition and libels against the government? Was this left in full force by the First Amendment, although it was the biggest of all the legal limitations on discussion of public matters before the Revolution? No doubt conditions in 1791 must be considered, but they do not arbitrarily fix the division between lawful and unlawful speech for all time.

Clearly, we must look further and find a rational test of what is use and what is abuse. Saying that the line lies between them gets us nowhere. And "license" is too often "liberty" to the speaker, and what happens to be anathema to the judge.

One of the strongest reasons for the waywardness of trial judges during the war was their inability to get guidance from precedents. There were practically no satisfactory judicial discussions before 1917 about the meaning of the free speech clauses. The pre-war courts in construing such clauses did little more than place obvious cases on this or that side of the line. They told us, for instance, that libel and slander were actionable, or even punishable, that indecent books were criminal, that it was contempt to interfere with pending judicial proceedings, and that a permit could be required for street meetings; and on the other hand, that some criticism of the government must be allowed, that a temperate examination of a judge's opinion was not contempt, and that honest discussion of the merits of a painting caused no liability for damages. But when we asked where the line actually ran and how they knew on which side of it a given utterance belonged, we found little answer in their opinions.

Even frequently quoted statements by Justice Holmes in his first Espionage Act decisions are open to the same adverse criticism — they tell us that plainly unlawful utterances are, to be sure, unlawful:

> *The First Amendment . . . obviously was not intended to give im-*
> *munity for every possible use of language. . . . We venture to believe*
> *that neither Hamilton nor Madison, nor any other competent person*
> *then or later, ever supposed that to make criminal the counselling of*
> *a murder . . . would be an unconstitutional interference with free*
> *speech.*
>
> *The most stringent protection of free speech would not protect a*
> *man in falsely shouting fire in a theater and causing a panic.*

How about the man who gets up in a theater between the acts and informs the audience honestly, but perhaps mistakenly, that the fire exits are too few or locked? He is a much closer parallel to Frohwerk or Debs. How about James Russell Lowell when he counseled, not murder, but the cessation of murder, his name for war? The question whether such perplexing cases are within the First Amendment or not cannot be solved by the multiplication of obvious examples, but only by the development of a rational principle to mark the limits of constitutional protection.

"The gradual process of judicial inclusion and exclusion," which has served so well to define other clauses in the federal Constitution by blocking out concrete situations on each side of the line until the line itself becomes increasingly plain, was of very little use for the First Amendment before 1917. The pre-war cases were too few, too varied in their character, and often too easily solved to develop any definite boundary between lawful and unlawful speech.

Fortunately, we did get during the war years three very able judicial statements which take us far toward the ultimate solution of the problem of the limits of free speech, one by Judge Learned Hand in 1917 and two by Justice Holmes in 1919 . . .

For the moment, however, it may be worth while to forsake the purely judicial discussion of free speech, and obtain light upon its meaning from the history of the constitutional clauses and from the purpose free speech serves in social and political life.

The framers of the First Amendment make it plain that they regarded freedom of speech as very important; "absolutely necessary" is Luther Martin's phrase. But they say very little about its exact meaning. That should not surprise us if we recall our own vagueness about freedom of the seas. Men rarely define their inspirations until they are forced into doing so by sharp antagonism. Therefore, it is not until the Sedition Law of 1798 made the limits of liberty of the press a concrete and burning issue that we get much helpful expression of opinion on our problem. Before that time, however, we have a few important pieces of evidence to show that the words were used in the Constitution in a wide and liberal sense.

On October 26, 1774, the Continental Congress issued an address to the inhabitants of Quebec, declaring that the English colonists had five invaluable rights, representative government, trial by jury, liberty of the person, easy tenure of land, and freedom of the press:

> *The last right we shall mention regards the freedom of the press. The importance of this consists, besides the advancement of truth, science, morality and arts in general, in its diffusion of liberal sentiment on the administration of government, its ready communication of thoughts between subjects, and its consequential promotion of union among them, whereby oppressive officials are shamed or intimidated into more honorable and just modes of conducting affairs.*

In 1785 Virginia, which was the first state to insert a clause protecting the liberty of the press in its constitution (1776), enacted a statute drawn by Jefferson for Establishing Religious Freedom. This opened with a very broad principle of toleration: "Whereas, Almighty God hath created the mind free; that all attempts to influence it by temporal punishments or burthens, or by civil incapacitations, tend only to beget habits of hypocrisy and meanness." Though this relates specifically to religion, it shows the trend of men's thoughts, and the meaning which "liberty" had to Jefferson long before the bitter controversy of 1798.

Benjamin Franklin, in discussing the brief "freedom of speech" clause in the Pennsylvania Constitution of 1776, said in 1789 that if by the liberty of the press were to be understood merely the liberty of discussing the propriety of public measures and political opinions, let us have as much of it as you please. On the other hand, if it means liberty to calumniate another, there ought to be some limit.

The reason given by the Maryland convention of 1788 to the people for including a free speech clause in the proposed federal Bill of Rights was: "In prosecutions in the federal courts, for libels, the constitutional preservation of this great and fundamental right may prove invaluable."

The contemporaneous evidence in the passages just quoted shows that in the years before the First Amendment freedom of speech was conceived as giving a wide and genuine protection for all sorts of discussion of public matters. These various statements are, of course, absolutely inconsistent with any Blackstonian theory that liberty of the press forbids nothing except censorship. The men of 1791 went as far as Blackstone, and much farther.

If we apply Coke's test of statutory construction, and consider what mischief in the existing law the framers of the First Amendment wished to remedy by a new safeguard, we can be sure that it was not the censorship. This had expired in England in 1695, and in the colonies by 1725. They knew from books that it destroyed liberty of the press; and if they ever thought of its revival as within the range of practical possibilities, they must have regarded it as clearly prohibited by the First Amendment. But there was no need to go to all the trouble of pushing through a constitutional amendment just to settle an issue that had been dead for decades. What the framers did have plenty of reason to fear was an entirely different danger to political writers and speakers.

For years the government here and in England had substituted for the censorship rigorous and repeated prosecutions for seditious libel, which were directed against political discussion, and for years these prosecutions were opposed by liberal opinion and popular agitation. Primarily the controversy raged around two legal contentions of the great advocates for the defense, such as Erskine and Andrew Hamilton. They argued, first, that the jury and not the judge ought to decide whether the writing was seditious, and secondly, that the truth of the charge ought to prevent conviction. The real issue, however, lay much deeper. Two different views of the relation of rulers and people were in conflict. According to one view, the rulers were the superiors of the people, and therefore must not be subjected to any censure that would tend to diminish their authority. The people could not make adverse criticism in newspapers or pamphlets, but only through their lawful representatives in the legislature, who might be petitioned in an orderly manner. According to the other view, the rulers were agents and servants of the people, who might therefore find fault with their servants and discuss questions of their punishment or dismissal, and of governmental policy.

Under the first view, which was officially accepted until the close of the eighteenth century, developed the law of seditious libel. This was defined as "the intentional publication, without lawful excuse or justification, of written blame of any public man, or of the law, or of any institution established by law." There was no need to prove any intention on the part of the defendant to produce disaffection or excite an insurrection. It was enough if he intended to publish the blame, because it was unlawful in him merely to find fault with his masters and betters. Such, in the opinion of the best authorities, was the common law of sedition.

It is obvious that under this law liberty of the press was nothing more than absence of the censorship, as Blackstone said. All through the eighteenth century, however, there existed beside this definite legal meaning of liberty of the press, a definite popular meaning: the right of unrestricted discussion of public affairs. There can be no doubt that this was in a general way what freedom of speech meant to the framers of the Constitution. Thus Madison, who drafted the First Amendment, bases his explanation of it in 1799 on "the essential difference between the British Government and the American constitutions." In the United States the people and not the government possess the absolute sovereignty, and the legislature as well as the executive is under limitations of power. Hence, Congress is not free to punish anything which was criminal at English common law. A government which is "elective, limited and responsible" in all its branches may well be supposed to require "a greater freedom of animadversion" than might be tolerated by one that is composed of an irresponsible hereditary king and upper house, and an omnipotent legislature.

This contemporary testimony corroborates the conclusion of Professor Schofield:

> One of the objects of the Revolution was to get rid of the English common law on liberty of speech and of the press. . . . Liberty of the press as declared in the First Amendment, and the English common-law crime of sedition, cannot co-exist.

There are a few early judicial decisions to the contrary, but they ought not to weigh against the statements of Madison and the general temper of the time. These judges were surely wrong in holding as they did that sedition was a common-law crime in the federal courts, and in other respects they drew their inspiration from British precedents and the British bench instead of being in close contact with the new ideas of this country. "Indeed," as Senator Beveridge says, "some of them were more British than they were American." "Let a stranger go into our courts," wrote one observer, "and he would almost believe himself in the Court of the King's Bench." Great as was the service of these judges in establishing the common law as to private rights, their testimony as to its place in public affairs is of much less value than the other contemporary evidence of the men who sat in the conventions and argued over the adoption of the Constitution. The judges forgot the truth emphasized by Maitland: "The law of a nation can only be studied in relation to the whole national life." I must therefore strongly dissent, with Justice Holmes, from the position sometimes taken in arguments on the Espionage Act, that the founders of our government left the common law as to seditious libel in force and merely intended by the First Amendment "to limit the new government's statutory powers to penalize utterances as seditious, to those which were seditious under the then accepted common-law rule." The founders had seen seventy English prosecutions for libel since 1760, and fifty convictions under that common-law rule, which made conviction easy. That rule had been detested in this country ever since it was repudiated by jury and populace in the famous trial of Peter Zenger, the New York printer, the account of which went through fourteen editions before 1791. The close relation between the Zenger trial and the prosecutions under George III in England and America is shown by the quotations on reprints of the trial and the dedication of the 1784 London edition to Erskine, as well as by reference to Zenger in the discussions preceding the First Amendment. Nor was this the only colonial sedition prosecution under the common law, and many more were threatened. All the American cases before 1791 prove that our common law of sedition was exactly like that of England, and it would be extraordinary if the First Amendment enacted the English sedition law of that time, which was repudiated by every American and every liberal Englishman, and altered through Fox's Libel Act by Parliament itself in the very next year, 1792. We might well fling at the advocates of this common law view the challenge of Randolph of Roanoke, "whether the common law of libels which attaches to this Constitution be the doctrine laid down by Lord Mansfield, or that which has immortalized Mr. Fox?" The First Amendment was written by men to whom Wilkes and Junius were household words, who intended to wipe out the common law of sedition, and make further prosecutions for criticism of the government, without any incitement to law-breaking, forever impossible in the United States of America.

It must not be forgotten that the controversy over liberty of the press was a conflict between two views of government, that the law of sedition was a product of the view that the government was master, and that the American Revolution transformed into a working reality the second view that the government was servant, and therefore subjected to blame from its master, the people. Consequently, the words of Sir James Fitzjames Stephen about this second view have a vital application to American law.

> To those who hold this view fully and carry it out to all its consequences there can be no such offense as sedition. There may indeed be breaches of the peace which may destroy or endanger life, limb, or property, and there may be incitements to such offenses, but no imaginable censure of the government, short of a censure which has an immediate tendency to produce such a breach of the peace, ought to be regarded as criminal.

In short, the framers of the First Amendment sought to preserve the fruits of the old victory abolishing the censorship, and to achieve a new victory abolishing sedition prosecutions.

The repudiation by the constitutions of the English common law of sedition, which was also the common law of the American colonies, has been obscured by some judicial retention of the two technical incidents of the old law after the adoption of the free speech clauses. Many judges, rightly or wrongly, continued to pass on the criminality of the writing and to reject its truth as a defense, until statutes or new constitutional provisions embodying the popular view on these two points were enacted. Doubtless, a jury will protect a popular attack on the government better than a judge, and the admission of truth as a defense lessens the evils of suppression. These procedural changes help to substitute the modern view of rulers for the old view, but they are not enough by themselves to establish freedom of speech. Juries can suppress much-needed political discussion in times of intolerance, so long as the substantive common law or a statute defines criminal utterances in sweeping and loose terms. Sedition prosecutions went on with shameful severity in England after Fox's Libel Act had given the jury power to determine criminality. The American Sedition Act of 1798, which President Wilson declares to have "cut perilously near the root of freedom of speech and of the press," entrusted criminality to the jury and admitted truth as a defense. On the other hand, freedom of speech might exist without these two technical safeguards.

The essential question is not, who is judge of the criminality of an utterance, but what is the test of its criminality. The common law and the Sedition Act of 1798 made the test blame of the government and its officials, because to bring them into disrepute tended to overthrow the state. The real issue in every free speech controversy is this: whether the state can punish all words which have some tendency, however remote, to bring about acts in violation of law, or only words which directly incite to acts in violation of law.

If words do not become criminal until they have "an immediate tendency to produce a breach of the peace," there is no need for a law of sedition, since the ordinary standards of criminal solicitation and attempt apply. Under those standards the words must bring the speaker's unlawful intention reasonably near to success. Such a limited power to punish utterances rarely satisfies the zealous in times of excitement like a war. They realize that all condemnation of the war or of conscription may conceivably lead to active resistance or insubordination. Is it not better to kill the serpent in the egg? All writings that have even a remote tendency to hinder the war must be suppressed.

Such has always been the argument of the opponents of free speech. And the most powerful weapon in their hands, since the abolition of the censorship, is this doctrine of indirect causation, under which words can be punished for a supposed bad tendency long before there is any probability that they will break out into unlawful acts. Closely related to it is the doctrine of constructive intent, which regards the intent of the defendant to cause violence as immaterial so long as he intended to write the words, or else presumes the violent intent from the bad tendency of the words on the ground that a man is presumed to intend the consequences of his acts. When rulers are allowed to possess these weapons, they can by the imposition of severe sentences create an *ex post facto* censorship of the press. The transference of that censorship from the judge to the jury is indeed important when the attack on the government which is prosecuted expresses a widespread popular sentiment, but the right to jury trial is of much less value in times of war or threatened disorder when the herd instinct runs strong, if the opinion of the defendant is highly objectionable to the majority of the population, or even to the particular class of men from whom or by whom the jury are drawn.

Under Charles II trial by jury was a blind and cruel system. During the last part of the reign of George III it was, to say the least, quite as severe as the severest judge without a jury could have been. The revolutionary tribunal during the Reign of Terror tried by a jury. It is worth our frank consideration, whether in a country where the doctrine of indirect causation is recognized by the courts twelve small property-holders, who have been through an uninterrupted series of patriotic campaigns and are sufficiently middle-aged to be in no personal danger of compulsory military service, are fitted to decide whether there is a tendency to obstruct the draft in the writings of a pacifist, who also happens to be a Socialist and in sympathy with the Russian Revolution. This, however, is perhaps a problem for the psychologist rather than the lawyer.

Another significant fact in sedition prosecutions is the well-known probability that juries will acquit, after the excitement is over, for words used during the excitement, which are as bad in their tendency as other writings prosecuted and severely punished during the critical period. This was very noticeable during the reign of George III. It is also interesting to find two juries in different parts of the country differing as to the criminal character of similar publications or even the same publication. Thus Leigh Hunt was acquitted for writing an article, for the printing of which John Drakard was convicted. The acquittal of Scott Nearing and the conviction by the same jury of the American Socialist Society for publishing his book form an interesting parallel.

The manner in which juries in time of excitement may be used to suppress writings in opposition to the government, if bad tendency is recognized as a test of criminality, is illustrated by the numerous British sedition trials during the wars with Revolutionary France and Napoleon, after the passage of Fox's Libel Act. For instance, in the case just mentioned,

Drakard was convicted for printing an article on the shameful amount of flogging in the army, under a charge in which Baron Wood emphasized the formidable foe with whom England was fighting, and the general belief that Napoleon was using the British press to carry out his purpose of securing her downfall.

> *It is to be feared, there are in this country many who are endeavoring to aid and assist him in his projects, by crying down the establishment of the country, and breeding hatred against the government. Whether that is the source from whence the paper in question springs, I cannot say, but I advise you to consider whether it has not that tendency. You will consider whether it contains a fair discussion — whether it has not a manifest tendency to create disaffection in the country and prevent men enlisting into the army — whether it does not tend to induce the soldier to desert from the service of his country. And what considerations can be more awful than these? . . .*
>
> *The House of Parliament is the proper place for the discussion of subjects of this nature . . . It is said that we have a right to discuss the acts of our legislature. That would be a large permission indeed. Is there, gentlemen, to be a power in the people to counteract the acts of the parliament, and is the libeller to come and make the people dissatisfied with the government under which he lives? This is not to be permitted to any man — it is unconstitutional and seditious.*

The same emphasis on bad tendency appears in Lord Ellenborough's charge at Leigh Hunt's trial, although it failed to secure his conviction.

> *Can you conceive that the exhibition of the words "One Thousand Lashes," with strokes underneath to attract attention, could be for any other purpose than to excite disaffection? Could it have any other tendency than that of preventing men from entering the army?*

The same desire to nip revolution in the bud was shown by the Scotch judges who secured the conviction of Muir and Palmer for advocating reform of the rotten boroughs which chose the House of Commons and the extension of the franchise, sentences of transportation for seven and fourteen years being imposed.

> *The right of universal suffrage, the subjects of this country never enjoyed; and were they to enjoy it, they would not long enjoy either liberty or a free constitution. You will, therefore, consider whether telling the people that they have a just right to what would unquestionably be tantamount to a total subversion of this constitution, is such a writing as any person is entitled to compose, to print, and to publish.*

American sentiment about sedition trials was decisively shown by an expedition to New South Wales to rescue Muir, a sort of reverse deportation.

In the light of such prosecutions it is plain that the most vital indication that the popular definition of liberty of the press, unpunishable criticism of officials and laws, has become a reality, is the disappearance of these doctrines of bad tendency and presumptive intent. In Great Britain they lingered until liberalism triumphed in 1832, but in this country they disappeared with the adoption of the free speech clauses.

The revival of those doctrines is a sure symptom of an attack upon the liberty of the press.

Only once in our history prior to 1917 has an attempt been made to apply these doctrines. In 1798 the impending war with France, the spread of revolutionary doctrines by foreigners in our midst, and the spectacle of the disastrous operation of those doctrines abroad — facts that have a familiar sound today — led to the enactment of the Alien and Sedition Laws. The Alien Law allowed the President to compel the departure of aliens whom he judged dangerous to the peace and safety of the United States, or suspected, on reasonable grounds, of treasonable or secret machinations against our government. The Sedition Law punished false, scandalous, and malicious writings against the government, either House of Congress, or the President, if published with intent to defame any of them, or to excite against them the hatred of the people, or to stir up sedition or to excite resistance of law, or to aid any hostile designs of any foreign nation against the United States. The maximum penalty was a fine of two thousand dollars and two years' imprisonment. Truth was a defense, and the jury had power to determine criminality as under Fox's Libel Act. Despite the inclusion of the two legal rules for which reformers had contended, and the requirement of an actual intention to cause over injury, the Sedition Act was bitterly resented as invading the liberty of the press. Its constitutionality was assailed on that ground by Jefferson, who pardoned all prisoners when he became President; Congress eventually repaid all the fines; and popular indignation at the Act and the prosecutions wrecked the Federalist party. In those prosecutions words were once more made punishable for their judicially supposed bad tendency, and the judges reduced the test of intent to a fiction by inferring the bad intent from this bad tendency.

Whether or not the Sedition Act was unconstitutional, and on that question Jefferson seems right, it surely defeated the fundamental policy of the First Amendment, the open discussion of public affairs. Like the British trials, the American sedition cases showed, as Professor Schofield demonstrates, "the great danger . . . that men will be fined and imprisoned, under the guise of being punished for their bad motives, or bad intent and ends, simply because the powers that be do not agree with their opinions, and spokesmen of minorities may be terrorized and silenced when they are most needed by the community and most useful to it, and when they stand most in need of the protection of the law against a hostile, arrogant majority." When the Democrats got into power, a common-law prosecution for seditious libel was brought in New York against a Federalist who had attacked Jefferson. Hamilton conducted the defense in the name of the liberty of the press. This testimony from Jefferson and Hamilton, the leaders of both parties, leaves the Blackstonian interpretation of free speech in America without a leg to stand on. And the brief attempt of Congress and the Federalist judges to revive the crime of sedition had proved so disastrous that it was not repeated during the next century.

The lesson of the prosecutions for sedition in Great Britain and the United States during this revolutionary period, that the most essential element of free speech is the rejection of bad tendency as the test of a criminal utterance, was never more clearly recognized than in Jefferson's preamble to the Virginia Act for establishing Religious Freedom. His words about religious liberty hold good of political and speculative freedom, and the portrayal of human life in every form of art.

> *To suffer the civil Magistrate to intrude his powers into the field of opinion, and to restrain the profession or propagation of principles on supposition of their ill tendency, is a dangerous fallacy, which at once destroys all religious liberty, because he being of course judge of that tendency, will make his opinions the rule of judgment, and approve or condemn the sentiments of others only as they shall square with or differ from his own.*

Although the free speech clauses were directed primarily against the sedition prosecutions of the immediate past, it must not be thought that they would permit unlimited previous restraint. They must also be interpreted in the light of more remote history. The framers of those clauses did not invent the conception of freedom of speech as a result of their own experience of the last few years. The idea had been gradually molded in men's minds by centuries of conflict. It was the product of a people of whom the framers were merely the mouthpiece. Its significance was not fixed by their personality, but was the endless expression of a civilization. It was formed out of past resentment against the royal control of the press under the Tudors, against the Star Chamber and the pillory, against the Parliamentary censorship which Milton condemned in his *Areopagitica*, by recollections of heavy newspaper taxation, by hatred of the suppression of thought which went on vigorously on the Continent during the eighteenth century. Blackstone's views also had undoubted influence to bar out previous restraint. The censor is the most dangerous of all the enemies of liberty of the press, and ought not to exist in this country unless made necessary by extraordinary perils.

Moreover, the meaning of the First Amendment did not crystallize in 1791. The framers would probably have been horrified at the thought of protecting books by Darwin or Bernard Shaw, but "liberty of speech" is no more confined to the speech they thought permissible than "commerce" in another clause is limited to the sailing vessels and horse-drawn vehicles of 1787. Into the making of the constitutional conception of free speech have gone, not only men's bitter experience of the censorship and sedition prosecutions before 1791, but also the subsequent development of the law of fair comment in civil defamation, and the philosophical speculations of John Stuart Mill. Justice Holmes phrases the thought with even more than his habitual felicity. "The provisions of the Constitution are not mathematical formulas having their essence in their form; they are organic living institutions transplanted from English soil."

It is now clear that the First Amendment fixes limits upon the power of Congress to restrict speech either by a censorship or by a criminal statute, and if the Espionage Act exceeds those limits it is unconstitutional. It is sometimes argued that the Constitution gives Congress the power to declare war, raise armies, and support a navy, that one provision of the Constitution cannot be used to break down another provision, and consequently freedom of speech cannot be invoked to break down the war power. I would reply that the First Amendment is just as much a part of the Constitution as the war clauses, and that it is equally accurate to say that the war clauses cannot be invoked to break down freedom of speech. The truth is that all provisions of the Constitution must be construed together so as to limit each other. In a war as in peace, this process of mutual adjustment must include the Bill of Rights. There are those who believe that the Bill of Rights can be set aside in war time at the uncontrolled will of the government. The first ten amendments were drafted by men who had just been through a war. The Third and Fifth Amendments expressly apply in war. A majority of the Supreme Court declared the war power of Congress to be restricted by the Bill of Rights in Ex parte *Milligan*. If the First Amendment is to mean anything, it must restrict powers which are expressly granted by the Constitution to Congress, since Congress has no other powers. It must apply to those activities of government which are most liable to interfere with free discussion, namely, the postal service and the conduct of war.

The true meaning of freedom of speech seems to be this. One of the most important purposes of society and government is the discovery and spread of truth on subjects of general concern. This is possible only through absolutely unlimited discussion, for, as Bagehot points out, once force is thrown into the argument, it becomes a matter of chance whether it is thrown on the false side or the true, and truth loses all its natural advantage in the contest. Nevertheless, there are other purposes of government, such as order, the training of the young, protection against external aggression. Unlimited discussion sometimes interferes with these purposes, which must then be balanced against freedom of speech, but freedom of speech ought to weigh very heavily in the scale. The First Amendment gives binding force to this principle of political wisdom.

Or to put the matter another way, it is useless to define free speech by talk about rights. The agitator asserts his constitutional right to speak, the government asserts its constitutional right to wage war. The result is a deadlock. Each side takes the position of the man who was arrested for swinging his arms and hitting another in the nose, and asked the judge if he did not have a right to swing his arms in a free country. "Your right to swing your arms ends just where the other man's nose begins." To find the boundary line of any right, we must get behind rules of law to human facts. In our problem, we must regard the desires and needs of the individual human being who wants to speak and those of the great group of human beings among whom he speaks. That is, in technical language, there are individual interests and social interests, which must be balanced against each other, if they conflict, in order to determine which interest shall be sacrificed under the circumstances and which shall be protected and become the foundation of a legal right. It must never be forgotten that the balancing cannot be properly done unless all the interests involved are adequately ascertained, and the great evil of all this talk about rights is that each side is so busy denying the other's claim to rights that it entirely overlooks the human desires and needs behind that claim.

The rights and powers of the Constitution, aside from the portions which create the machinery of the federal system, are largely means of protecting important individual and social interests, and because of this necessity of balancing such interests the clauses cannot be construed with absolute literalness. The Fourteenth Amendment and the obligation of contracts clause, maintaining important individual interests, are modified by the police power of the states, which protects health and other social interests. The Thirteenth Amendment is subject to many implied exceptions, so that temporary involuntary servitude is permitted to secure social interests in the construction of roads, the prevention of vagrancy, the training of the militia or national army. It is common to rest these implied exceptions to the Bill of Rights upon the ground that they existed in 1791 and long before, but a less arbitrary explanation is desirable. Not everything old is good. Thus the antiquity of peonage does not constitute it an exception to the Thirteenth Amendment; it is not now demanded by any strong social interest. It is significant that the social interest in shipping which formerly required the compulsory labor of articled sailors is no longer recognized in the United States as sufficiently important to outweigh the individual interest in free locomotion and choice of occupation. Even treaties providing for the apprehension in our ports of deserting foreign seamen have been abrogated by the La Follette Seamen's Act. The Bill of Rights does not crystallize antiquity. It seems better to say that long usage does not create an exception to the absolute language of the Constitution, but demonstrates the importance of the social interest behind the exception.

The First Amendment protects two kinds of interests in free speech. There is an individual interest, the need of many men to express their opinions on matters vital to them if life is to be worth living, and a social interest in the attainment of truth, so that the country may not only adopt the wisest course of action but carry it out in the wisest way. This social interest is especially important in war time. Even after war has been declared there is bound to be a confused mixture of good and bad arguments in its support, and a wide difference of opinion as to its objects. Truth can be sifted out from falsehood only if the government is vigorously and constantly cross-examined, so that the fundamental issues of the struggle may be clearly defined, and the war may not be diverted to improper ends, or conducted with an undue sacrifice of life and liberty, or prolonged after its just purposes are accomplished. Legal proceedings prove that an opponent makes the best cross-examiner. Consequently it is a disastrous mistake to limit criticism to those who favor the war. Men bitterly hostile to it may point out evils in its management like the secret treaties, which its supporters have been too busy to unearth. If a free canvassing of the aims of the war by its opponents is crushed by the menace of long imprisonment, such evils, even though made public in one or two newspapers, may not come to the attention of those who had power to counteract them until too late.

The history of the years between 1914 and 1919 shows how the objects of a war may change completely during its progress, and it is well that those objects should be steadily reformulated under the influence of open discussion not only by those who demand a military victory, but by pacifists who take a different view of the national welfare. Further argument for the existence of this social interest becomes unnecessary if we recall the national value of the opposition in former wars.

The great trouble with most judicial construction of the Espionage Act is that this social interest has been ignored and free speech has been regarded as merely an individual interest, which must readily give way like other personal desires the moment it interferes with the social interest in national safety. The judge [Oliver Wendell Holmes, Jr.] who has done most to bring social interests into legal thinking said years ago, "I think that the judges themselves have failed adequately to recognize their duty of weighing considerations of social advantage. The duty is inevitable, and the result of the often proclaimed judicial aversion to deal with such considerations is simply to leave the very ground and foundation of judgments inarticulate and often unconscious." The failure of the courts in the past to formulate any principle for drawing a boundary line around the right of free speech not only threw the judges into the difficult questions of the Espionage Act without any well-considered standard of criminality, but also allowed some of them to impose standards of their own and fix the line at a point which makes all opposition to this or any future war impossible. For example:

> *No man should be permitted, by deliberate act, or even unthinkingly, to do that which will in any way detract from the efforts which the United States is putting forth or serve to postpone for a single moment the early coming of the day when the success of our arms shall be a fact.*

The true boundary line of the First Amendment can be fixed only when Congress and the courts realize that the principle on which speech is classified as lawful or unlawful involves the balancing against each other of two very important social interests, in public safety and in the search for truth. Every reasonable attempt should be made to maintain both interests unimpaired, and the great interest in free speech should be sacrificed only when the interest in public safety is really imperiled, and not, as most men believe, when it is barely conceivable that it may be slightly affected. In war time, therefore, speech should be unrestricted by the censorship or by punishment, unless it is clearly liable to cause direct and dangerous interference with the conduct of the war.

Thus our problem of locating the boundary line of free speech is solved. It is fixed close to the point where words will give rise to unlawful acts. We cannot define the right of free speech with the precision of the Rule against Perpetuities or the Rule in Shelley's Case, because it involves national policies which are much more flexible than private property, but we can establish a workable principle of classification in this method of balancing and this broad test of certain danger. There is a similar balancing in the determination of what is "due process of law." We can insist upon various procedural safeguards which make it more probable that a tribunal will give the value of open discussion its proper weight in the balance. Fox's Libel Act is such a safeguard . . . And we can with certitude declare that the First Amendment forbids the punishment of words merely for their injurious tendencies. The history of the Amendment and the political function of free speech corroborate each other and make this conclusion plain.

1894—1915

REGENTS OF THE UNIVERSITY OF WISCONSIN

Bronze Tablet

In 1894 Richard T. Ely, Professor of Economics at the University of Wisconsin, was attacked by Oliver E. Wells, a state official, as an heretical and seditious teacher who had interfered in a strike of the printing trade. A hearing held by the Board of Regents of the University of Wisconsin not only cleared Dr. Ely but also resulted in a statement of principle. In 1910 the final sentence of this statement was ordered placed on a bronze tablet set in the wall of Bascom Hall, the main building of the university. The tablet was dedicated in 1915.

WHATEVER MAY BE THE LIMITATIONS WHICH TRAMMEL INQUIRY ELSEWHERE, WE BELIEVE THAT THE GREAT STATE UNIVERSITY OF WISCONSIN SHOULD EVER ENCOURAGE THAT CONTINUAL AND FEARLESS SIFTING AND WINNOWING BY WHICH ALONE THE TRUTH CAN BE FOUND.

1892

KARL PEARSON

The Scope and Method of Science

In November 1890 a young man of thirty-three named Karl Pearson, a fighter against what seemed to him misdirected authority, was appointed Lecturer in Geometry at Gresham College, in London, founded by that Sir Thomas Gresham who gave his name to "Gresham's Law." Determined to modernize the foundation, Pearson delivered in March and April, 1891, the lectures which he later published as The Grammar of Science *in 1892 (revised in 1900 and, partially, in 1911). This great statement of the theory of scientific investigation had an influence as far away as the University of Kharkov, where, one of the professors informs us, it was, in his experience, "the first attempt we had met to construct a 'Weltanschauung' not on any kind of dogmatic basis, but on reason." The first chapter, here reprinted in part, remained virtually unaltered in the various editions. Pearson begins by pointing to the rapidity of change in modern society, a fact which throws special responsibility upon the citizen to pass judgment upon facts objectively; he then argues that "the classification of facts, the recognition of their sequence and relative significance is the function of science," says that training in science is an "education specially fitted to promote sound citizenship," and insists that "the unity of all science consists alone in its method, not in its material." A section on the "scope of science" argues that the goal of science is "nothing short of the complete interpretation of the universe," but says also that the goal is "an ideal one — it marks the direction in which we move and strive, but never a stage we shall actually reach." At this point in the argument our selections begin. Besides the omissions indicated by the usual sign (. . .), almost all of Pearson's footnotes have been omitted. The text is that of the 1900 edition.*

Science and Metaphysics

NOW I WANT TO DRAW THE READER'S ATTENTION to two results which flow from the above considerations, namely: that the material of science is co-extensive with the whole life, physical and mental, of the universe, and furthermore that the limits to our perception of the universe are only apparent, not real. It is no exaggeration to say that the universe was not the same for our great-grandfathers as it is for us, and that in all probability it will be utterly different for our great-grandchildren. The universe is a variable quantity, which depends upon the keenness and structure of our organs of sense, and upon the fineness of our powers and instruments of observation. We [should] see more clearly the important bearing of this latter remark [were we to discuss more closely] how the universe is largely the construction of each individual mind. For the present we must briefly consider the former remark, which defines the unlimited scope of science. To say that there are certain fields — for example, *metaphysics* — from which science is excluded, wherein its methods have no application, is merely to say that the rules of methodical observation and the laws of logical thought do not apply to the facts, if any, which lie within such fields. These fields, if indeed such exist, must lie outside any intelligible definition which can be given of the word *knowledge*. If there are facts, and sequences to be observed among those facts, then we have all the requisites of scientific classification and knowledge. If there are no facts, or no sequences to be observed among them, then the possibility of *all* knowledge disappears. The greatest assumption of everyday life — the inference which the metaphysicians tell us is wholly beyond science — namely, that other beings have consciousness as well as ourselves, seems to have just as much or as little *scientific* validity as the statement that an earth-grown apple would fall to the ground if carried to the planet of another star. Both are beyond the range of experimental demonstration, but to assume uniformity in the characteristics of brain "matter" under certain conditions seems as scientific as to assume uniformity in the characteristics of stellar "matter." Both are only working hypotheses and valuable in so far as they simplify our description of the universe. Yet the distinction between science and metaphysics is often insisted upon, and not unadvisedly, by the devotees of both. If we take any group of physical or biological facts — say, for example, electrical phenomena or the development of the ovum — we shall find that, though physicists or biologists may differ to some extent in their measurements or in their hypotheses, yet in the fundamental principles and sequences the professors of each individual science are in practical agreement among themselves. A similar if not yet so complete agreement is rapidly springing up in both mental and social science, where the facts are more difficult to classify and the bias of individual opinion is much stronger. Our more thorough classification, however, of the facts of human development, our more accurate knowledge of the early history of human societies, of primitive customs, laws, and religions, our application of the principle of natural selection to man and his communities, are converting anthropology, folklore, sociology, and psychology into true sciences. We begin to see indisputable sequences in groups of both mental and social facts. The causes which favour the growth or decay of human societies become more obvious and more the subject of scientific investigation. Mental and social facts are thus not beyond the range of scientific treatment, but their classification has not been so complete, nor for obvious reasons so unprejudiced, as those of physical or biological phenomena.

The case is quite different with metaphysics and those other supposed branches of human knowledge which claim exemption from scientific control. Either they are based on an accurate classification of facts, or they are not. But if their classification of the facts were accurate, the application of the scientific method ought to lead their professors to a practically identical system. Now one of the idiosyncrasies of metaphysicians lies in this: that each metaphysician has his own system, which to a large extent excludes that of his predecessors and colleagues. Hence we must conclude that metaphysics are built either on air or on quicksands — either they start from no foundation in facts at all, or the superstructure has been raised before a basis has been found in the accurate classification of facts. I want to lay special stress on this point. There is no short cut to truth, no way to gain a knowledge of the universe except through the gateway of scientific method. The hard and stony path of classifying facts and reasoning upon them is the only way to ascertain truth. It is the reason and not the imagination which must ultimately be appealed to. The poet may give us in sublime language an account of the origin and purport of the universe, but in the end it will not satisfy our æsthetic judgment, our idea of harmony and beauty, like the few facts which the scientist may venture to tell us in the same field. The one will agree with all our experiences past and present, the other is sure, sooner or later, to contradict our observation because it propounds a dogma, where we are yet far from knowing the whole truth. Our æsthetic judgment demands harmony between the representation and the represented, and in this sense science is often more artistic than modern art.

The poet is a valued member of the community, for he is known to be a poet; his value will increase as he grows to recognise the deeper insight into nature with which modern science provides him. The metaphysician is a poet, often a very great one, but unfortunately he is not known to be a poet, because he strives to clothe his poetry in the language of reason, and hence it follows that he is liable to be a dangerous member of the community. The danger at the present time that metaphysical dogmas may check scientific research is, perhaps, not very great. The day has gone by when the Hegelian philosophy threatened to strangle infant science in Germany; — that it begins to languish at Oxford is a proof that it is practically dead in the country of its birth. The day has gone by when philosophical or theological dogmas of any kind can throw back for generations the progress of scientific investigation. There is no restriction now on research in any field, or on the publication of the truth when it has been reached. But there is nevertheless a danger which we cannot afford to disregard, a danger which retards the spread of scientific knowledge among the unenlightened, and which flatters obscurantism by discrediting the scientific method. There is a certain school of thought which finds the laborious process by which science reaches truth too irksome; the temperament of this school is such that it demands a short and easy cut to knowledge, where knowledge can only be gained, if at all, by the long and patient toiling of many groups of workers, perhaps through several centuries. There are various fields at the present day wherein mankind is ignorant, and the honest course for us is simply to confess our ignorance. This ignorance may arise from the want of any proper classification of facts, or because supposed facts are themselves inconsistent, unreal creations of untrained minds. But because this ignorance is frankly admitted by science, an attempt is made to fence off these fields as ground which science cannot profitably till, to shut them up as a preserve whereon science has no business to trespass. Wherever science has succeeded in ascertaining the truth, there, according to the school we have referred to, are the "legitimate problems of science." Wherever science is yet ignorant, there, we are told, its method is inapplicable; there some other relation than cause and effect (than the same sequence recurring with the like grouping of phenomena), some new but undefined relationship rules. In these fields, we are told, problems become philosophical and can only be treated by the method of philosophy. The philosophical method is opposed to the scientific method; and here, I think, the danger I have referred to arises. We have defined the scientific method to consist in the orderly classification of facts followed by the recognition of their relationship and recurring sequences. The scientific judgment is the judgment based upon this recognition and free from personal bias. If this were the philosophical method there would be no need of further discussion, but as we are told the subject-matter of philosophy is not the "legitimate problem of science," the two methods are presumably not identical. Indeed the philosophical method seems based upon an analysis which does not start with the classification of facts, but reaches its judgments by some obscure process of internal cogitation. It is therefore dangerously liable to the influence of individual bias; it results, as experience shows us, in an needless number of competing and contradictory systems. It is because the so-called philosophical method does not, when different individuals approach the same range of facts, lead, like the scientific, to practical unanimity of judgment, that science, rather than philosophy, offers the better training for modern citizenship.

The Ignorance of Science

It must not be supposed that science for a moment denies the existence of some of the problems which have hitherto been classed as philosophical or metaphysical. On the contrary, it recognises that a great variety of physical and biological phenomena lead directly to these problems. But it asserts that the methods hitherto applied to these problems have been futile, because they have been unscientific. The classifications of facts hitherto made by the system-mongers have been hopelessly inadequate or hopelessly prejudiced. Until the scientific study of psychology, both by observation and experiment, has advanced immensely beyond its present limits — and this may take generations of work — science can only answer to the great majority of "metaphysical" problems, "I am ignorant." Meanwhile it is idle to be impatient or to indulge in system-making. The cautious and laborious classification of facts must have proceeded much further than at present before the time will be ripe for drawing conclusions.

Science stands now with regard to the problems of life and mind in much the same position as it stood with regard to cosmical problems in the seventeenth century. Then the system-mongers were the theologians, who declared that cosmical problems were not the "legitimate problems of science." It was vain for Galilei to assert that the theologians' classification of facts was hopelessly inadequate. In solemn congregation assembled they settled that: —

> *"The doctrine that the earth is neither the centre of the universe nor immovable, but moves even with a daily rotation, is absurd, and both philosophically and theologically false, and at the least an error of faith."*

It took nearly two hundred years to convince the whole theological world that cosmical problems were the legitimate problems of science and science alone, for in 1819 the books of Galilei, Copernicus, and Keppler were still upon the index of forbidden books, and not till 1822 was a decree issued allowing books teaching the motion of the earth about the sun to be printed and published in Rome!

I have cited this memorable example of the absurdity which arises from trying to pen science into a limited field of thought, because it seems to me exceedingly suggestive of what must follow again, if any attempt, philosophical or theological, be made to define the "legitimate problems of science." Wherever there is the slightest possibility for the human mind to *know*, there is a legitimate problem of science. Outside the field of actual knowledge can only lie a region of the vaguest opinion and imagination, to which unfortunately men too often, but still with decreasing prevalence, pay higher respect than to knowledge.

We must here investigate a little more closely what the man of science means when he says, *"Here I am ignorant."* In the first place, he does not mean that the method of science is necessarily inapplicable, and accordingly that some other method is to be sought for. In the next place, if the ignorance really arises from the inadequacy of the scientific method, then we may be quite sure that no other method whatsoever will reach the truth. The ignorance of science means the enforced ignorance of mankind. I should be sorry myself to assert that there is any field of either mental or physical perceptions which science may not in the long course of centuries enlighten. Who can give us the assurance that the fields already occupied by science are alone those in which knowledge is possible? Who, in the words of Galilei, is willing to set limits to the human intellect? It is true that this view is not held by several leading scientists, both in this country and Germany. They are not content with saying, "We *are* ignorant," but they add, with regard to certain classes of facts, "Mankind must *always* be ignorant." Thus in England Professor Huxley has invented the term *Agnostic*, not so much for those who are ignorant as for those who limit the possibility of knowledge in certain fields. In Germany Professor E. du Bois-Reymond has raised the cry, *"Ignorabimus"* ("We shall be ignorant"), and both his brother and he have undertaken the difficult task of demonstrating that with regard to certain problems human knowledge is impossible. We must, however, note that in these cases we are not concerned with the limitation of the scientific method, but with the denial of the possibility that any method whatever can lead to knowledge. Now I venture to think that there is great danger in this cry, "We *shall* be ignorant." To cry "We are ignorant" is safe and healthy, but the attempt to demonstrate an endless futurity of ignorance appears a modesty which approaches despair. Conscious of the past great achievements and the present restless activity of science, may we not do better to accept as our watchword that sentence of Galilei: "Who is willing to set limits to the human intellect?" — interpreting it by what evolution has taught us of the continual growth of man's intellectual powers . . .

Do we now know how the stars influence human lives, or how witches turn milk blue? Not in the least. We have learnt to look upon the facts themselves as unreal, as vain imaginings of the untrained human mind; we have learnt that they could not be described scientifically because they involved notions which were in themselves contradictory and absurd. With alchemy the case was somewhat different. Here a false classification of real facts was combined with inconsistent sequences — that is, sequences not deduced by a rational method. So soon as science entered the field of alchemy with a true classification and a true method, alchemy was converted into chemistry and became an important branch of human knowledge. Now it will, I think, be found that the fields of inquiry, where science has not yet penetrated and where the scientist still confesses ignorance, are very like the alchemy, astrology, and witchcraft of the Middle Ages. Either they involve facts which are in themselves unreal — conceptions which are self-contradictory and absurd, and therefore incapable of analysis by the scientific or any other method, — or, on the other hand, our ignorance arises from an inadequate classification and a neglect of scientific method . . .

If on inquiry we ascertain that the facts cannot possibly be of this class, we must then remember that it may require long ages of increasing toil and investigation before the classification of the facts can be so complete that science can express a definite judgment on their relationship. Let us suppose that the Emperor Karl V. had said to the learned of his day: "I want a method by which I can send a message in a few seconds to that new world, which my mariners take weeks in reaching. Put your heads together and solve the problem." Would they not undoubtedly have replied that the problem was impossible? To propose it would have seemed as ridiculous to them as the suggestion that science should straightway solve many problems of life and mind seems to the learned of to-day. It required centuries spent in the discovery and classification of new facts before the Atlantic cable became a possibility. It may require the like or even a longer time to unriddle those psychical and biological enigmas to which I have referred; but he who declares that they can never be solved by the scientific method is to my mind as rash as the man of the early sixteenth century would have been had he declared it utterly impossible that the problem of talking across the Atlantic Ocean should ever be solved.

The Wide Domain of Science

If I have put the case of science at all correctly, the reader will have recognised that modern science does much more than demand that it shall be left in undisturbed possession of what the theologian and metaphysician please to term its "legitimate field." It claims that the whole range of phenomena, mental as well as physical — the entire universe — is its field. It asserts that the scientific method is the sole gateway to the whole region of knowledge. The word science is here used in no narrow sense, but applies to all reasoning about facts which proceeds, from their accurate classification, to the appreciation of their relationship and sequence. The touchstone of science is the universal validity of its results for all normally constituted and duly instructed minds. Because the glitter of the great metaphysical systems becomes dross when tried by this touchstone, we are compelled to classify them as interesting works of the imagination, and not as solid contributions to human knowledge.

Although science claims the whole universe as its field, it must not be supposed that it has reached, or ever can reach, complete knowledge in every department. Far from this, it confesses that its ignorance is more widely extended than its knowledge. In this very confession of ignorance, however, it finds a safeguard for future progress. Science cannot give its consent to man's development being some day again checked by the barriers which dogma and myth are ever erecting round territory that science has not yet effectually occupied. It cannot allow theologian or metaphysician, those Portuguese of the intellect, to establish a right to the foreshore of our present ignorance, and so hinder the settlement in due time of vast and yet unknown continents of thought. In the like barriers erected in the past science finds some of the greatest difficulties in the way of intellectual progress and social advance at the present. It is the want of impersonal judgment, of scientific method, and of accurate insight into facts, a want largely due to a non-scientific training, which renders clear thinking so rare, and random and irresponsible judgments so common, in the mass of our citizens to-day. Yet these citizens, owing to the growth of democracy, have graver problems to settle than probably any which have confronted their forefathers since the days of the Revolution.

The Second Claim of Science

Hitherto the sole ground on which we have considered the appeal of modern science to the citizen is the *indirect* influence it has upon conduct owing to the more efficient mental training which it provides. But we have further to recognise that science can on occasion adduce facts having far more *direct* bearing on social problems than any theory of the state propounded by the philosophers from the days of Plato to those of Hegel. I cannot bring home to the reader the possibility of this better than by citing some of the conclusions to which the theory of heredity elaborated by the German biologist Weismann introduces us. Weismann's theory lies on the borderland of scientific knowledge; his results are still open to discussion, his conclusions to modification. But to indicate the manner in which science can directly influence conduct, we will assume for the time being Weismann's main conclusion to be correct. One of the chief features of his theory is the non-inheritance by the offspring of characteristics acquired by the parents in the course of life. Thus good or bad habits acquired by the father or mother in their lifetime are not inherited by their children. The effects of special training or of education on the parents have no direct influence on the child before birth. The parents are merely trustees who hand down their commingled stocks to their offspring. From a bad stock can come only bad offspring, and if a member of such a stock is, owing to special training and education, an exception to his family, his offspring will still be born with the old taint. Now this conclusion of Weismann's — if it be valid, and all we can say at present is that the arguments in favour of it are remarkably strong — radically affects our judgment on the moral conduct of the individual, and on the duties of the state and society towards their degenerate members. No degenerate and feeble stock will ever be converted into healthy and sound stock by the accumulated effects of education, good laws, and sanitary surroundings. Such means may render the individual members of the stock passable if not strong members of society, but the same process will have to be gone through again and again with their offspring, and this in ever-widening circles, if the stock, owing to the conditions in which society has placed it, is able to increase in numbers. The suspension of that process of natural selection which in an earlier struggle for existence crushed out feeble and degenerate stocks, may be a real danger to society, if society relies solely on changed environment for converting its inherited bad into an inheritable good. If society is to shape its own future — if we are to replace the stern processes of natural law, which have raised us to our present high standard of civilisation, by milder methods of eliminating the unfit — then we must be peculiarly cautious that in following our strong social instincts we do not at the same time weaken society by rendering the propagation of bad stock more and more easy.

If the views of Weismann be correct — if the bad man can by the influence of education and surroundings be made good, but the bad stock can never be converted into good stock — then we see how grave a responsibility is cast at the present day upon every citizen, who directly or indirectly has to consider problems relating to the state endowment of education, the revision and administration of the Poor Law, and above all, the conduct of public and private charities annually disposing of immense resources. In all problems of this kind the blind social instinct and the individual bias at present form extremely strong factors of our judgment. Yet these very problems are just those which, affecting the whole future of our society, its stability and its efficiency, require us, as good citizens, above all to understand and obey the laws of healthy social development.

The example we have considered will not be futile, nor its lessons worthless, should Weismann's views after all be inaccurate. It is clear that in social problems of the kind I have referred to, the laws of heredity, whatever they may be, must profoundly influence our judgment. The conduct of parent to child, and of society to its antisocial members, can never be placed on sound and permanent bases without regard be paid to what science has to tell us on the fundamental problems of inheritance. The "philosophical" method can never lead to a real theory of morals. Strange as it may seem, the laboratory experiments of a biologist may have greater weight than all the theories of the state from Plato to Hegel! The scientific classification of facts, biological or historical, the observation of their correlation and sequence, the resulting absolute, as opposed to the individual judgment — these are the sole means by which we can reach truth in such a vital social question as that of heredity. In these considerations alone there appears to be sufficient justification for the national endowment of science, and for the universal training of our citizens in scientific methods of thought. Each one of us is now called upon to give a judgment upon an immense variety of problems, crucial for our social existence. If that judgment confirms measures and conduct tending to the increased welfare of society, then it may be termed a moral, or, better, a social judgment. It follows, then, that to ensure a judgment's being moral, method and knowledge are essential to its formation. It cannot be too often insisted upon that the formation of a moral judgment — that is, one which the individual is reasonably certain will tend to social welfare — does not depend solely on the readiness to sacrifice individual gain or comfort, or on the impulse to act unselfishly: it depends in the first place on knowledge and method. The first demand of the state upon the individual is not for self-sacrifice, but for self-development. The man who gives a thousand pounds to a vast and vague scheme of charity may or may not be acting socially; his self-sacrifice, if it be such, proves nothing; but the man who gives a vote, either directly or even indirectly, in the choice of a representative, after forming a judgment based upon *knowledge*, is undoubtedly acting socially, and is fulfilling a higher standard of citizenship.

The Third Claim of Science

Thus far I have been more particularly examining the influence of science on our treatment of social problems. I have endeavoured to point out that science cannot legitimately be excluded from any field of investigation after truth, and that, further, not only is its *method* essential to good citizenship, but that its *results* bear closely on the practical treatment of many social difficulties. In this I have endeavoured to justify the state endowment and teaching of pure science as apart from its technical applications. If in this justification I have laid most stress on the advantages of scientific method — on the training which science gives us in the appreciation of evidence, in the classification of facts, and in the elimination of personal bias, in all that may be termed exactness of mind — we must still remember that ultimately the *direct* influence of pure science on practical life is enormous. The observations of Newton on the relation between the motions of a falling stone and the moon, of Galvani on the convulsive movements of frogs' legs in contact with iron and copper, of Darwin on the adaptation of woodpeckers, of tree-frogs, and of seeds to their surroundings, of Kirchhoff on certain lines which occur in the spectrum of sunlight, of other investigators on the life-history of bacteria — these and kindred observations have not only revolutionised our conception of the universe, but they have revolutionised, or are revolutionising, our practical life, our means of transit, our social conduct, our treatment of disease. What at the instant of its discovery appears to be only a sequence of purely theoretical interest, becomes the basis of discoveries which in the end profoundly modify the conditions of human life. It is impossible to say of any result of pure science that it will not some day be the starting-point of wide-reaching technical applications. The frogs' legs of Galvani and the Atlantic cable seem wide enough apart, but the former was the starting-point of the series of investigations which ended in the latter. In the recent discovery of Hertz that the action of electro-magnetism is propagated in waves like light — in his confirmation of Maxwell's theory that light is only a special phase of electro-magnetic action — we have a result which, if of striking interest to pure science, seems yet to have no immediate practical application.* But that man would indeed be a bold dogmatist who would venture to assert that the results which may ultimately flow from this discovery of Hertz's will not, in a generation or two, do more to revolutionise life than the frogs' legs of Galvani achieved when they led to the perfection of the electric telegraph.

Science and the Imagination

There is another aspect from which it is right that we should regard pure science — one that makes no appeal to its utility in practical life, but touches a side of our nature which the reader may have thought that I have entirely neglected. There is an element in our being which is not satisfied by the formal processes of reasoning; it is the imaginative or æsthetic side, the side to which the poets and philosophers appeal, and one which science cannot, to be scientific, disregard. We have seen that the imagination must not replace the reason in the deduction of relation and law from classified facts. But, none the less, disciplined imagination has been at the bottom of all great scientific discoveries. All great scientists have, in a certain sense, been great artists; the man with no imagination may collect facts, but he cannot make great discoveries. If I were compelled to name the Englishmen who during our generation have had the widest imaginations and exercised them most beneficially, I think I should put the novelists and poets on one side

* Even since this sentence was written a first and initially quite unexpected application to practical life has arisen in wireless telegraphy!

and say Michael Faraday and Charles Darwin. Now it is very needful to understand the exact part imagination plays in pure science. We can, perhaps, best achieve this result by considering the following proposition: Pure science has a further strong claim upon us on account of the exercise it gives to the imaginative faculties and the gratification it provides for the æsthetic judgment. The exact meaning of the terms "scientific fact" and "scientific law" will be considered in later chapters, but for the present let us suppose an elaborate classification of such facts has been made, and their relationships and sequences carefully traced. What is the next stage in the process of scientific investigation? Undoubtedly it is the use of the imagination. The discovery of some single statement, some brief *formula* from which the whole group of facts is seen to flow, is the work, not of the mere cataloguer, but of the man endowed with creative imagination. The single statement, the brief formula, the few words of which replace in our minds a wide range of relationships between isolated phenomena, is what we term a scientific *law*. Such a law, relieving our memory from the burden of individual sequences, enables us, with the minimum of intellectual fatigue, to grasp a vast complexity of natural or social phenomena. The discovery of law is therefore the peculiar function of the creative imagination. But this imagination has to be a *disciplined* one. It has in the first place to appreciate the whole range of facts, which require to be resumed in a single statement; and then when the law is reached — often by what seems solely the inspired imagination of genius — it must be tested and criticised by its discoverer in every conceivable way, till he is certain that the imagination has not played him false, and that his law is in real agreement with the whole group of phenomena which it resumes. Herein lies the key-note to the scientific use of the imagination. Hundreds of men have allowed their imagination to solve the universe, but the men who have contributed to our real understanding of natural phenomena have been those who were unstinting in their application of criticism to the product of their imaginations. It is such criticism which is the essence of the scientific use of the imagination, which is, indeed, the very life-blood of science . . .

In two sections here omitted Pearson illustrates the "method of science" from the work of Darwin; and argues that there is a beauty in science satisfactory to the aesthetic judgment. He then concludes:

The Fourth Claim of Science

There is an insatiable desire in the human breast to resume in some short formula, some brief statement, the facts of human experience. It leads the savage to "account" for all natural phenomena by deifying the wind and

the stream and the tree. It leads civilised man, on the other hand, to express
his emotional experience in works of art, and his physical and mental experience in the formulæ or so-called laws of science. Both works of art and
laws of science are the product of the creative imagination, both afford
material for the gratification of the æsthetic judgment. It may seem at first
sight strange to the reader that the laws of science should thus be associated
with the creative imagination in man rather than with the physical world
outside him. But . . . the laws of science are products of the human mind
rather than factors of the external world. Science endeavours to provide a
mental *résumé* of the universe, and its last great claim to our support is the
capacity it has for satisfying our cravings for a brief description of the history of the world. Such a brief description, a formula resuming all things,
science has not yet found and may probably never find, but of this we may
feel sure, that its method of seeking for one is the sole possible method, and
that the truth it has reached is the only form of truth which can perma-
nently satisfy the æsthetic judgment. For the present, then, it is better to be
content with the fraction of a right solution than to beguile ourselves with
the whole of a wrong solution. The former is at least a step towards the
truth, and shows us the direction in which other steps may be taken. The
latter cannot be in entire accordance with our past or future experience, and
will therefore ultimately fail to satisfy the æsthetic judgment. Step by step
that judgment, restless under the growth of positive knowledge, has dis-
carded creed after creed, and philosophic system after philosophic system.
Surely we might now be content to learn from the pages of history that only
little by little, slowly line upon line, man, by the aid of organised observation
and careful reasoning, can hope to reach knowledge of the truth, that science,
in the broadest sense of the word, is the sole gateway to a knowledge which
can harmonise with our past as well as with our possible future experience.
As Clifford puts it, "Scientific thought is not an accompaniment or condition of human progress, but human progress itself."

1874

WALTER BAGEHOT

The Metaphysical Basis of Toleration

Walter Bagehot's essay was originally published in the Contemporary Review *for April 1874 and was later collected into volume three of his* Literary Studies *(new edition, 1895), from which the present text, with a few omissions, has been taken. It was not written for a particular occasion. But in March 1873 the Gladstone Ministry resigned over the Irish University Bill, a question involving education and religion; and in the years 1873–1875 Bagehot interested himself in such theological topics as revelation and the higher criticism and was about to interest himself in the case of the Vatican Decrees. As a member of the Metaphysical Society, moreover, he was accustomed to participating in discussions of the widest intellectual range. The present essay was probably written for that society. It is reprinted here because of the clarity of its discussion of social health and toleration of dissident opinion.*

ONE OF THE MOST MARKED PECULIARITIES of recent times in England is the increased liberty in the expression of opinion. Things are now said constantly and without remark, which even ten years ago would have caused a hubbub, and have drawn upon those who said them much obloquy. But already I think there are signs of a reaction. In many quarters of orthodox opinion I observe a disposition to say, "Surely this is going too far; really we cannot allow such things to be said." And what is more curious, some writers, whose pens are just set at liberty, and who would, not at all long ago, have been turned out of society for the things that they say, are setting themselves to explain the "weakness" of liberty, and to extol the advantages of persecution. As it appears to me that the new practice of this country is a great improvement on its old one, and as I conceive that the doctrine of Toleration rests on what may be called a metaphysical basis, I wish shortly to describe what that basis is.

I should say that, except where it is explained to the contrary, I use the word "Toleration" to mean toleration by law. Toleration by Society of matters not subject to legal penalty is a kindred subject on which, if I have room, I will add a few words, but in the main I propose to deal with the simpler subject, — toleration by law. And by toleration, too, I mean, when it is not otherwise said, toleration in the public expression of opinions. Toleration of acts and practices is another allied subject on which I can, in a paper like this, but barely hope to indicate what seems to me to be the truth. And I should add, that I deal only with the discussion of impersonal doctrines. The law of libel, which deals with accusations of living persons, is a topic requiring consideration by itself.

Meaning this by "toleration," I do not think we ought to be surprised at a reaction against it. What was said long ago of slavery seems to be equally true of persecution, — it "exists by the law of nature." It is so congenial to human nature, that it has arisen everywhere in past times, as history shows; that the cessation of it is a matter of recent times in England; that even now, taking the world as a whole, the practice and the theory of it are in a triumphant majority. Most men have always much preferred persecution, and do so still; and it is therefore only natural that it should continually reappear in discussion and argument.

One mode in which it tempts human nature is very obvious. Persons of strong opinions wish, above all things, to propagate those opinions. They find close at hand what seems an immense engine for that propagation; they find the *State*, which has often in history interfered for and against opinions, — which has had a great and undeniable influence in helping some and hindering others, — and in their eagerness they can hardly understand why they should not make use of this great engine to crush the errors which they hate, and to replace them with the tenets they approve. So long as there are earnest believers in the world, they will always wish to punish opinions, even if their judgment tells them it is unwise, and their conscience that it is wrong. They may not gratify their inclination, but the inclination will not be the less real.

Since the time of Carlyle, "earnestness" has been a favourite virtue in literature, and it is customary to treat this wish to twist other people's belief into ours as if it were a part of the love of truth. And in the highest minds so it may be. But the mass of mankind have, as I hold, no such fine motive. Independently of truth or falsehood, the spectacle of a different belief from ours is disagreeable to us, in the same way that the spectacle of a different form of dress and manners is disagreeable. A set of schoolboys will persecute a new boy with a new sort of jacket; they will hardly let him have a new-shaped penknife. Grown-up people are just as bad, except when culture has softened them. A mob will hoot a foreigner who looks very unlike themselves. Much of the feeling of "earnest believers" is, I believe, altogether the same. They wish others to think as they do, not only because they wish to diffuse doctrinal truth, but also and much more because they cannot bear to hear the words of a creed different from their own. At any rate, without further analysing the origin of the persecuting impulse, its deep root in human nature, and its great power over most men, are evident.

But this natural impulse was not the only motive — perhaps was not the principal one — of historical persecutions. The main one, or a main one, was a most ancient political idea which once ruled the world, and of which deep vestiges are still to be traced on many sides. The most ancient conception of a State is that of a "religious partnership," in which any member may by his acts bring down the wrath of the gods on the other members, and, so to speak, on the whole company. This danger was, in the conception of the time, at once unlimited and inherited; in any generation, partners A, C, D, etc., might suffer loss of life, or health, or goods — the whole association even might perish, because in a past generation the ancestors of Z had somehow offended the gods. Thus the historian of Athens tells us that after a particular act of sacrilege — a breach of the local privileges of sanctuary — the perpetrators were compelled "to retire into banishment"; and that those who had died before the date he is speaking of were "disinterred and cast beyond the borders." "Yet," he adds, "their exile continuing, as it did, only for a time, was not held sufficient to expiate the impiety for which they have been condemned. The Alkmoônids, one of the most powerful families in Attica, long continued to be looked upon as a tainted race, and in cases of public calamity were liable to be singled out as having by their sacrilege drawn down the judgment of the gods upon their countrymen." And as false opinions about the gods have almost always been thought to be peculiarly odious to them, the misbeliever, the "miscreant," has been almost always thought to be likely not only to impair hereafter the salvation of himself and others in a future world, but also to bring on his neighbours and his nation grievous calamities immediately in this. He has been persecuted to stop political danger more than to arrest intellectual error.

But it will be said: Put history aside, and come to things now. Why should not those who are convinced that certain doctrines are errors, that they are most dangerous, that they may ruin man's welfare here and his salvation hereafter, use the power of the State to extirpate those errors? Experience seems to show that the power of the State can be put forth in that way effectually. Why, then, should it not be put forth? If I had room, I should like for a moment to criticise the word "effectually." I should say that the State, in the cases where it is most wanted, is not of the use which is thought. I admit that it extirpates error, but I doubt if it creates belief — at least, if it does so in cases where the persecuted error is suitable to the place and time. In such cases, I think the effect has often been to eradicate a heresy among the few, at the cost of creating a scepticism among the many; to kill the error no doubt, but also to ruin the general belief. And this is the cardinal point, for the propagation of the "truth" is the end of persecution; all else is only a means. But I have not space to discuss this, and will come to the main point.

I say that the State power should not be used to arrest discussion, because the State power may be used equally for truth or error, for Mohammedanism or Christianity, for belief or no-belief, but in discussion truth has an advantage. Arguments always tell for truth as such, and against error as such; if you let the human mind alone, it has a preference for good argument over bad; it oftener takes truth than not. But if you do not let it alone, you give truth no advantage at all; you substitute a game of force, where all doctrines are equal, for a game of logic, where the truer have the better chance.

The process by which truth wins in discussion is this, — certain strong and eager minds embrace original opinions, seldom all wrong, never quite true, but of a mixed sort, part truth, part error. These they inculcate on all occasions, and on every side, and gradually bring the cooler sort of men to a hearing of them. These cooler people serve as quasi-judges, while the more eager ones are a sort of advocates; a Court of Inquisition is sitting perpetually, investigating, informally and silently, but not ineffectually, what, on all great subjects of human interest, is truth and error. There is no sort of infallibility about the court; often it makes great mistakes, most of its decisions are incomplete in thought and imperfect in expression. Still, on the whole, the force of evidence keeps it right. The truth has the best of the proof, and therefore wins most of the judgments. The process is slow, far more tedious than the worst Chancery suit. Time in it is reckoned not by days, but by years, or rather by centuries. Yet, on the whole, it creeps along, if you do not stop it. But all is arrested, if persecution begins — if you have a *coup d'état*, and let loose soldiers on the court; for it is perfect chance which litigant turns them in, or what creed they are used to compel men to believe.

This argument, however, assumes two things. In the first place, it presupposes that we are speaking of a state of society in which discussion is possible. And such societies are not very common. Uncivilised man is not capable of discussion: savages have been justly described as having "the intellect of children with the passions and strength of men." Before anything like speculative argument can be used with them, their intellect must be strengthened and their passions restrained. There was, as it seems to me, a long preliminary period before human nature, as we now see it, existed, and while it was being formed. During that preliminary period, persecution, like slavery, played a most considerable part. Nations mostly became nations by having a common religion. It was a necessary condition of the passage from a loose aggregate of savages to a united polity, that they should believe in the same gods and worship these gods in the same way. What was necessary was, that they should for a long period — for centuries, perhaps — lead the same life and conform to the same usages. They believed that the "gods of their fathers" had commanded these usages. Early law is hardly to be separated from religious ritual: it is more like the tradition of a Church than the enactments of a statute-book. It is a thing essentially immemorial and sacred. It is not conceived of as capable either of addition or diminution; it is a body of holy customs which no one is allowed either to break or to impugn. The use of these is to aid in creating a common national character, which in after-times may be tame enough to bear discussion, and which may suggest common axioms upon which discussion can be founded. Till that common character has been formed, discussion is impossible; it cannot be used to find out truth, for it cannot exist; it is not that we have to forego its efficacy on purpose, we have not the choice of it, for its prerequisites cannot be found. The case of civil liberty is, as I conceive, much the same. Early ages need a coercive despotism more than they need anything else. The age of debate comes later. An omnipotent power to enforce the sacred law is that which is then most required. A constitutional opposition would be born before its time. It would be dragging the wheel before the horses were harnessed. The strongest advocates both of Liberty and Toleration may consistently hold that there were unhappy ages before either became possible, and when attempts at either would have been pernicious.

The case is analogous to that of education. Every parent wisely teaches his child his own creed, and till the child has attained a certain age, it is better that he should not hear too much of any other. His mind will in the end be better able to weigh arguments, because it does not begin to weigh them so early. He will hardly comprehend any creed unless he has been taught some creed. But the restrictions of childhood must be relaxed in youth, and abandoned in manhood. One object of education is to train us for discussion, and as that training gradually approaches to completeness, we should gradually begin to enter into and to take part in discussion. The restrictions that are useful at nine years old are pernicious at nineteen.

This analogy would have seemed to me obvious, but there are many most able persons who turn the matter just the other way. They regard the discipline of education as a precedent for persecution. They say, "I would no sooner let the nation at large read that bad book than I would let my children read it." They refuse to admit that the age of the children makes any difference. At heart they think that they are wiser than the mass of mankind, just as they are wiser than their children, and would regulate the studies of both unhesitatingly. But experience shows that no man is on all points so wise as the mass of men are after a good discussion, and that if the ideas of the very wisest were by miracle to be fixed on the race, the certain result would be to stereotype monstrous error. If we fixed the belief of Bacon, we should believe that the earth went around the sun; if we fixed that of Newton, we should believe "that the Argonautic expedition was a real event, and occurred B.C. 937; that Hercules was a real person, and delivered Theseus, another real person, B.C. 936; that in the year 1036 Ceres, a woman of Sicily, in seeking her daughter who was stolen, came into Attica, and there taught the Greeks to sow corn." And the worst is, that the minds of most would-be persecutors are themselves unfixed: their opinions are in a perpetual flux; they would persecute all others for tenets which yesterday they had not heard of and which they will not believe to-morrow.

But it will be said, the theory of Toleration is not so easy as that of education. We know by a certain fact when a young man is grown up and can bear discussion. We judge by his age, as to which every one is agreed. But we cannot tell by any similar patent fact when a State is mature enough to bear discussion. There may be two opinions about it. And I quite agree that the matter of fact is more difficult to discover in one case than in the other; still it is a matter of fact which the rulers of the State must decide upon their responsibility, and as best they can . . . Of course, most Governments are wholly unequal to so high a morality and so severe a self-command. The Governments of most countries are composed of persons who wish everybody to believe as they do, merely because they do. Some here and there, from a higher motive, so eagerly wish to propagate their opinions, that they are unequal to consider the problem of toleration impartially. They persecute till the persecuted become strong enough to make them desist. But the delicacy of a rule and the unwillingness of Governments to adopt it, do not prove that it is not the best and the right one. There are already in inevitable jurisprudence many lines of vital importance just as difficult to draw. The line between sanity and insanity has necessarily to be drawn, and it is as nice as anything can be. The competency of people to bear discussion is not intrinsically more difficult than their competency to manage their own affairs, though perhaps a Government is less likely to be impartial and more likely to be biassed in questions of discussion than in pecuniary ones.

Secondly, the doctrine that rulers are to permit discussion, assumes not only, as we have seen, that discussion is possible, but also that discussion will not destroy the Government. No Government is bound to permit a controversy which will annihilate itself. It is a trustee for many duties, and if possible, it must retain the power to perform those duties. The controversies which may ruin it are very different in different countries. The Government of the day must determine in each case what those questions are. If the Roman Emperors who persecuted Christianity really did so because they imagined that Christianity would destroy the Roman Empire, I think they are to be blamed not for their misconception of duty, but for their mistake of fact. The existence of Christianity was not really more inconsistent with the existence of the Empire in the time of Diocletian than in that of Constantine; but if Diocletian thought that it was inconsistent, it was his duty to preserve the Empire.

It will be asked, "What do you mean by preserving a society? All societies are in a state of incipient change; the best of them are often the most changing; what is meant, then, by saying you will 'preserve' any? You admit that you cannot keep them unaltered, what then do you propose to do?" I answer that, in this respect, the life of societies is like the life of the individuals composing them. You cannot interfere so as to keep a man's body unaltered; you can interfere so as to keep him alive. What changes in such cases will be fatal, is a question of fact. The Government must determine what will, so to say, "break up the whole thing" and what will not. No doubt it may decide wrong . . . Here, as before, the practical difficulties in the application of a rule do not disprove its being the true and the only one.

It will be objected that this principle is applicable only to truths which are gained by discussion. "We admit," such objectors say, "that where discussion is the best or the only means of proving truth, it is unadvisable to prohibit that discussion, but there are other means besides discussion of arriving at truth, which are sometimes better than discussion even where discussion is applicable, and sometimes go beyond it and attain regions in which it is inapplicable; and where those more efficient means are applicable, it may be wise to prohibit discussion, for in these instances discussion may confuse the human mind and impede it in the use of those higher means. The case is analogous to that of the eyes. For the most part it is a sound rule to tell persons who want to see things, that they must necessarily use *both* their eyes, and rely on them. But there are cases in which that rule is wrong. If a man wants to see things too distant for the eyes, as the satellites of Jupiter and the ring of Saturn, you must tell him, on the contrary, to shut one eye and look through a telescope with the other. The ordinary mode of using the common instruments may, in exceptional cases, interfere with the right use of the supplementary instruments." And I quite admit that there are such exceptional cases and such additional means; but I say that their existence introduces no new difficulty into the subject, and that it is no reason for prohibiting discussion except in the cases in which we have seen already that it was advisable to prohibit it.

Putting the matter in the most favourable way for these objectors, and making all possible concessions to them, I believe the exceptions which they contend for must come at last to three.

First, there are certain necessary propositions which the human mind *will* think, must think, and cannot help thinking. For example, we must believe that things which are equal to the same thing are equal to each other, — that a thing cannot *both* be and not be, — that it must *either* be or not be. These truths are not gained by discussion; on the contrary, discussion presupposes at least some of them, for you cannot argue without first principles any more than you can use a lever without a fulcrum. The prerequisites of reasoning must somehow be recognized by the human mind before we begin to reason. So much is obvious, but then it is obvious also that in such cases attempts at discussion cannot do any harm. If the human mind has in it certain first principles which it cannot help seeing, and which it accepts of itself, there is no harm in arguing against those first principles. You may contend as long as you like, that things which are equal to the same thing are *not* equal to each other, or that a thing *can* both exist and not exist at the same time, but you will not convince any one. If you could convince any one you would do him irreparable harm, for you would hurt the basis of his mind and destroy the use of his reason. But happily you cannot convince him. That which the human mind cannot help thinking it cannot help thinking, and discussion can no more remove the primary perceptions than it can produce them. The multiplication table will remain the multiplication table, neither more nor less, however much we may argue either for it or against it.

But, though the denial of the real necessary perceptions of the human mind cannot possibly do any harm, the denial of alleged necessary perceptions is often essential to the discovery of truth. The human mind, as experience shows, is apt to manufacture sham self-evidences. The most obvious case is, that men perpetually "do sums" wrong. If we dwell long enough and intently enough on the truths of arithmetic they are in each case self-evident; but, if we are too quick, or let our minds get dull, we may make any number of mistakes. A certain deliberation and a certain intensity are both essential to correctness in the matter. Fictitious necessities of thought will be imposed on us without end unless we are careful. The greatest minds are not exempt from the risk of such mistakes even in matters most familiar to them. On the contrary, the history of science is full of cases in which the ablest men and the most experienced assumed that it was impossible to think things which are in matter of fact true, and which it has since been found possible to think quite easily. The mode in which these sham self-evidences are distinguished from the real ones is by setting as many minds as possible to try as often as possible whether they can help thinking the thing or not. But such trials will never exist without discussion. So far, therefore, the existence of self-evidences in the human mind is not a reason for discouraging discussion, but a reason for encouraging it.

Next, it is certainly true that many conclusions which are by no means self-evident and which are gradually obtained, nevertheless, are not the result of discussion. For example, the opinion of a man as to the characters of his friends and acquaintances is not the result of distinct argument, but the aggregate of distinct impressions: it is not the result of an investigation consciously pursued, but the effect of a multiplicity of facts involuntarily presented; it is a definite thing and has a most definite influence on the mind, but its origin is indefinite and not to be traced; it is like a great fund raised in very small subscriptions and of which the subscribers' names are lost. But here again, though these opinions too were not gained by discussion, their existence is a reason for promoting discussion, not for preventing it. Every-day experience shows that these opinions as to character are often mistaken in the last degree. Human character is a most complex thing, and the impressions which different people form of it are as various as the impressions which the inhabitants of an impassable mountain have of its shape and size. Each observer has an aggregate idea derived from certain actions and certain sayings, but the real man has always or almost always said a thousand sayings of a kind quite different and in a connection quite different; he has done a vast variety of actions among "other men" and "other minds"; a mobile person will often seem hardly the same if you meet him in very different societies. And how, except by discussion, is the true character of such a person to be decided? Each observer must bring his contingent to the list of *data*; those data must be arranged and made use of. The certain and positive facts as to which every one is agreed must have their due weight; they must be combined and compared with the various impressions as to which no two people exactly coincide. A rough summary must be made of the whole. In no other way is it possible to arrive at the truth of the matter. Without discussion each mind is dependent on its own partial observation. A great man is one image — one thing, so to speak — to his valet, another to his son, another to his wife, another to his greatest friend. None of these must be stereotyped; all must be compared. To prohibit discussion is to prohibit the corrective process.

Lastly, I hold that there are first principles or first perceptions which are neither the result of constant though forgotten trials like those last spoken of, nor common to all the race like the first. The most obvious seem to me to be the principles of taste. The primary perceptions of beauty vary much in different persons, and for different persons at different times, but no one can say that they are not most real and most influential parts of human nature. There is hardly a thing made by human hands which is not affected more or less by the conception of beauty felt by the maker; and there is hardly a human life which would not have been different if the idea of beauty in the mind of the man who lived it had been different.

But certainly it would not answer to exclude subjects of taste from discussion, and to allow one school of taste-teachers to reign alone, and to prohibit the teaching of all rival schools. The effect would be to fix on all ages the particular ideas of one age on a matter which is beyond most others obscure and difficult to reduce to a satisfactory theory. The human mind evidently differs at various times immensely in its conclusions upon it, and there is nothing to show that the era of the persecutor is wiser than any other era, or that his opinion is better than any one else's.

The case of these variable first principles is much like that of the "personal equation," as it is called in the theory of observations. Some observers, it is found, habitually see a given phenomenon, say the star coming to the meridian, a little sooner than most others; some later; no two persons exactly coincide. The first thing done when a new man comes into an observatory for practical work is to determine whether he sees quick or slow; and this is called the "personal equation." But, according to the theory of persecution, the national astronomer in each country would set up his own mind as the standard; in one country he would be a quick man, and would not let the slow people contest what he said; in another he would be a slow man, and would not tolerate the quick people, or let men speak their minds; and so the astronomical observations — the astronomical *creeds* if I may say so — of different countries would radically differ. But as toleration and discussion are allowed, no such absurd result follows. The observations of different minds are compared with those of others, and truth is assumed to lie in the mean between the errors of the quick people and the errors of the slow ones.

No such accurate result can be expected in more complex matters. The phenomena of astronomical observation relate only to very simple events, and to a very simple fact about these events. But perceptions of beauty have an infinite complexity: they are all subtle aggregates of countless details, and about each of these details probably every mind in some degree differs from every other one. But in a rough way the same sort of agreement is possible. Discussion is only an organised mode by which various minds compare their conclusions with those of various others. Bold and strong minds describe graphic and definite impressions: at first sight these impressions seem wholly different. Writers of the last century thought classical architecture altogether superior to Gothic; many writers now put it just the other way, and maintain a mediæval cathedral to be a thing altogether superior in kind and nature to anything classical. For years the world thought Claude's landscapes perfect. Then came Mr. Ruskin, and by his ability and eloquence he has made a whole generation depreciate them, and think Turner's altogether superior. The extrication of truth by such discussions is very slow; it is often retarded; it is often thrown back; it often seem to pause for ages. But upon the whole it makes progress, and the principle of that progress is this: Each mind which is true to itself, and which draws its own impressions carefully, and which compares those impressions with the impressions of others, arrives at certain conclusions, which as far as that mind is concerned are ultimate, and are its highest conclusions. These it sets down as expressively as it can on paper, or communicates by word of mouth, and these again form data which other minds can contrast with their own. In this incessant comparison eccentric minds fall off on every side; some like Milton, some Wordsworth, some can see nothing in Dryden, some find Racine intolerably dull, some think Shakespeare barbarous, others consider the contents of the Iliad "battles and schoolboy stuff." With history it is the same; some despise one great epoch, some another. Each epoch has its violent partisans, who will listen to nothing else, and who think every other epoch in comparison mean and wretched. These violent minds are always faulty and sometimes absurd, but they are almost always useful to mankind. They compel men to hear neglected truth. They uniformly exaggerate their gospel; but it generally *is* a gospel. Carlyle said many years since of the old Poor-law in England: "It being admitted then that outdoor relief should at once cease, what means did great Nature take to make it cease? She created various men who thought the cessation of outdoor relief the one thing needful." In the same way, it being desirable that the taste of men should be improved on some point, Nature's instrument on that point is some man of genius, of attractive voice and limited mind, who declaims and insists, not only that the special improvement is a good thing in itself, but the best of all things, and the root of all other good things. Most useful, too, are others less apparent; shrinking, sensitive, testing minds, of whom often the world knows nothing, but each of whom is in the circle just near him an authority on taste, and communicates by personal influence the opinions he has formed. The human mind of a certain maturity, if left alone, prefers real beauty to sham beauty, and prefers it the sooner if original men suggest new charms, and quiet men criticise and judge of them.

But an æsthetical persecution would derange all this, for generally the compulsive power would be in the hands of the believers in some tradition. The State represents "the rough force of society," and is little likely to be amendable to new charms or new ideas; and therefore the first victim of the persecution would be the original man who was proposing that which in the end would most improve mankind; and the next would be the testing and discerning critic who was examining these ideas and separating the chaff from the wheat in them. Neither would conform to the old tradition. The inventor would be too eager; the critic too scrupulous; and so a heavy code of ancient errors would be chained upon mankind. Nor would the case be at all the better if by some freak of events the propounder of the new doctrine were to gain full control, and were to prohibit all he did not like. He would try, and try in vain, to make the inert mass of men accept or care for his new theory, and his particular enemy would be the careful critic who went with him a little way and then refused to go any further. If you allow persecution, the partisans of the new sort of beauty will, if they can, attack those of the old sort; and the partisans of the old sort will attack those of the new sort; while both will turn on the quiet and discriminating person who is trying to select what is good from each. Some chance taste will be fixed for ages.

But it will be said, "Whoever heard of such nonsense as an æsthetical persecution? Everybody knows such matters of taste must be left to take care of themselves; as far as they are concerned, nobody wants to persecute or prohibit." But I have spoken of matters of taste because it is sometimes best to speak in parables. The case of morals and religion, in which people have always persecuted and still wish to persecute, is the very same. If there are (as I myself think there are) ultimate truths of morals and religion which more or less vary for each mind, some sort of standard and some kind of agreement can only be arrived at about it in the very same way. The same comparison of one mind with another if necessary; the same discussion; the same use of criticising minds; the same use of original ones. The mode of arriving at truth is the same, and also the mode of stopping it.

We now see the reason why, as I said before, religious persecution often extirpates new doctrines, but commonly fails to maintain the belief in old tenets. You can prevent whole classes of men from hearing of the religion which is congenial to them, but you cannot make men believe a religion which is uncongenial. You can prevent the natural admirers of Gothic architecture from hearing anything of it, or from seeing it; but you cannot make them admire classical architecture. You may prevent the admirers of

Claude from seeing his pictures, or from praising them; but you cannot make them admirers of Turner. Just so, you may by persecution prevent minds prone to be Protestant from being Protestant; but you will not make men real Catholics: you may prevent naturally Catholic minds from being Catholic; but you will not make them genuine Protestants. You will not make those believe your religion who are predisposed by nature in favour of a different kind of religion; you will make of them, instead, more or less conscious sceptics. Being denied the sort of religion of which the roots are in their minds and which they could believe, they will for ever be conscious of an indefinite want. They will constantly feel after something which they are never able to attain; they will never be able to settle upon anything; they will feel an instinctive repulsion from everything; they will be sceptics at heart, because they were denied the creed for which their heart craves; they will live as indifferentists, because they were withheld by force from the only creed to which they would not be indifferent. Persecution in intellectual countries produces a superficial conformity, but also underneath an intense, incessant, implacable doubt.

Upon examination, therefore, the admission that certain truths are not gained by discussion introduces no new element into the subject. The discussion of such truths is as necessary as of all other truths. The only limitations are that men's minds shall in the particular society be mature enough to bear the discussion, and that the discussion shall not destroy the society.

I acknowledge these two limitations to the doctrine that discussion should be free, but I do not admit another which is often urged. It is said that those who write against toleration should not be tolerated; that discussion should not aid the enemies of discussion. But why not? If there is a strong Government and a people fit for discussion, why should not the cause be heard? We must not assume that the liberty of discussion has no case of exception. We have just seen that there are, in fact, several such. In each instance, let the people decide whether the particular discussion shall go on or not. Very likely, in some cases, they may decide wrong; but it is better that they should so decide, than that we should venture to anticipate all experience, and to make sure that they cannot possibly be right.

It is plain, too, that the argument here applied to the toleration of opinion has no application to that of actions. The human mind in the cases supposed, learns by freely hearing all arguments, but in no case does it learn by trying freely all practices. Society, as we now have it, cannot exist at all unless certain acts are prohibited. It goes on much better because many other acts are prohibited also. The Government must take the responsibility of saying what actions it will allow; that is its first business, and the allowance of all would be the end of civilisation. But it must, under the conditions specified, hear all opinions, for the tranquil discussion of all more than anything else promotes the progressive knowledge of truth, which is the mainspring of civilisation.

Nor does the argument that the law should not impose a penalty on the expression of any opinion equally prove that society should not in many cases apply a penalty to that expression. Society can deal much more severely than the law with many kinds of acts, because it need be far less strict in the evidence it requires. It can take cognisance of matters of common repute and of things of which every one is sure, but which nobody can prove. Particularly, it can fairly well compare the character of the doctrine with the character of the agent, which law can do but imperfectly, if at all. And it is certain that opinions are evidence of the character of those who hold them — not conclusive evidence, but still presumptive. Experience shows that every opinion is compatible with what every one would admit to be a life fairly approvable, a life far higher than that of the mass of men. Great scepticism and great belief have both been found in characters whom both sceptics and believers must admire. Still, on the whole, there is a certain kinship between belief and character; those who disagree with a man's fundamental creed will generally disapprove of his habitual character. If, therefore, society sees a man maintaining opinions which by experience it has been led to connect with actions such as it discountenances, it is justified in provisionally discountenancing the man who holds those opinions. Such a man should be put to the proof to show by his life that the opinions which he holds are not connected with really pernicious actions, as society thinks they are. If he is visibly leading a high life, society should discountenance him no longer; it is then clear that he did not lead a bad life, and the idea that he did or might lead such a life was the only reason for so doing. A doubt was suggested, but it also has been removed. This habit of suspicion does not, on the whole, impair free discussion; perhaps even it improves it. It keeps out the worst disputants, men of really bad character, whose opinions are the results of that character, and who refrain from publishing them, because they fear what society may say. If the law could similarly distinguish between good disputants and bad, it might usefully impose penalties on the bad. But, of course, this is impossible. Law cannot distinguish between the niceties of character; it must punish the publication of an opinion, if it punishes at all, no matter whether the publisher is a good man or whether he is a bad one. In such a matter, society is a discriminating agent: the law is but a blind one.

To most people I may seem to be slaying the slain, and proving what no one doubts. People, it will be said, no longer wish to persecute. But I say, they *do* wish to persecute. In fact, from their writings, and still better from their conversation, it is easy to see that very many believers would persecute sceptics, and that very many sceptics would persecute believers. Society may be wiser; but most earnest believers and most earnest unbelievers are not at all wiser.

1874

JOHN MORLEY

Intellectual Responsibility and the Political Spirit

In the 1870's British opinion was agitated by the problem of modernizing an obsolescent educational "system." This problem was complicated by the relation of Ireland to the United Kingdom and by the question whether, amid the alleged agnosticism springing from evolution, church control of education, either Anglican, or Roman Catholic, or Dissenting, should give way to secular control. Into this fray entered John Morley, one of the great Victorian liberals; and, reflecting on the problem of church, state, and education, he published in 1874 his remarkable volume, On Compromise, *of which a contemporary critic remarked that the only compromise was in the title. This book pleads for wide latitude in opinion, notably when religious opinion is brought to bear upon educational and political problems. Chapter II restates Mill's argument for the toleration of error, real or supposed, and is followed by the chapter here reprinted with the omission of a few digressive and illustrative passages, and of the footnotes.*

WE HAVE BEEN CONSIDERING the position of those who would fain divide the community into two great castes; the one of thoughtful and instructed persons using their minds freely, but guarding their conclusions in strict reserve; the other of the illiterate or unreflecting who should have certain opinions and practices taught them, not because they are true or are really what their votaries are made to believe them to be, but because the intellectual superiors of the community think the inculcation of such a belief useful in all cases save their own. Nor is this a mere theory. On the contrary, it is a fair description of an existing state of things. We have the old *disciplina arcani* among us in as full force as in the primitive church, but with an all-important difference. The Christian fathers practised reserve for the sake of leading the acolyte the more surely to the fulness of truth. The modern economiser keeps back his opinions, or dissembles the grounds of them, for the sake of leaving his neighbours the more at their ease in the peaceful sloughs of prejudice and superstition and low ideals. We quote Saint Paul when he talked of making himself all things to all men, and of becoming to the Jews a Jew, and as without the Law to the heathen. But then we do so with a view to justifying ourselves for leaving the Jew to remain a Jew, and the heathen to remain heathen. We imitate the same apostle in accepting old time-worn altars dedicated to the Unknown God. We forget that he made the ancient symbol the starting-point of a revolutionised doctrine. There is, as anybody can see, a whole world of difference between the reserve of sagacious apostleship, on the one hand, dealing tenderly with scruple and fearfulness and fine sensibility of conscience, and the reserve of intellectual cowardice on the other hand, dealing hypocritically with narrow minds in the supposed interests of social peace and quietness. The old *disciplina arcani* signified the disclosure of a little light with a view to the disclosure of more. The new means the dissimulation of truth with a view to the perpetuation of error. Consider the difference between these two fashions of compromise, in their effects upon the mind and character of the person compromising. The one is fully compatible with fervour and hopefulness and devotion to great causes. The other stamps a man with artifice, and hinders the free eagerness of his vision, and wraps him about with mediocrity, — not always of understanding, but that still worse thing, mediocrity of aspiration and purpose.

The coarsest and most revolting shape which the doctrine of conformity can assume, and its degrading consequences to the character of the conformer, may be conveniently illustrated by a passage in the life of Hume. He looked at things in a more practical manner than would find favour with the sentimental champions of compromise in nearer times. There is a well-known letter of Hume's, in which he recommends a young man to become a clergyman, on the ground that it was very hard to get any tolerable civil employment, and that as Lord Bute was then all powerful, his friend would be certain of preferment. In answer to the young man's scruples as to the Articles and the rest, Hume says: —

'It is putting too great a respect on the vulgar and their superstitions to pique one's self on sincerity with regard to them. If the thing were worthy of being treated gravely, I should tell him [the young man] that the Pythian oracle with the approbation of Xenophon advised every one to worship the gods — νόμῳπόλεως. I wish it were still in my power to be a hypocrite in this particular. The common duties of society usually require it; and the ecclesiastical profession only adds a little more to an innocent dissimulation, or rather simulation, without which it is impossible to pass through the world.'

This is a singularly straightforward way of stating a view which silently influences a much greater number of men than it is pleasant to think of. They would shrink from throwing their conduct into so gross a formula. They will lift up their hands at this quotation, so strangely blind are we to the hiding-places of our own hearts, even when others flash upon them the terrible illumination that comes of calling conduct and motives by plain names. Now it is not merely the moral improbity of these cases which revolts us — the improbity of making in solemn form a number of false statements for the sake of earning a livelihood; of saying in order to get money or social position that you accept a number of propositions which in fact you utterly reject; of declaring expressly that you trust you are inwardly moved to take upon you this office and ministration by the Holy Ghost, when the real motive is a desire not to miss the chance of making something out of the Earl of Bute. This side of such dissimulation is shocking enough. And it is not any more shocking to the most devout believer than it is to people who doubt whether there be any Holy Ghost or not. Those who no longer place their highest faith in powers above and beyond men, are for that very reason more deeply interested than others in cherishing the integrity and worthiness of man himself. Apart, however, from the immorality of such reasoned hypocrisy, which no man with a particle of honesty will attempt to blink, there is the intellectual improbity which it brings in its train, the infidelity to truth, the disloyalty to one's own intelligence. Gifts of understanding are numbed and enfeebled in a man, who has once played such a trick with his own conscience as to persuade himself that, because the vulgar are superstitious, it is right for the learned to earn money by turning themselves into the ministers and accomplices of superstition. If he is clever enough to see through the vulgar and their beliefs, he is tolerably sure to be clever enough from time to time and in his better moments to see through himself. He begins to suspect himself of being an impostor. That suspicion gradually unmans him when he comes to use his mind in the sphere of his own enlightenment. One of really superior power cannot escape these better moments and the remorse that they bring. As he advances in life, as his powers ought to be coming to fuller maturity and his intellectual productiveness to its prime, just in the same degree the increasing seriousness of life multiplies such moments and deepens their remorse, and so the light of intellectual promise slowly goes out in impotent endeavour, or else in taking comfort that much goods are laid up, or, what is deadliest of all, in a soulless cynicism.

We do not find out until it is too late that the intellect too, at least where it is capable of being exercised on the higher objects, has its sensitiveness. It loses its colour and potency and finer fragrance in an atmosphere of mean purpose and low conception of the sacredness of fact and reality. Who has not observed inferior original power achieving greater results even in the intellectual field itself, where the superior understanding happens to have been unequally yoked with a self-seeking character, ever scenting the expedient? If Hume had been in the early productive part of his life the hypocrite which he wished it were in his power to show himself in its latter part, we may be tolerably sure that European philosophy would have missed one of its foremost figures. It has been often said that he who begins life by stifling his convictions is in a fair way for ending it without any convictions to stifle. We may, perhaps, add that he who sets out with the notion that the difference between truth and falsehood is a thing of no concern to the vulgar, is very likely sooner or later to come to the kindred notion that it is not a thing of any supreme concern to himself.

Let thus much have been said as to those who deliberately and knowingly sell their intellectual birthright for a mess of pottage, making a brazen compromise with what they hold despicable, lest they should have to win their bread honourably. Men need to expend no declamatory indignation upon them. They have a hell of their own; words can add no bitterness to it. It is no light thing to have secured a livelihood on condition of going through life masked and gagged. To be compelled, week after week, and year after year, to recite the symbols of ancient faith and lift up his voice in the echoes of old hopes, with the blighting thought in his soul that the faith is a lie, and the hope no more than the folly of the crowd; to read hundreds of times in a twelvemonth with solemn unction as the inspired word of the Supreme what to him are meaningless as the Abracadabras of the conjuror in a booth; to go on to the end of his days administering to simple folk holy rites of commemoration and solace, when he has in his mind at each phrase what dupes are these simple folk and how wearisomely counterfeit their rites: and to know through all that this is really to be the one business of his prostituted life, that so dreary and hateful a piece of play-acting will make the desperate retrospect of his last hours — of a truth here is the very βδέλυγμα τῆς ἐρημώσεως, the abomination of desolation of the human spirit indeed.

No one will suppose that this is designed for the normal type of priest. But it is well to study tendencies in their extreme catastrophe. This is only the catastrophe, in one of its many shapes, of the fatal doctrine that money, position, power, philanthropy, or any of the thousand seductive masks of the pseudo-expedient, may carry a man away from love of truth and yet leave him internally unharmed. The depravation that follows the trucking for money of intellectual freedom and self-respect, attends in its degree each other departure from disinterested following of truth, and each other substitution of convenience, whether public or private, in its place. And both parties to such a compromise are losers. The world which offers gifts and tacitly undertakes to ask no questions as to the real state of the timeserver's inner mind, loses no less than the timeserver himself who receives the gifts and promises to hold his peace. It is as though a society placed penalties on mechanical inventions and the exploration of new material resources, and offered bounties for the steadiest adherence to all ancient processes in culture and production. The injury to wealth in the one case would not be any deeper than the injury to morality is in the other.

To pass on to less sinister forms of this abnegation of intellectual responsibility. In the opening sentences of the first chapter we spoke of a wise suspense in forming opinions, a wise reserve in expressing them, and a wise tardiness in trying to realise them. Thus we meant to mark out the three independent provinces of compromise, each of them being the subject of considerations that either do not apply at all to the other two, or else apply in a different degree. Disingenuousness or self-illusion, arising from a depressing deference to the existing state of things, or to what is immediately practicable, or to what other people would think of us if they knew our thoughts, is the result of compromising truth in the matter of forming and holding opinions. Secondly, positive simulation is what comes of an unlawful willingness to compromise in the matter of avowing and publishing them. Finally, pusillanimity or want of faith is the vice that belongs to unlawful compromise in the department of action and realisation. This is not merely a division arranged for convenience of discussion. It goes to the root of conduct and character, and is the key to the present mood of our society. It is always a hardy thing to attempt to throw a complex matter into very simple form, but we should say that the want of energy and definiteness in contemporary opinions, of which we first complained, is due mainly to the following notion; that if a subject is not ripe for practical treatment, you and I are therefore entirely relieved from the duty of having clear ideas about it. If the majority cling to an opinion, why should we ask whether that is the sound and right opinion or the reverse? Now this notion, which springs from a confusion of the three fields of compromise with one another, quietly reigns almost without dispute. The devotion to the practical aspect of truth is in such excess, as to make people habitually deny that it can be worth while to form an opinion, when it happens at the moment to be incapable of realisation, for the reason that there is no direct prospect of inducing a sufficient number of persons to share it. 'We are quite willing to think that your view is the right one, and would produce all the improvements for which you hope; but then there is not the smallest chance of persuading the only persons able to carry out such a view; why therefore discuss it?' No talk is more familiar to us than this. As if the mere possibility of the view being a right one did not obviously entitle it to discussion; discussion being the only process by which people are likely to be induced to accept it, or else to find good grounds for finally dismissing it.

It is precisely because we believe that opinion, and nothing but opinion, can effect great permanent changes, that we ought to be careful to keep this most potent force honest, wholesome, fearless, and independent. Take the political field. Politicians and newspapers almost systematically refuse to talk about a new idea, which is not capable of being at once embodied in a bill, and receiving the royal assent before the following August. There is something rather contemptible, seen from the ordinary standards of intellectual integrity, in the position of a minister who waits to make up his mind whether a given measure, say the disestablishment of the Irish Church, is in itself and on the merits desirable, until the official who runs diligently up and down the backstairs of the party, tells him that the measure is practicable and required in the interests of the band. On the one hand, a leader is lavishly panegyrised for his highmindedness, in suffering himself to be driven into his convictions by his party. On the other, a party is extolled for its political tact, in suffering itself to be forced out of its convictions by its leader. It is hard to decide which is the more discreditable and demoralising sight. The education of chiefs by followers, and of followers by chiefs, into the abandonment in a month of the traditions of centuries or the principles of a lifetime may conduce to the rapid and easy working of the machine. It certainly marks a triumph of the political spirit which the author of *The Prince* might have admired. It is assuredly mortal to habits of intellectual self-respect in the society which allows itself to be amused by the cajolery and legerdemain and self-sophistication of its rulers.

Of course there are excellent reasons why a statesman immersed in the actual conduct of affairs, should confine his attention to the work which his hands find to do. But the fact that leading statesmen are of necessity so absorbed in the tasks of the hour furnishes all the better reason why as many other people as possible should busy themselves in helping to prepare opinion for the practical application of unfamiliar but weighty and promising suggestions, by constant and ready discussion of them upon their merits. As a matter of fact it is not the men most occupied who are usually most deaf to new ideas. It is the loungers of politics, the quidnuncs, gossips, bustling idlers, who are most industrious in stifling discussion by protests against the waste of time and the loss of force involved in talking about proposals which are not exactly ready to be voted on. As it is, everybody knows that questions are inadequately discussed, or often not discussed at all, on the ground that the time is not yet come for their solution. Then when some unforeseen perturbation, or the natural course of things, forces on the time for their solution, they are settled in a slovenly, imperfect, and often downright vicious manner, from the fact that opinion has not been prepared for solving them in an efficient and perfect manner. The so-called settlement of the question of national education is the most recent and most deplorable illustration of what comes of refusing to examine ideas alleged to be impracticable. Perhaps we may venture to prophesy that the disendowment of the national church will supply the next illustration on an imposing scale. Gratuitous primary instruction, and the redistribution of electoral power, are other matters of signal importance, which comparatively few men will consent to discuss seriously and patiently, and for our indifference to which we shall one day surely smart. A judicious and cool writer has said that 'an opinion gravely professed by a man of sense and education demands always respectful consideration — demands and actually receives it from those whose own sense and education give them a correlative right; and whoever offends against this sort of courtesy may fairly be deemed to have forfeited the privileges it secures.' That is the least part of the matter. The serious mischief is the eventual miscarriage and loss and prodigal waste of good ideas.

The evil of which we have been speaking comes of not seeing the great truth, that it is worth while to take pains to find out the best way of doing a given task, even if you have strong grounds for suspecting that it will ultimately be done in a worse way. And so also in spheres of thought away from the political sphere, it is worth while 'to scorn delights and live laborious days' in order to make as sure as we can of having the best opinion, even if we know that this opinion has an infinitely small chance of being speedily or ever accepted by the majority, or by anybody but ourselves. Truth and wisdom have to bide their time, and then take their chance after all. The most that the individual can do is to seek them for himself, even if he seek alone. And if it is the most, it is also the least. Yet in our present mood we seem not to feel this. We misunderstand the considerations which should rightly lead us in practice to surrender some of what we desire, in order to secure the rest; and rightly make us acquiesce in a second-best course of action, in order to avoid stagnation or retrogression. We misunderstand all this, and go on to suppose that there are the same grounds why we should in our own minds acquiesce in second-best opinions; why we should mix a little alloy of conventional expression with the too fine ore of conviction; why we should adopt beliefs that we suspect in our hearts to be of more than equivocal authenticity, but into whose antecedents we do not greatly care to inquire, because they stand so well with the general public. This is compromise or economy or management of the first of the three kinds of which we are talking. It is economy applied to the formation of opinion; compromise or management in making up one's mind.

The lawfulness or expediency of it turns mainly, as with the other two kinds of compromise, upon the relative rights of the majority and the minority, and upon the respect which is owing from the latter to the former. It is a very easy thing for people endowed with the fanatical temperament, or demoralised by the habit of looking at society exclusively from the juridical point of view, to insist that no respect at all, except the respect that arises from being too weak to have your own way, is due from either to the other. This shallow and mischievous notion rests either on a misinterpretation of the experience of civilised societies, or else on nothing more creditable than an arbitrary and unreflecting temper. Those who have thought most carefully and disinterestedly about the matter, are agreed that in advanced societies the expedient course is that no portion of the community should insist on imposing its own will upon any other portion, except in matters which are vitally connected with the maintenance of the social union. The question where this vital connection begins is open to much discussion. The line defining the sphere of legitimate interference may be drawn variously, whether at self-regarding acts, or in some other condition and element of conduct. Wherever this line may be best taken, not only abstract speculation, but the practical and spontaneous tact of the world, has decided that there are limits, alike in the interest of majority and minority, to the rights of either to disturb the other. In other words, it is expedient in certain affairs that the will of the majority should be absolutely binding, while in affairs of a different order it should count for nothing, or as nearly nothing, as the sociable dependence of a man on his fellows will permit.

Our thesis is this. In the positive endeavour to realise an opinion, to convert a theory into practice, it may be, and very often is, highly expedient to defer to the prejudices of the majority, to move very slowly, to bow to the conditions of the *status quo*, to practise the very utmost sobriety, self-restraint, and conciliatoriness. The mere expression of opinion, in the next place, the avowal of dissent from received notions, the refusal to conform to language which implies the acceptance of such notions, — this rests on a different footing. Here the reasons for respecting the wishes and sentiments of the majority are far less strong, though, as we shall presently see, such reasons certainly exist, and will weigh with all well-considering men. Finally, in the formation of an opinion as to the abstract preferableness of one course of action over another, or as to the truth or falsehood or right significance of a proposition, the fact that the majority of one's contemporaries lean in the other direction is naught, and no more than dust in the balance. In making up our minds as to what would be the wisest line of policy if it were practicable, we have nothing to do with the circumstance that it is not practicable. And in settling with ourselves whether propositions purporting to state matters of fact are true or not, we have to consider how far they are conformable to the evidence. We have nothing to do with the comfort and solace which they would be likely to bring to others or ourselves, if they were taken as true . . .

Yet it is at least well, and more than that, it is an indispensable condition of social wellbeing, that the divorce between political responsibility and intellectual responsibility, between respect for what is instantly practicable and search after what is only important in thought, should not be too complete and universal. Even if there were no other objection, the undisputed predominance of the political spirit has a plain tendency to limit the subjects in which the men animated by it can take a real interest. All matters fall out of sight, or at least fall into a secondary place, which do not bear more or less directly and patently upon the material and structural welfare of the community. In this way the members of the community miss the most bracing, widening, and elevated of the whole range of influences that create great characters. First, they lose sincere concern about the larger questions which the human mind has raised up for itself. Second, they lose a fearless desire to reach the true answers to them, or if no certain answers should prove to be within reach, then at any rate to be satisfied on good grounds that this is so. Such questions are not immediately discerned by commonplace minds to be of social import. Consequently they, and all else that is not obviously connected with the machinery of society, give way in the public consideration to what is so connected with it, in a manner that cannot be mistaken.

Again, even minds that are not commonplace are affected for the worse by the same spirit. They are aware of the existence of the great speculative subjects and of their importance, but the pressure of the political spirit on such men makes them afraid of the conclusions to which free inquiry might bring them. Accordingly they abstain from inquiry, and dread nothing so much as making up their minds. They see reasons for thinking that, if they applied themselves seriously to the formation of true opinions in this or that department, they would come to conclusions which, though likely to make their way in the course of some centuries, are wholly unpopular now, and which might ruin the influence of anybody suspected of accepting, or even of so much as leaning towards, them. Life, they reflect, is short; missionaries do not pass for a very agreeable class, nor martyrs for a very sensible class; one can only do a trifling amount of good in the world, at best; it is moral suicide to throw away any chance of achieving even that trifle; and therefore it is best not only not to express, but not to take the trouble to acquire, right views in this quarter or that, and to draw clear away from such or such a region of thought, for the sake of keeping peace on earth and superficial good will among men.

It would be too harsh to stigmatise such a train of thought as self-seeking and hypocritical. It is the natural product of the political spirit, which is incessantly thinking of present consequences and the immediately feasible. There is nothing in the mere dread of losing it, to hinder influence from being well employed, so far as it goes. But one can hardly overrate the ill consequences of this particular kind of management, this unspoken bargaining with the little circle of his fellows which constitutes the world of a man. If he may retain his place among them as preacher or teacher, he is willing to forego his birthright of free explanation; he consents to be blind to the duty which attaches to every intelligent man of having some clear ideas, even though only provisional ones, upon the greatest subjects of human interest, and of deliberately preferring these, whatever they may be, to their opposites. Either an individual or a community is fatally dwarfed by any such limitation of the field in which one is free to use his mind. For it is a limitation, not prescribed by absorption in one set of subjects rather than another, nor by insufficient preparation for the discussion of certain subjects, nor by indolence nor incuriousness, but solely by apprehension of the conclusions to which such use of the mind might bring the too courageous seeker. If there were no other ill effect, this kind of limitation would at least have the radical disadvantage of dulling the edge of responsibility, of deadening the sharp sense of personal answerableness either to a God, or to society, or to a man's own conscience and intellectual self-respect.

How momentous a disadvantage this is, we can best know by contemplating the characters which have sometimes lighted up the old times. Men were then devoutly persuaded that their eternal salvation depended on their having true beliefs. Any slackness in finding out which beliefs are the true ones would have to be answered for before the throne of Almighty God, at the sure risk and peril of everlasting damnation. To what quarter in the large historic firmament can we turn our eyes with such certainty of being stirred and elevated, of thinking better of human life and the worth of those who have been most deeply penetrated by its seriousness, as to the annals of the intrepid spirits whom the protestant doctrine of indefeasible personal responsibility brought to the front in Germany in the sixteenth century, and in England and Scotland in the seventeenth? It is not their fanaticism, still less is it their theology, which makes the great Puritan chiefs of England and the stern Covenanters of Scotland so heroic in our sight. It is the fact that they sought truth and ensued it, not thinking of the practicable nor cautiously counting majorities and minorities, but each man pondering and searching so 'as ever in the great Taskmaster's eye.'

It is no adequate answer to urge that this awful consciousness of a divine presence and supervision has ceased to be the living fact it once was. That partly explains, but it certainly does not justify, our present lassitude. For the ever-wakeful eye of celestial power is not the only conceivable stimulus to responsibility. To pass from those grim heroes of protestantism to the French philosophers of the last century is a wide leap in a hundred respects, yet they too were pricked by the œstrus of intellectual responsibility. Their doctrine was dismally insufficient, and sometimes, as the present writer has often pointed out, it was directly vicious. Their daily lives were surrounded by much shabbiness and many meannesses. But, after all, no temptation and no menace, no pains or penalties for thinking about certain subjects, and no rewards for turning to think about something else, could divert such men as Voltaire and Diderot from their alert and strenuous search after such truth as could be vouchsafed to their imperfect lights. A catastrophe followed, it is true, but the misfortunes which attended it were due more to the champions of tradition and authority than to the soldiers of emancipation. Even in the case of the latter, they were due to an inadequate doctrine, and not at all either to their sense of the necessity of free speculation and inquiry, or to the intrepidity with which they obeyed the promptings of that ennobling sense . . .

It may be urged that if, as it is the object of the present chapter to state, there are opinions which a man should form for himself, and which it may yet be expedient that he should not only be slow to attempt to realise in practical life, but sometimes even slow to express, — then we are demanding from him the performance of a troublesome duty, while we are taking from him the only motives which could really induce him to perform it. If, it may be asked, I am not to carry my notions into practice, nor try to induce others to accept them, nor even boldly publish them, why in the name of all economy of force should I take so much pains in forming opinions which are, after all, on these conditions so very likely to come to naught? The answer to this is that opinions do not come to naught, even if the man who holds them should never think fit to publish them. For one thing, as we shall see in our next division, the conditions which make against frank declaration of our convictions are of rare occurrence. And, apart from this, convictions may well exert a most decisive influence over our conduct, even if reasons exist, or seem to exist, for not pressing them on others. Though themselves invisible to the outer world, they may yet operate with magnetic force both upon other parts of our belief which the outer world does see, and upon the whole of our dealings with it. Whether we are good or bad, it is only a broken and incoherent fragment of our whole personality that even those who are intimate with us, much less the common world, can ever come into contact with. The important thing is that the personality itself should be as little as possible broken, incoherent, and fragmentary; that reasoned and consistent opinions should back a firm will, and independent convictions inspire the intellectual self-respect and strenuous self-possession which the clamour of majorities and the silent yet ever-pressing force of the *status quo* are equally powerless to shake.

Character is doubtless of far more importance than mere intellectual opinion. We only too often see highly rationalised convictions in persons of weak purpose or low motives. But while fully recognising this, and the sort of possible reality which lies at the root of such a phrase as 'godless intellect' or 'intellectual devils' — though the phrase has no reality when it is used by self-seeking politicians or prelates — yet it is well to remember the very obvious truth that opinions are at least an extremely important part of character. As it is sometimes put, what we think has a prodigiously close connection with what we are. The consciousness of having reflected seriously and conclusively on important questions, whether social or spiritual, augments dignity while it does not lessen humility. In this sense, taking thought can and does add a cubit to our stature. Opinions which we may not feel bound or even permitted to press on other people, are not the less forces for being latent. They shape ideals, and it is ideals that inspire conduct. They do this, though from afar, and though he who possesses them may not presume to take the world into his confidence. Finally, unless a man follows out ideas to their full conclusion without fear what the conclusion may be, whether he thinks it expedient to make his thought and its goal fully known or not, it is impossible that he should acquire a commanding grasp of principles. And a commanding grasp of principles, whether they are public or not, is at the very root of coherency of character. It raises mediocrity near to a level with the highest talents, if these talents are in company with a disposition that allows the little prudences of the hour incessantly to obscure the persistent laws of things. These persistencies, if a man has once satisfied himself of their direction and mastered their bearings and application, are just as cogent and valuable a guide to conduct, whether he publishes them *ad urbem et orbem*, or esteems them too strong meat for people who have, through indurated use and wont, lost the courage of facing unexpected truths.

One conspicuous result of the failure to see that our opinions have roots to them, independently of the feelings which either majorities or other portions of the people around us may entertain about them, is that neither political matters nor any other serious branches of opinion, engage us in their loftiest or most deep-reaching forms. The advocate of a given theory of government or society is so misled by a wrong understanding of the practice of just and wise compromise in applying it, as to forget the noblest and most inspiring shape which his theory can be made to assume. It is the worst of political blunders to insist on carrying an ideal set of principles into execution, where others have rights of dissent, and those others persons whose assent is as indispensable to success, as it is impossible to attain. But to be afraid or ashamed of holding such an ideal set of principles in one's mind in their highest and most abstract expression, does more than any one other cause to stunt or petrify those elements in character to which life should owe most of its savour.

If a man happens to be a Conservative, for instance, it is pitiful that he should think so much more of what other people on his side or the other think, than of the widest and highest of the ideas on which a conservative philosophy of life and human society reposes. Such ideas are these, — that the social union is the express creation and ordering of the Deity: that its movements follow his mysterious and fixed dispensation: that the church and the state are convertible terms, and each citizen of the latter is an incorporated member of the former: that conscience, if perversely and misguidedly self-asserting, has no rights against the decrees of the conscience of the nation: that it is the most detestable of crimes to perturb the pacific order of society either by active agitation or speculative restlessness: that descent from a long line of ancestors in great station adds an element of dignity to life, and imposes many high obligations. We do not say that these and the rest of the propositions which make up the true theoretic basis of a conservative creed, are proper for the hustings, or expedient in an election address or a speech in parliament. We do say that if these high and not unintelligible principles, which alone can give to reactionary professions any worth or significance, were present in the minds of men who speak reactionary language, the country would be spared the ignominy of seeing certain real truths of society degraded at the hands of aristocratic adventurers and plutocratic parasites into some miserable process of 'dishing Whigs.'

This impoverishment of aims and depravation of principles by the triumph of the political spirit outside of its proper sphere, cannot unfortunately be restricted to any one set of people in the state. It is something in the very atmosphere, which no sanitary cordon can limit. Liberalism, too, would be something more generous, more attractive — yes, and more practically effective, if its professors and champions could allow their sense of what is feasible to be refreshed and widened by a more free recognition, however private and undemonstrative, of the theoretic ideas which give their social creed whatever life and consistency it may have. Such ideas are these: That the conditions of the social union are not a mystery, only to be touched by miracle, but the results of explicable causes, and susceptible of constant modification: that the thoughts of wise and patriotic men should be perpetually turned towards the improvement of these conditions in every direction: that contented acquiescence in the ordering that has come down to us from the past is selfish and anti-social, because amid the ceaseless change that is inevitable in a growing organism, the institutions of the past demand progressive re-adaptations: that such improvements are most likely to be secured in the greatest abundance by limiting the sphere of authority, extending that of free individuality, and steadily striving after the bestowal, so far as the nature of things will ever permit it, of equality of opportunity: that while there is dignity in ancestry, a modern society is only safe in proportion as it summons capacity to its public counsels and enterprises: that such a society to endure must progress: that progress on its political side means more than anything else the substitution of Justice as a governing idea, instead of Privilege, and that the best guarantee for justice in public dealings is the participation in their own government of the people most likely to suffer from injustice. This is not an exhaustive account of the progressive doctrine, and we have here nothing to say as to its soundness. We only submit that if those who use the watchwords of Liberalism were to return upon its principles, instead of dwelling exclusively on practical compromises, the tone of public life would be immeasurably raised. The cause of social improvement would be less systematically balked of the victories that are best worth gaining. Progress would mean something more than mere entrances and exits on the theatre of office. We should not see in the mass of parliamentary candidates — and they are important people, because nearly every Englishman with any ambition is a parliamentary candidate, actual or potential — that grave anxiety, that sober rigour, that immense caution, which are all so really laughable, because so many of these men are only anxious lest they should make a mistake in finding out what the majority of their constituents would like them to think; only rigorous against those who are indiscreet enough to press a principle against the beck of a whip or a wire-puller; and only very cautious not so much lest their opinion should be wrong, as lest it should not pay.

Indolence and timidity have united to popularise among us a flaccid latitudinarianism, which thinks itself a benign tolerance for the opinions of others. It is in truth only a pretentious form of being without settled opinions of our own, and without any desire to settle them. No one can complain of the want of speculative activity at the present time in a certain way. The air, at a certain social elevation, is as full as it has ever been of ideas, theories, problems, possible solutions, suggested questions, and proffered answers. But then they are at large, without cohesion, and very apt to be the objects even in the more instructed minds of not much more than dilettante interest. We see in solution an immense number of notions, which people think it quite unnecessary to precipitate in the form of convictions. We constantly hear the age lauded for its tolerance, for its candour, for its openness of mind, for the readiness with which a hearing is given to ideas that forty years ago, or even less that that, would have excluded persons suspected of holding them from decent society, and in fact did so exclude them. Before, however, we congratulate ourselves too warmly on this, let us be quite sure that we are not mistaking for tolerance what is really nothing more credit- able than indifference. These two attitudes of mind, which are so vitally unlike in their real quality, are so hard to distinguish in their outer seem- ing . . .

Ambrose's famous saying, that 'it hath not pleased the Lord to give his people salvation in dialectic,' has a profound meaning far beyond its applica- tion to theology. It is deeply true that our ruling convictions are less the product of ratiocination than of sympathy, imagination, usage, tradition. But from this it does not follow that the reasoning faculties are to be further discouraged. On the contrary, just because the other elements are so strong that they can be trusted to take care of themselves, it is expedient to give special countenance to the intellectual habits, which alone can check and rectify the constantly aberrating tendencies of sentiment on the one side, and custom on the other. This remark brings us to another type, of whom it is not irrelevant to speak shortly in this place. The consequences of the strength of the political spirit are not all direct, nor does its strength by any means spring solely from its indulgence to the less respectable elements of character, such as languor, extreme pliableness, superficiality. On the con- trary, it has an indirect influence in removing the only effective restraint on the excesses of some qualities which, when duly directed and limited, are among the most precious parts of our mental constitution. The political spirit is the great force in throwing love of truth and accurate reasoning into a secondary place. The evil does not stop here. This achievement has indirectly countenanced the postponement of intellectual methods, and the diminution of the sense of intellectual responsibility, by a school that is anything rather than political.

Theology has borrowed, and coloured for her own use, the principles which were first brought into vogue in politics. If in the one field it is the fashion to consider convenience first and truth second, in the other there is a corresponding fashion of placing truth second and emotional comfort first. If there are some who compromise their real opinions, or the chance of reaching truth, for the sake of gain, there are far more who shrink from giving their intelligence free play, for the sake of keeping undisturbed cer- tain luxurious spiritual sensibilities. This choice of emotional gratification before truth and upright dealing with one's own understanding, creates a character that is certainly far less unlovely than those who sacrifice their intellectual integrity to mere material convenience. The moral flaw is less palpable and less gross. Yet here too there is the stain of intellectual improbity, and it is perhaps all the more mischievous for being partly hidden under the mien of spiritual exaltation . . .

We only desire to state the evil of the notion that a man is warranted in comforting himself with dogmas and formularies, which he has first to empty of all definite, precise, and clearly determinable significance, before he can get them out of the way of his religious sensibilities. Whether Reason or Affection is to have the empire in the society of the future, when Reason may possibly have no more to discover for us in the region of morals and religion, and so will have become *emeritus* and taken a lower place, as of a tutor whose services the human family, being now grown up, no longer requires, — however this may be, it is at least certain that in the meantime the spiritual life of man needs direction quite as much as it needs impulse, and light quite as much as force. This direction and light can only be safely procured by the free and vigorous use of the intelligence. But the intelligence is not free in the presence of a mortal fear lest its conclusions should trouble soft tranquillity of spirit. There is always hope of a man so long as he dwells in the region of the direct categorical proposition and the unambiguous term; so long as he does not deny the rightly drawn conclusion after accepting the major and minor premises. This may seem a scanty virtue and very easy grace. Yet experience shows it to be too hard of attainment for those who tamper with disinterestedness of conviction, for the sake of luxuriating in the softness of spiritual transport without interruption from a syllogism. It is true that there are now and then in life as in history noble and fair natures, that by the silent teaching and unconscious example of their inborn purity, star-like constancy, and great devotion, do carry the world about them to further heights of living than can be attained by ratiocination. But these, the blameless and loved saints of the earth, rise too rarely on our dull horizons to make a rule for the world. The law of things is that they who tamper with veracity, from whatever motive, are tampering with the vital force of human progress. Our comfort and the delight of the religious imagination are no better than forms of self-indulgence, when they are secured at the cost of that love of truth on which, more than on anything else, the increase of light and happiness among men must depend. We have to fight and do lifelong battle against the forces of darkness, and anything that turns the edge of reason blunts the surest and most potent of our weapons.

1859

JOHN STUART MILL

On the Liberty of Thought and Discussion

Two great forces operated in the life of John Stuart Mill to produce his classic work, On Liberty *(1859), the second chapter of which is here reprinted, the footnotes being omitted. Born into a utilitarian family, educated for the business of being a genius, and touched by the humanitarianism of his age, he reshaped political and social theory in the Victorian world. In 1830 he met a Mrs. Taylor, whose husband seems to have been philosophical about being away from home when Mill dined with his wife. Mill's connection with Mrs. Taylor (whom he married in 1851 upon the death of her husband) estranged Mill's family and embarrassed his friends. In his capacity as a political theorist demanding the widest latitude for the discussion of social reform, and in his capacity as a private person experiencing the pressures of social prejudice, he came to believe that the individual should be let alone, free to make his mistakes, within the broadest boundaries of tolerance. The first chapter of the book declares that modern society must protect the right of private opinion. Then follows the famous explication of the nature of intellectual liberty given below.*

THE TIME, IT IS TO BE HOPED, is gone by, when any defence would be necessary of the "liberty of the press" as one of the securities against corrupt or tyrannical government. No argument, we may suppose, can now be needed, against permitting a legislature or an executive, not identified in interest with the people, to prescribe opinions to them, and determine what doctrines or what arguments they shall be allowed to hear. This aspect of the question, besides, has been so often and so triumphantly enforced by preceding writers, that it needs not be specially insisted on in this place. Though the law of England, on the subject of the press, is as servile to this day as it was in the time of the Tudors, there is little danger of its being actually put in force against political discussion, except during some temporary panic, when fear of insurrection drives ministers and judges from their propriety; and, speaking generally, it is not, in constitutional countries, to be apprehended, that the government, whether completely responsible to the people or not, will often attempt to control the expression of opinion, except when in doing so it makes itself the organ of the general intolerance of the public. Let us suppose, therefore, that the government is entirely at one with the people, and never thinks of exerting any power of coercion unless in agreement with what it conceives to be their voice. But I deny the right of the people to exercise such coercion, either by themselves or by their government. The power itself is illegitimate. The best government has no more title to it than the worst. It is as noxious, or more noxious, when exerted in accordance with public opinion, than when in opposition to it. If all mankind minus one were of one opinion, and only one person were of the contrary opinion, mankind would be no more justified in silencing that one person, than he, if he had the power, would be justified in silencing mankind. Were an opinion a personal possession of no value except to the owner; if to be obstructed in the enjoyment of it were simply a private injury, it would make some difference whether the injury was inflicted only on a few persons or on many. But the peculiar evil of silencing the expression of an opinion is, that it is robbing the human race; posterity as well as the existing generation; those who dissent from the opinion, still more than those who hold it. If the opinion is right, they are deprived of the opportunity of exchanging error for truth: if wrong, they lose, what is almost as great a benefit, the clearer perception and livelier impression of truth, produced by its collision with error.

It is necessary to consider separately these two hypotheses, each of which has a distinct branch of the argument corresponding to it. We can never be sure that the opinion we are endeavouring to stifle is a false opinion; and if we were sure, stifling it would be an evil still.

First: the opinion which it is attempted to suppress by authority may possibly be true. Those who desire to suppress it, of course deny its truth; but they are not infallible. They have no authority to decide the question for all mankind, and exclude every other person from the means of judging. To refuse a hearing to an opinion, because they are sure that it is false, is to assume that *their* certainty is the same thing as *absolute* certainty. All silencing of discussion is an assumption of infallibility. Its condemnation may be allowed to rest on this common argument, not the worse for being common.

Unfortunately for the good sense of mankind, the fact of their fallibility is far from carrying the weight in their practical judgment which is always allowed to it in theory; for while every one well knows himself to be fallible, few think it necessary to take any precautions against their own fallibility, or admit the supposition that any opinion, of which they feel very certain, may be one of the examples of the error to which they acknowledge themselves to be liable. Absolute princes, or others who are accustomed to unlimited deference, usually feel this complete confidence in their own opinions on nearly all subjects. People more happily situated, who sometimes hear their opinions disputed, and are not wholly unused to be set right when they are wrong, place the same unbounded reliance only on such of their opinions as are shared by all who surround them, or to whom they habitually defer; for in proportion to a man's want of confidence in his own solitary judgment, does he usually repose, with implicit trust, on the infallibility of "the world" in general. And the world, to each individual, means the part of it with which he comes in contact; his party, his sect, his church, his class of society; the man may be called, by comparison, almost liberal and large-minded to whom it means anything so comprehensive as his own country or his own age. Nor is his faith in this collective authority at all shaken by his being aware that other ages, countries, sects, churches, classes, and parties have thought, and even now think, the exact reverse. He devolves upon his own world the responsibility of being in the right against the dissentient worlds of other people; and it never troubles him that mere accident has decided which of these numerous worlds is the object of his reliance, and that the same causes which make him a Churchman in London, would have made him a Buddhist or a Confucian in Pekin. Yet it is as evident in itself, as any amount of argument can make it, that ages are no more infallible than individuals; every age having held many opinions which subsequent ages have deemed not only false but absurd; and it is as certain that many opinions now general will be rejected by future ages, as it is that many, once general, are rejected by the present.

The objection likely to be made to this argument would probably take some such form as the following. There is no greater assumption of infallibility in forbidding the progagation of error, than in any other thing which is done by public authority on its own judgment and responsibility. Judgment is given to men that they may use it. Because it may be used erroneously, are men to be told that they ought not to use it at all? To prohibit what they think pernicious, is not claiming exemption from error, but fulfilling the duty incumbent on them, although fallible, of acting on their conscientious conviction. If we were never to act on our opinions, because those opinions may be wrong, we should leave all our interests uncared for, and all our duties unperformed. An objection which applies to all conduct can be no valid objection to any conduct in particular. It is the duty of governments, and of individuals, to form the truest opinions they can; to form them carefully, and never impose them upon others unless they are quite sure of being right. But when they are sure (such reasoners may say), it is not conscientiousness but cowardice to shrink from acting on their opinions, and allow doctrines which they honestly think dangerous to the welfare of mankind, either in this life or in another, to be scattered abroad without restraint, because other people, in less enlightened times, have persecuted opinions now believed to be true. Let us take care, it may be said, not to make the same mistake: but governments and nations have made mistakes in other things, which are not denied to be fit subjects for the exercise of authority: they have laid on bad taxes, made unjust wars. Ought we therefore to lay on no taxes, and, under whatever provocation, make no wars? Men, and governments, must act to the best of their ability. There is no such thing as absolute certainty, but there is assurance sufficient for the purposes of human life. We may, and must, assume our opinion to be true for the guidance of our own conduct: and it is assuming no more when we forbid bad men to pervert society by the propagation of opinions which we regard as false and pernicious.

I answer, that it is assuming very much more. There is the greatest difference between presuming an opinion to be true, because, with every opportunity for contesting it, it has not been refuted, and assuming its truth for the purpose of not permitting its refutation. Complete liberty of contradicting and disproving our opinion is the very condition which justifies us in assuming its truth for purposes of action; and on no other terms can a being with human faculties have any rational assurance of being right.

When we consider either the history of opinion, or the ordinary conduct of human life, to what is it to be ascribed that the one and the other are no worse than they are? Not certainly to the inherent force of the human understanding; for, on any matter not self-evident, there are ninety-nine persons totally incapable of judging of it for one who is capable; and the capacity of the hundredth person is only comparative; for the majority of the eminent men of every past generation held many opinions now known to be erroneous, and did or approved numerous things which no one will now justify. Why is it, then, that there is on the whole a preponderance among mankind of rational opinions and rational conduct? If there really is this preponderance — which there must be unless human affairs are, and have always been, in an almost desperate state — it is owing to a quality of the human mind, the source of everything respectable in man either as an intellectual or as a moral being, namely, that his errors are corrigible. He is capable of rectifying his mistakes, by discussion and experience. Not by experience alone. There must be discussion, to show how experience is to be interpreted. Wrong opinions and practices gradually yield to fact and argument; but facts and arguments, to produce any effect on the mind, must be brought before it. Very few facts are able to tell their own story, without comments to bring out their meaning. The whole strength and value, then, of human judgment, depending on the one property, that it can be set right when it is wrong, reliance can be placed on it only when the means of setting it right are kept constantly at hand. In the case of any person whose judg-

ment is really deserving of confidence, how has it become so? Because he
has kept his mind open to criticism of his opinions and conduct. Because it
has been his practice to listen to all that could be said against him; to profit
by as much of it as was just, and expound to himself, and upon occasion to
others, the fallacy of what was fallacious. Because he has felt, that the only
way in which a human being can make some approach to knowing the
whole of a subject, is by hearing what can be said about it by persons of
every variety of opinion, and studying all modes in which it can be looked
at by every character of mind. No wise man ever acquired his wisdom in
any mode but this; nor is it in the nature of human intellect to become wise
in any other manner. The steady habit of correcting and completing his own
opinion by collating it with those of others, so far from causing doubt and
hesitation in carrying it into practice, is the only stable foundation for a just
reliance on it: for, being cognisant of all that can, at least obviously, be said
against him, and having taken up his position against all gainsayers —
knowing that he has sought for objections and difficulties, instead of avoid-
ing them, and has shut out no light which can be thrown upon the subject
from any quarter — he has a right to think his judgment better than that of
any person, or any multitude, who have not gone through a similar process.

It is not too much to require that what the wisest of mankind, those who
are best entitled to trust their own judgment, find necessary to warrant their
relying on it, should be submitted to by that miscellaneous collection of a
few wise and many foolish individuals, called the public. The most intoler-
ant of churches, the Roman Catholic Church, even at the canonisation of a
saint, admits, and listens patiently to, a "devil's advocate." The holiest of
men, it appears, cannot be admitted to posthumous honours, until all that
the devil could say against him is known and weighed. If even the Newtonian philosophy were not permitted to be questioned, mankind could not
feel as complete assurance of its truth as they now do. The beliefs which we
have most warrant for have no safeguard to rest on, but a standing invita-
tion to the whole world to prove them unfounded. If the challenge is not
accepted, or is accepted and the attempt fails, we are far enough from certainty still; but we have done the best that the existing state of human
reason admits of; we have neglected nothing that could give the truth a
chance of reaching us: if the lists are kept open, we may hope that if there
be a better truth, it will be found when the human mind is capable of
receiving it; and in the meantime we may rely on having attained such
approach to truth as is possible in our own day. This is the amount of certainty attainable by a fallible being, and this the sole way of attaining it.

Strange it is, that men should admit the validity of the arguments for free
discussion, but object to their being "pushed to an extreme"; not seeing that

unless the reasons are good for an extreme case, they are not good for any case. Strange that they should imagine that they are not assuming infallibility, when they acknowledge that there should be free discussion on all subjects which can possibly be *doubtful*, but think that some particular principle or doctrine should be forbidden to be questioned because it is so *certain*, that is, because *they are certain* that it is certain. To call any proposition certain, while there is any one who would deny its certainty if permitted, but who is not permitted, is to assume that we ourselves, and those who agree with us, are the judges of certainty, and judges without hearing the other side.

In the present age — which has been described as "destitute of faith, but terrified at scepticism" — in which people feel sure, not so much that their opinions are true, as that they should not know what to do without them — the claims of an opinion to be protected from public attack are rested not so much on its truth, as on its importance to society. There are, it is alleged, certain beliefs so useful, not to say indispensable, to well-being that it is as much the duty of governments to uphold those beliefs, as to protect any other of the interests of society. In a case of such necessity, and so directly in the line of their duty, something less than infallibility may, it is maintained, warrant, and even bind, governments to act on their own opinion, confirmed by the general opinion of mankind. It is also often argued, and still oftener thought, that none but bad men would desire to weaken these salutary beliefs; and there can be nothing wrong, it is thought, in restraining bad men, and prohibiting what only such men would wish to practise. This mode of thinking makes the justification of restraints on discussion not a question of the truth of doctrines, but of their usefulness; and flatters itself by that means to escape the responsibility of claiming to be an infallible judge of opinions. But those who thus satisfy themselves, do not perceive that the assumption of infallibility is merely shifted from one point to another. The usefulness of an opinion is itself matter of opinion: as disputable, as open to discussion, and requiring discussion as much as the opinion itself. There is the same need of an infallible judge of opinions to decide an opinion to be noxious, as to decide it to be false, unless the opinion condemned has full opportunity of defending itself. And it will not do to say that the heretic may be allowed to maintain the utility or harmlessness of his opinion, though forbidden to maintain its truth. The truth of an opinion is part of its utility. If we would know whether or not it is desirable that a proposition should be believed, is it possible to exclude the consideration of whether or not it is true? In the opinion, not of bad men, but of the best men, no belief which is contrary to truth can be really useful: and can you prevent such men from urging that plea, when they are charged with culpability for denying some doctrine which they are told is useful, but which they believe to be false? Those who are on the side of received opinions never fail to take all possible advantage of this plea; you do not find *them* handling the question of utility as if it could be completely abstracted from that of truth: on the contrary, it is, above all, because their doctrine is "the truth," that the knowledge or the belief of it is held to be so indispensable. There can be no fair discussion of the question of usefulness when an argument so vital may be employed on one side, but not on the other. And in point of fact, when law or public feeling do not permit the truth of an opinion to be disputed, they are just as little tolerant of a denial of its usefulness. The utmost they allow is an extenuation of its absolute necessity, or of the positive guilt of rejecting it.

In order more fully to illustrate the mischief of denying a hearing to opinions because we, in our own judgment, have condemned them, it will be desirable to fix down the discussion to a concrete case; and I choose, by preference, the cases which are least favourable to me — in which the argument against freedom of opinion, both on the score of truth and on that of utility, is considered the strongest. Let the opinions impugned be the belief in a God and in a future state, or any of the commonly received doctrines of morality. To fight the battle on such ground gives a great advantage to an unfair antagonist; since he will be sure to say (and many who have no desire to be unfair will say it internally), Are these the doctrines which you do not deem sufficiently certain to be taken under the protection of law? Is the belief in a God one of the opinions to feel sure of which you hold to be assuming infallibility? But I must be permitted to observe, that it is not the feeling sure of a doctrine (be it what it may) which I call an assumption of infallibility. It is the undertaking to decide that question *for others*, without allowing them to hear what can be said on the contrary side. And I denounce and reprobate this pretension not the less, if put forth on the side of my most solemn convictions. However positive any one's persuasion may be, not only of the falsity but of the pernicious consequences — not only of the pernicious consequences, but (to adopt expressions which I altogether condemn) the immorality and impiety of an opinion; yet if, in pursuance of that private judgment, though backed by the public judgment of his country or his contemporaries, he prevents the opinion from being heard in its defence, he assumes infallibility. And so far from the assumption being less objectionable or less dangerous because the opinion is called immoral or impious, this is the case of all others in which it is most fatal. These are exactly the occasions on which the men of one generation commit those dreadful mistakes which excite the astonishment and horror of posterity. It is among such that we find the instances memorable in history, when the arm of the law has been employed to root out the best men and the noblest doctrines; with deplorable success as to the men, though some of the doctrines have survived to be (as if in mockery) invoked in defence of similar conduct towards those who dissent from *them*, or from their received interpretation.

Mankind can hardly be too often reminded, that there was once a man named Socrates, between whom and the legal authorities and public opinion of his time there took place a memorable collision. Born in an age and country abounding in individual greatness, this man has been handed down to us by those who best knew both him and the age, as the most virtuous man in it; while *we* know him as the head and prototype of all subsequent teachers of virtue, the source equally of the lofty inspiration of Plato and the judicious utilitarianism of Aristotle, "*i maestri di color che sanno*," the two headsprings of ethical as of all other philosophy. This acknowledged master of all the eminent thinkers who have since lived — whose fame, still growing after more than two thousand years, all but outweighs the whole remainder of the names which make his native city illustrious — was put to death by his countrymen, after a judicial conviction, for impiety and immorality. Impiety, in denying the gods recognised by the State; indeed his accuser asserted (see the "Apologia") that he believed in no gods at all. Immorality, in being, by his doctrines and instructions, a "corruptor of youth." Of these charges the tribunal, there is every ground for believing, honestly found him guilty, and condemned the man who probably of all then born had deserved best of mankind to be put to death as a criminal.

To pass from this to the only other instance of judicial iniquity, the mention of which, after the condemnation of Socrates, would not be an anticlimax: the event which took place on Calvary rather more than eighteen hundred years ago. The man who left on the memory of those who witnessed his life and conversation such an impression of his moral grandeur that eighteen subsequent centuries have done homage to him as the Almighty in person, was ignominiously put to death, as what? As a blasphemer. Men did not merely mistake their benefactor; they mistook him for the exact contrary of what he was, and treated him as that prodigy of impiety which they themselves are now held to be for their treatment of him. The feelings with which mankind now regard these lamentable transactions, especially the later of the two, render them extremely unjust in their judgment of the unhappy actors. These were, to all appearance, not bad men — not worse than men commonly are, but rather the contrary; men who possessed in a full, or somewhat more than a full measure, the religious, moral, and patriotic feelings of their time and people: the very kind of men who, in all times, our own included, have every chance of passing through life blameless and respected. The high-priest who rent his garments when the words were pronounced, which, according to all the ideas of his country, constituted the blackest guilt, was in all probability quite as sincere in his horror and indignation as the generality of respectable and pious men now are in the religious and moral sentiments they profess; and most of those who now shudder at his conduct, if they had lived in his time, and been born Jews, would have acted precisely as he did. Orthodox Christians who are tempted to think that those who stoned to death the first martyrs must have been worse men than they themselves are, ought to remember that one of those persecutors was Saint Paul.

Let us add one more example, the most striking of all, if the impressiveness of an error is measured by the wisdom and virtue of him who falls into it. If ever any one, possessed of power, had grounds for thinking himself the best and most enlightened among his contemporaries, it was the Emperor Marcus Aurelius. Absolute monarch of the whole civilised world, he preserved through life not only the most unblemished justice, but what was less to be expected from his Stoical breeding, the tenderest heart. The few failings which are attributed to him were all on the side of indulgence: while his writings, the highest ethical product of the ancient mind, differ scarcely perceptibly, if they differ at all, from the most characteristic teachings of Christ. This man, a better Christian in all but the dogmatic sense of the word than almost any of the ostensibly Christian sovereigns who have since reigned, persecuted Christianity. Placed at the summit of all the previous attainments of humanity, with an open, unfettered intellect, and a character which led him of himself to embody in his moral writings the Christian ideal, he yet failed to see that Christianity was to be a good and not an evil to the world, with his duties to which he was so deeply penetrated. Existing society he knew to be in a deplorable state. But such as it was, he saw, or thought he saw, that it was held together, and prevented from being worse, by belief and reverence of the received divinities. As a ruler of mankind, he deemed it his duty not to suffer society to fall in pieces; and saw not how, if its existing ties were removed, any others could be formed which could again knit it together. The new religion openly aimed at dissolving these ties: unless, therefore, it was his duty to adopt that religion, it seemed to be his duty to put it down. Inasmuch then as the theology of Christianity did not appear to him true or of divine origin; inasmuch as this strange history of a crucified God was not credible to him, and a system which purported to rest entirely upon a foundation to him so wholly unbelievable, could not be foreseen by him to be that renovating agency which, after all abatements, it has in fact proved to be; the gentlest and most amiable of philosophers and rulers, under a solemn sense of duty, authorised the persecution of Christianity. To my mind this is one of the most tragical facts in all history. It is a bitter thought, how different a thing the Christianity of the world might have been, if the Christian faith had been adopted as the religion of the empire under the auspices of Marcus Aurelius instead of those of Constantine. But it would be equally unjust to him and false to truth to deny, that no one plea which can be urged for punishing anti-Christian teaching was wanting to Marcus Aurelius for punishing, as he did, the propagation of Christianity. No Christian more firmly believes that Atheism is false, and tends to the dissolution of society, than Marcus Aurelius believed the same things of Christianity; he who, of all men then living, might have been thought the most capable of appreciating it. Unless any one who approves of punishment for the promulgation of opinions, flatters himself that he is a wiser and better man than Marcus Aurelius — more deeply versed in the wisdom of his time, more elevated in his intellect above it — more earnest in his search for truth, or more single-minded in his devotion to it when found; let him abstain from that assumption of the joint infallibility of himself and the multitude, which the great Antoninus made with so unfortunate a result.

Aware of the impossibility of defending the use of punishment for restraining irreligious opinions by any argument which will not justify Marcus Antoninus, the enemies of religious freedom, when hard pressed, occasionally accept this consequence, and say, with Dr. Johnson, that the persecutors of Christianity were in the right; that persecution is an ordeal through which truth ought to pass, and always passes successfully, legal penalties being, in the end, powerless against truth, though sometimes beneficially effective against mischievous errors. This is a form of the argument for religious intolerance sufficiently remarkable not to be passed without notice.

A theory which maintains that truth may justifiably be persecuted because persecution cannot possibly do it any harm, cannot be charged with being intentionally hostile to the reception of new truths; but we cannot commend the generosity of its dealing with the persons to whom mankind are indebted for them. To discover to the world something which deeply concerns it, and of which it was previously ignorant; to prove to it that it had been mistaken on some vital point of temporal or spiritual interest, is as important a service as a human being can render to his fellow-creatures, and in certain cases, as in those of the early Christians and of the Reformers, those who think with Dr. Johnson believe it to have been the most precious gift which could be bestowed on mankind. That the authors of such splendid benefits should be requited by martyrdom; that their reward should be to be dealt with as the vilest of criminals, is not, upon this theory, a deplorable error and misfortune, for which humanity should mourn in sackcloth and ashes, but the normal and justifiable state of things. The propounder of a new truth, according to this doctrine, should stand, as stood, in the legislation of the Locrians, the proposer of a new law, with a halter round his neck, to be instantly tightened if the public assembly did not, on hearing his reasons, then and there adopt his proposition. People who defend this mode of treating benefactors cannot be supposed to set much value on the benefit; and I believe this view of the subject is mostly confined to the sort of persons who think that new truths may have been desirable once, but that we have had enough of them now.

But, indeed, the dictum that truth always triumphs over persecution is one of those pleasant falsehoods which men repeat after one another till they pass into commonplaces, but which all experience refutes. History teems with instances of truth put down by persecution. If not suppressed for ever, it may be thrown back for centuries. To speak only of religious opinions: the Reformation broke out at least twenty times before Luther, and was put down. Arnold of Brescia was put down. Fra Dolcino was put down. Savonarola was put down. The Albigeois were put down. The Vaudois were put down. The Lollards were put down. The Hussites were put down. Even after the era of Luther, wherever persecution was persisted in, it was successful. In Spain, Italy, Flanders, the Austrian empire, Protestantism was rooted out; and, most likely, would have been so in England, had Queen Mary lived, or Queen Elizabeth died. Persecution has always succeeded, save where the heretics were too strong a party to be effectually persecuted. No reasonable person can doubt that Christianity might have been extirpated in the Roman Empire. It spread, and became predominant, because the persecutions were only occasional, lasting but a short time, and separated by long intervals of almost undisturbed propagandism. It is a piece of idle sentimentality that truth, merely as truth, has any inherent power denied to error of prevailing against the dungeon and the stake. Men are not more zealous for truth than they often are for error, and a sufficient application of legal or even of social penalties will generally succeed in stopping the propagation of either. The real advantage which truth has consists in this, that when an opinion is true, it may be extinguished once, twice, or many times, but in the course of ages there will generally be found persons to rediscover it, until some one of its reappearances falls on a time when from favourable circumstances it escapes persecution until it has made such head as to withstand all subsequent attempts to suppress it.

It will be said, that we do not now put to death the introducers of new opinions: we are not like our fathers who slew the prophets, we even build sepulchres to them. It is true we no longer put heretics to death; and the amount of penal infliction which modern feeling would probably tolerate, even against the most obnoxious opinions, is not sufficient to extirpate them. But let us not flatter ourselves that we are yet free from the stain even of legal persecution. Penalties for opinion, or at least for its expression, still exist by law; and their enforcement is not, even in these times, so unexampled as to make it at all incredible that they may some day be revived in full force. In the year 1857, at the summer assizes of the county of Cornwall, an unfortunate man, said to be of unexceptionable conduct in all relations of life, was sentenced to twenty-one months' imprisonment, for uttering, and writing on a gate, some offensive words concerning Christianity. Within a month of the same time, at the Old Bailey, two persons, on two separate occasions, were rejected as jurymen, and one of them grossly insulted by the judge and by one of the counsel, because they honestly declared that they had no theological belief; and a third, a foreigner, for the same reason, was denied justice against a thief. This refusal of redress took place in virtue of the legal doctrine, that no person can be allowed to give evidence in a court of justice who does not profess belief in a God (any god is sufficient) and in a future state; which is equivalent to declaring such persons to be outlaws, excluded from the protection of the tribunals; who may not only be robbed or assaulted with impunity, if no one but themselves, or persons of similar opinions, be present, but any one else may be robbed or assaulted with impunity, if the proof of the fact depends on their evidence. The assumption on which this is grounded is that the oath is worthless of a person who does not believe in a future state; a proposition which betokens much ignorance of history in those who assent to it (since it is historically true that a large proportion of infidels in all ages have been persons of distinguished integrity and honour); and would be maintained by no one who had the smallest conception how many of the persons in greatest repute with the world, both for virtues and attainments, are well known, at least to their intimates, to be unbelievers. The rule, besides, is suicidal, and cuts away its own foundation. Under pretence that atheists must be liars, it admits the testimony of all atheists who are willing to lie, and rejects only those who brave the obloquy of publicly confessing a detested creed rather than affirm a falsehood. A rule thus self-convicted of absurdity so far as regards its professed purpose, can be kept in force only as a badge of hatred, a relic of persecution; a persecution, too, having the peculiarity that the qualification for undergoing it is the being clearly proved not to deserve it. The rule, and the theory it implies, are hardly less insulting to believers than to infidels. For if he who does not believe in a future state necessarily lies, it follows that they who do believe are only prevented from lying, if prevented they are, by the fear of hell. We will not do the authors and abettors of the rule the injury of supposing that the conception which they have formed of Christian virtue is drawn from their own consciousness.

These, indeed, are but rags and remnants of persecution, and may be thought to be not so much an indication of the wish to persecute, as an example of that very frequent infirmity of English minds, which makes them take a preposterous pleasure in the assertion of a bad principle, when they are no longer bad enough to desire to carry it really into practice. But unhappily there is no security in the state of the public mind that the suspension of worse forms of legal persecution, which has lasted for about the space of a generation, will continue. In this age the quiet surface of routine is as often ruffled by attempts to resuscitate past evils, as to introduce new benefits. What is boasted of at the present time as the revival of religion, is always, in narrow and uncultivated minds, at least as much the revival of bigotry; and where there is the strong permanent leaven of intolerance in the feelings of a people, which at all times abides in the middle classes of this country, it needs but little to provoke them into actively persecuting those whom they have never ceased to think proper objects of persecution. For it is this — it is the opinions men entertain, and the feelings they cherish, respecting those who disown the beliefs they deem important, which makes this country not a place of mental freedom. For a long time past, the chief mischief of the legal penalties is that they strengthen the social stigma. It is that stigma which is really effective, and so effective is it, that the profession of opinions which are under the ban of society is much less common in England than is, in many other countries, the avowal of those which incur risk of judicial punishment. In respect to all persons but those whose pecuniary circumstances make them independent of the good will of other people, opinion, on this subject, is as efficacious as law; men might as well be imprisoned, as excluded from the means of earning their bread. Those whose bread is already secured, and who desire no favours from men in power, or from bodies of men, or from the public, have nothing to fear from the open avowal of any opinions, but to be ill-thought of and ill-spoken of, and this it ought not to require a very heroic mould to enable them to bear. There is no room for any appeal *ad misericordiam* in behalf of such persons. But though we do not now inflict so much evil on those who think differently from us as it was formerly our custom to do, it may be that we do ourselves as much evil as ever by our treatment of them. Socrates was put to death, but the Socratic philosophy rose like the sun in heaven, and spread its illumination over the whole intellectual firmament. Christians were cast to the lions, but the Christian church grew up a stately and spreading tree, overtopping the older and less vigorous growths, and stifling them by its shade. Our merely social intolerance kills no one, roots out no opinions, but induces men to disguise them, or to abstain from any active effort for their diffusion. With us, heretical opinions do not perceptibly gain, or even lose, ground in each decade or generation; they never blaze out far and wide, but continue to smoulder in the narrow circles of thinking and studious persons among whom they originate, without ever lighting up the general affairs of mankind with either a true or a deceptive light. And thus is kept up a state of things very satisfactory to some minds, because, without the unpleasant process of fining or imprisoning anybody, it maintains all prevailing opinions outwardly undisturbed, while it does not absolutely interdict the exercise of reason by dissentients afflicted with the malady of thought. A convenient plan for having peace in the intellectual world, and keeping all things going on therein very much as they do already. But the price paid for this sort of intellectual pacification is the sacrifice of the entire moral courage of the human mind. A state of things in which a large portion of the most active and inquiring intellects find it advisable to keep the general principles and grounds of their convictions within their own breasts, and attempt, in what they address to the public, to fit as much as they can of their own conclusions to premises which they have internally renounced, cannot send forth the open, fearless characters, and logical, consistent intellects who once adorned the thinking world. The sort of men who can be looked for under it, are either mere conformers to common-place, or time-servers for truth, whose arguments on all great subjects are meant for their hearers, and are not those which have convinced themselves. Those who avoid this alternative, do so by narrowing their thoughts and interest to things which can be spoken of without venturing within the region of principles, that is, to small practical matters, which would come right of themselves, if but the minds of mankind were strengthened and enlarged, and which will never be made effectually right until then: while that which would strengthen and enlarge men's minds, free and daring speculation on the highest subjects, is abandoned.

Those in whose eyes this reticence on the part of heretics is no evil should consider, in the first place, that in consequence of it there is never any fair and thorough discussion of heretical opinions; and that such of them as could not stand such a discussion, though they may be prevented from spreading, do not disappear. But it is not the minds of heretics that are deteriorated most by the ban placed on all inquiry which does not end in the orthodox conclusions. The greatest harm done is to those who are not heretics, and whose whole mental development is cramped, and their reason cowed, by the fear of heresy. Who can compute what the world loses in the multitude of promising intellects combined with timid characters, who dare not follow out any bold, vigorous, independent train of thought, lest it should land them in something which would admit of being considered irreligious or immoral? Among them we may occasionally see some man of deep conscientiousness, and subtle and refined understanding, who spends a life in sophisticating with an intellect which he cannot silence, and exhausts the resources of ingenuity in attempting to reconcile the promptings of his conscience and reason with orthodoxy, which yet he does not, perhaps, to the end succeed in doing. No one can be a great thinker who does not recognize, that as a thinker it is his first duty to follow his intellect to whatever conclusions it may lead. Truth gains more even by the errors of one who, with due study and preparation, thinks for himself, than by the true opinions of those who only hold them because they do not suffer themselves to think. Not that it is solely, or chiefly, to form great thinkers, that freedom of thinking is required. On the contrary, it is as much and even more indispensable to enable average human beings to attain the mental stature which they are capable of. There have been, and may again be, great individual thinkers in a general atmosphere of mental slavery. But there never has been, nor ever will be, in that atmosphere an intellectually active people. Where any people has made a temporary approach to such a character, it has been because the dread of heterodox speculation was for a time suspended. Where there is a tacit convention that principles are not to be disputed; where the discussion of the greatest questions which can occupy humanity is considered to be closed, we cannot hope to find that generally high scale of mental activity which has made some periods of history so remarkable. Never when controversy avoided the subjects which are large and important enough to kindle enthusiasm, was the mind of a people stirred up from its foundations, and the impulse given which raised even persons of the most ordinary intellect to something of the dignity of thinking beings. Of such we have had an example in the condition of Europe during the times immediately following the Reformation; another, though limited to the Continent and to a more cultivated class, in the speculative movement of the latter half of the eighteenth century; and a third, of still briefer duration, in the intellectual fermentation of Germany during the Goethian and Fichtean period. These periods differed widely in the particular opinions which they developed; but were alike in this, that during all three the yoke of authority was broken. In each, an old mental despotism had been thrown off, and no new one had yet taken its place. The impulse given at these three periods has made Europe what it now is. Every single improvement which has taken place either in the human mind or in institutions, may be traced distinctly to one or other of them. Appearances have for some time indicated that all three impulses are well nigh spent; and we can expect no fresh start until we again assert our mental freedom.

Let us now pass to the second division of the argument, and dismissing the supposition that any of the received opinions may be false, let us assume them to be true, and examine into the worth of the manner in which they are likely to be held, when their truth is not freely and openly canvassed. However unwillingly a person who has a strong opinion may admit the possibility that his opinion may be false, he ought to be moved by the consideration that, however true it may be, if it is not fully, frequently, and fearlessly discussed, it will be held as a dead dogma, not a living truth.

There is a class of persons (happily not quite so numerous as formerly) who think it enough if a person assents undoubtingly to what they think true, though he has no knowledge whatever of the grounds of the opinion, and could not make a tenable defence of it against the most superficial objections. Such persons, if they can once get their creed taught from authority, naturally think that no good, and some harm, comes of its being allowed to be questioned. Where their influence prevails, they make it nearly impossible for the received opinion to be rejected wisely and considerately, though it may still be rejected rashly and ignorantly; for to shut out discussion entirely is seldom possible, and when it once gets in, beliefs not grounded on conviction are apt to give way before the slightest semblance of an argument. Waiving, however, this possibility — assuming that the true opinion abides in the mind, but abides as a prejudice, a belief independent of, and proof against, argument — this is not the way in which truth ought to be held by a rational being. This is not knowing the truth. Truth, thus held, is but one superstition the more, accidentally clinging to the words which enunciate a truth.

If the intellect and judgment of mankind ought to be cultivated, a thing which Protestants at least do not deny, on what can these faculties be more appropriately exercised by any one, than on the things which concern him so much that it is considered necessary for him to hold opinions on them? If the cultivation of the understanding consists in one thing more than in another, it is surely in learning the grounds of one's own opinions. Whatever people believe, on subjects on which it is of the first importance to believe rightly, they ought to be able to defend against at least the common objections. But, some one may say, "Let them be *taught* the grounds of their opinions. It does not follow that opinions must be merely parroted because they are never heard controverted. Persons who learn geometry do not simply commit the theorems to memory, but understand and learn likewise the demonstrations; and it would be absurd to say that they remain ignorant of the grounds of geometrical truths, because they never hear any one deny, and attempt to disprove them." Undoubtedly: and such teaching suffices on a subject like mathematics, where there is nothing at all to be said on the wrong side of the question. The peculiarity of the evidence of mathematical truths is that all the argument is on one side. There are no objections, and no answers to objections. But on every subject on which difference of opinion is possible, the truth depends on a balance to be struck between two sets of conflicting reasons. Even in natural philosophy, there is always some other explanation possible of the same facts; some geocentric theory instead of heliocentric, some phlogiston instead of oxygen; and it has to be shown why that other theory cannot be the true one: and until this is shown, and until we know how it is shown, we do not understand the grounds of our opinion. But when we turn to subjects infinitely more complicated, to morals, religion, politics, social relations, and the business of life, three-fourths of the arguments for every disputed opinion consist in dispelling the appearances which favour some opinion different from it. The greatest orator, save one, of antiquity, has left it on record that he always studied his adversary's case with as great, if not still greater, intensity than even his own. What Cicero practised as the means of forensic success requires to be imitated by all who study any subject in order to arrive at the truth. He who knows only his own side of the case, knows little of that. His reasons may be good, and no one may have been able to refute them. But if he is equally unable to refute the reasons on the opposite side; if he does not so much as know what they are, he has no ground for preferring either opinion. The rational position for him would be suspension of judgment, and unless he contents himself with that, he is either led by authority, or adopts, like the generality of the world, the side to which he feels most inclination. Nor is it enough that he should hear the arguments of adversaries from his own teachers, presented as they state them, and accompanied by what they offer as refutations. That is not the way to do justice to the arguments, or bring them into real contact with his own mind. He must be able to hear them from persons who actually believe them; who defend them in earnest, and do their very utmost for them. He must know them in their most plausible and persuasive form; he must feel the whole force of the difficulty which the true view of the subject has to encounter and dispose of; else he will never really possess himself of the portion of truth which meets and removes that difficulty. Ninety-nine in a hundred of what are called educated men are in this condition; even of those who can argue fluently for their opinions. Their conclusion may be true, but it might be false for anything they know: they have never thrown themselves into the mental position of those who think differently from them, and considered what such persons may have to say; and consequently they do not, in any proper sense of the word, know the doctrine which they themselves profess. They do not know those parts of it which explain and justify the remainder; the considerations which show that a fact which seemingly conflicts with another is reconcilable with it, or that, of two apparently strong reasons, one and not the other ought to be preferred. All that part of the truth which turns the scale, and decides the judgment of a completely informed mind, they are strangers to; nor is it ever really known, but to those who have attended equally and impartially to both sides, and endeavoured to see the reasons of both in the strongest light. So essential is this discipline to a real understanding of moral and human subjects, that if opponents of all important truths do not exist, it is indispensable to imagine them, and supply them with the strongest arguments which the most skilful devil's advocate can conjure up.

To abate the force of these considerations, an enemy of free discussion may be supposed to say, that there is no necessity for mankind in general to know and understand all that can be said against or for their opinions by philosophers and theologians. That it is not needful for common men to be able to expose all the misstatements of fallacies of an ingenious opponent. That it is enough if there is always somebody capable of answering them, so that nothing likely to mislead uninstructed persons remains unrefuted. That simple minds, having been taught the obvious grounds of the truths inculcated on them, may trust to authority for the rest, and being aware that they have neither knowledge nor talent to resolve every difficulty which can be raised, may repose in the assurance that all those which have been raised have been or can be answered, by those who are specially trained to the task.

Conceding to this view of the subject the utmost that can be claimed for it by those most easily satisfied with the amount of understanding of truth which ought to accompany the belief of it; even so, the argument for free discussion is no way weakened. For even this doctrine acknowledges that mankind ought to have a rational assurance that all objections have been satisfactorily answered; and how are they to be answered if that which requires to be answered is not spoken? or how can the answer be known to be satisfactory, if the objectors have no opportunity of showing that it is unsatisfactory? If not the public, at least the philosophers and theologians who are to resolve the difficulties, must make themselves familiar with those difficulties in their most puzzling form; and this cannot be accomplished unless they are freely stated, and placed in the most advantageous light which they admit of. The Catholic Church has its own way of dealing with this embarrassing problem. It makes a broad separation between those who can be permitted to receive its doctrines on conviction, and those who must accept them on trust. Neither, indeed, are allowed any choice as to what they will accept; but the clergy, such at least as can be fully confided in, may admissibly and meritoriously make themselves acquainted with the arguments of opponents, in order to answer them, and may, therefore, read heretical books; the laity, not unless by special permission, hard to be obtained. This discipline recognizes a knowledge of the enemy's case as beneficial to the teachers, but finds means, consistent with this, of denying it to the rest of the world: thus giving to the *élite* more mental culture, though not more mental freedom, than it allows to the mass. By this device it succeeds in obtaining the kind of mental superiority which its purposes require; for though culture without freedom never made a large and liberal mind, it can make a clever *nisi prius* advocate of a cause. But in countries professing Protestantism, this resource is denied; since Protestants hold, at least in theory, that the responsibility for the choice of a religion must be borne by each for himself, and cannot be thrown off upon teachers. Besides, in the present state of the world, it is practically impossible that writings which are read by the instructed can be kept from the uninstructed. If the teachers of mankind are to be cognisant of all that they ought to know, everything must be free to be written and published without restraint.

If, however, the mischievous operation of the absence of free discussion, when the received opinions are true, were confined to leaving men ignorant of the grounds of those opinions, it might be thought that this, if an intellectual, is no moral evil, and does not affect the worth of the opinions, regarded in their influence on the character. The fact, however, is, that not only the grounds of the opinion are forgotten in the absence of discussion, but too often the meaning of the opinion itself. The words which convey it cease to suggest ideas, or suggest only a small portion of those they were originally employed to communicate. Instead of a vivid conception and a living belief, there remain only a few phrases retained by rote; or, if any part, the shell and husk only of the meaning is retained, the finer essence being lost. The great chapter in human history which this fact occupies and fills, cannot be too earnestly studied and meditated on.

It is illustrated in the experience of almost all ethical doctrines and religious creeds. They are all full of meaning and vitality to those who originate them, and to the direct disciples of the originators. Their meaning continues to be felt in undiminished strength, and is perhaps brought out into even fuller consciousness, so long as the struggle lasts to give the doctrine or creed an ascendancy over other creeds. At last it either prevails, and becomes the general opinion, or its progress stops; it keeps possession of the ground it has gained, but ceases to spread further. When either of these results has become apparent, controversy on the subject flags, and gradually dies away. The doctrine has taken its place, if not as a received opinion, as one of the admitted sects or divisions of opinion: those who hold it have generally inherited, not adopted it; and conversion from one of these doctrines to another, being now an exceptional fact, occupies little place in the thoughts of their professors. Instead of being, as at first, constantly on the alert either to defend themselves against the world, or to bring the world over to them, they have subsided into acquiescence, and neither listen, when they can help it, to arguments against their creed, nor trouble dissentients (if there be such) with arguments in its favour. From this time may usually be dated the decline in the living power of the doctrine. We often hear the teachers of all creeds lamenting the difficulty of keeping up in the minds of believers a lively apprehension of the truth which they nominally recognise, so that it may penetrate the feelings, and acquire a real mastery over the conduct. No such difficulty is complained of while the creed is still fighting for its existence: even the weaker combatants then know and feel what they are fighting for, and the difference between it and other doctrines; and in that period of every creed's existence, not a few persons may be found, who have realised its fundamental principles in all the forms of thought, have weighed and considered them in all their important bearings, and have experienced the full effect on the character which belief in that creed ought to produce in a mind thoroughly imbued with it. But when it has come to be an hereditary creed, and to be received passively, not actively — when the mind is no longer compelled, in the same degree as at first, to exercise its vital powers on the questions which its belief presents to it, there is a progressive tendency to forget all of the belief except the formularies, or to give it a dull and torpid assent, as if accepting it on trust dispensed with the necessity of realising it in consciousness, or testing it by personal experience, until it almost ceases to connect itself at all with the inner life of the human being. Then are seen the cases, so frequent in this age of the world as almost to form the majority, in which the creed remains as it were outside the mind, incrusting and petrifying it against all other influences addressed to the higher parts of our nature; manifesting its power by not suffering any fresh and living conviction to get in, but itself doing nothing for the mind or heart, except standing sentinel over them to keep them vacant.

To what an extent doctrines intrinsically fitted to make the deepest impression upon the mind may remain in it as dead beliefs, without being ever realised in the imagination, the feelings, or the understanding, is exemplified by the manner in which the majority of believers hold the doctrines of Christianity. By Christianity I here mean what is accounted such by all churches and sects — the maxims and precepts contained in the New Testament. These are considered sacred, and accepted as laws, by all professing Christians. Yet it is scarcely too much to say that not one Christian in a thousand guides or tests his individual conduct by reference to those laws. The standard to which he does refer it, is the custom of his nation, his class, or his religious profession. He has thus, on the one hand, a collection of ethical maxims, which he believes to have been vouchsafed to him by infallible wisdom as rules for his government; and on the other a set of every-day judgments and practices, which go a certain length with some of those maxims, not so great a length with others, stand in direct opposition to some, and are, on the whole, a compromise between the Christian creed and the interests and suggestions of worldly life. To the first of these standards he gives his homage; to the other his real allegiance. All Christians believe that the blessed are the poor and humble, and those who are ill-used by the world; that it is easier for a camel to pass through the eye of a needle than for a rich man to enter the kingdom of heaven; that they should judge not, lest they be judged; that they should swear not at all; that they should love their neighbour as themselves; that if one take their cloak, they should give him their coat also; that they should take no thought for the morrow; that if they would be perfect they should sell all that they have and give it to the poor. They are not insincere when they say that they believe these things. They do believe them, as people believe what they have always heard lauded and never discussed. But in the sense of that living belief which regulates conduct, they believe these doctrines just up to the point to which it is usual to act upon them. The doctrines in their integrity are serviceable to pelt adversaries with; and it is understood that they are to be put forward (when possible) as the reasons for whatever people do that they think laudable. But any one who reminded them that the maxims require an infinity of things which they never even think of doing, would gain nothing but to be classed among those very unpopular characters who affect to be better than other people. The doctrines have no hold on ordinary believers — are not a power in their minds. They have an habitual respect for the sound of them, but no feeling which spreads from the words to the things signified, and forces the mind to take *them* in, and make them conform to the formula. Whenever conduct is concerned, they look round for Mr. A and B to direct them how far to go in obeying Christ.

Now we may be well assured that the case was not thus, but far otherwise, with the early Christians. Had it been thus, Christianity never would have expanded from an obscure sect of the despised Hebrews into the religion of the Roman empire. When their enemies said, "See how these Christians love one another" (a remark not likely to be made by anybody now), they assuredly had a much livelier feeling of the meaning of their creed than they have ever had since. And to this cause, probably, it is chiefly owing that Christianity now makes so little progress in extending its domain, and after eighteen centuries is still nearly confined to Europeans and the descendants of Europeans. Even with the strictly religious, who are much in earnest about their doctrines, and attach a greater amount of meaning to many of them than people in general, it commonly happens that the part which is thus comparatively active in their minds is that which was made by Calvin, or Knox, or some such person much nearer in character to themselves. The sayings of Christ coexist passively in their minds, producing hardly any effect beyond what is caused by mere listening to words so amiable and bland. There are many reasons, doubtless, why doctrines which are the badge of a sect retain more of their vitality than those common to all recognised sects, and why more pains are taken by teachers to keep their meaning alive; but one reason certainly is, that the peculiar doctrines are more questioned, and have to be oftener defended against open gainsayers. Both teachers and learners go to sleep at their post, as soon as there is no enemy in the field.

The same thing holds true, generally speaking, of all traditional doctrines — those of prudence and knowledge of life, as well as of morals or religion. All languages and literatures are full of general observations on life, both as to what it is, and how to conduct oneself in it; observations which everybody knows, which everybody repeats, or hears with acquiescence, which are received as truisms, yet of which most people first truly learn the meaning when experience, generally of a painful kind, has made it a reality to them. How often, when smarting under some unforeseen misfortune or disappointment, does a person call to mind some proverb or common saying, familiar to him all his life, the meaning of which, if he had ever before felt it as he does now, would have saved him from the calamity. There are indeed reasons for this, other than the absence of discussion; there are many truths of which the full meaning *cannot* be realised until personal experience has brought it home. But much more of the meaning even of these would have been understood, and what was understood would have been far more deeply impressed on the mind, if the man had been accustomed to hear it argued *pro* and *con* by people who did understand it. The fatal tendency of mankind to leave off thinking about a thing when it is no longer doubtful, is the cause of half their errors. A contemporary author has well spoken of "the deep slumber of a decided opinion."

But what! (it may be asked) Is the absence of unanimity an indispensable condition of true knowledge? Is it necessary that some part of mankind should persist in error to enable any to realise the truth? Does a belief cease to be real and vital as soon as it is generally received — and is a proposition never thoroughly understood and felt unless some doubt it of remains? As soon as mankind have unanimously accepted a truth, does the truth perish within them? The highest aim and best result of improved intelligence, it has hitherto been thought, is to unite mankind more and more in the acknowledgment of all important truths; and does the intelligence only last as long as it has not achieved its object? Do the fruits of conquest perish by the very completeness of the victory?

I affirm no such thing. As mankind improve, the number of doctrines which are no longer disputed or doubted will be constantly on the increase: and the well-being of mankind may almost be measured by the number and gravity of the truths which have reached the point of being uncontested. The cessation, on one question after another, of serious controversy, is one of the necessary incidents of the consolidation of opinion; a consolidation as salutary in the case of true opinions, as it is dangerous and noxious when the opinions are erroneous. But though this gradual narrowing of the bounds of diversity of opinion is necessary in both senses of the term, being at once inevitable and indispensable, we are not therefore obliged to conclude that all its consequences must be beneficial. The loss of so important an aid to the intelligent and living apprehension of a truth, as is afforded by the necessity of explaining it to, or defending it against, opponents, though not sufficient to outweigh, is no trifling drawback from, the benefit of its universal recognition. Where this advantage can no longer be had, I confess I should like to see the teachers of mankind endeavouring to provide a substitute for it; some contrivance for making the difficulties of the question as present to the learner's consciousness, as if they were pressed upon him by a dissentient champion, eager for his conversion.

But instead of seeking contrivances for this purpose, they have lost those they formerly had. The Socratic dialectics, so magnificently exemplified in the dialogues of Plato, were a contrivance of this description. They were essentially a negative discussion of the great question of philosophy and life, directed with consummate skill to the purpose of convincing any one who had merely adopted the commonplaces of received opinion that he did not understand the subject — that he as yet attached no definite meaning to the doctrines he professed; in order that, becoming aware of his ignorance, he might be put in the way to obtain a stable belief, resting on a clear apprehension both of the meaning of doctrines and of their evidence. The school disputations of the Middle Ages had a somewhat similar object. They were intended to make sure that the pupil understood his own opinion, and (by necessary correlation) the opinion opposed to it, and could enforce the grounds of the one and confute those of the other. These last-mentioned contests had indeed the incurable defect, that the premises appealed to were taken from authority, not from reason; and, as a discipline to the mind, they were in every respect inferior to the powerful dialectics which formed the intellects of the "Socratici viri"; but the modern mind owes far more to both than it is generally willing to admit, and the present modes of education contain nothing which in the smallest degree supplies the place either of the one or of the other. A person who derives all his instruction from teachers or books, even if he escape the besetting temptation of contenting himself with cram, is under no compulsion to hear both sides; accordingly it is far from a frequent accomplishment, even among thinkers, to know both sides; and the weakest part of what everybody says in defence of his opinion is what he intends as a reply to antagonists. It is the fashion of the present time to disparage negative logic — that which points out weaknesses in theory or errors in practice, without establishing positive truths. Such negative criticism would indeed be poor enough as an ultimate result; but as a means to attaining any positive knowledge or conviction worthy the name, it cannot be valued too highly; and until people are again systematically trained to it, there will be few great thinkers, and a low general average of intellect, in any but the mathematical and physical departments of speculation. On any other subject no one's opinions deserve the name of knowledge, except so far as he has either had forced upon him by others, or gone through of himself, the same mental process which would have been required of him in carrying on an active controversy with opponents. That, therefore, which when absent, it is so indispensable, but so difficult, to create, how worse than absurd it is to forego, when spontaneously offering itself! If there are any persons who contest a received opinion, or who will do so if law or opinion will let them, let us thank them for it, open our minds to listen to them, and rejoice that there is some one to do for us what we otherwise ought, if we have any regard for either the certainty or the vitality of our convictions, to do with much greater labour for ourselves.

It still remains to speak of one of the principal causes which make diversity of opinion advantageous, and will continue to do so until mankind shall have entered a stage of intellectual advancement which at present seems at an incalculable distance. We have hitherto considered only two possibilities: that the received opinion may be false, and some other opinion, consequently, true; or that, the received opinion being true, a conflict with the opposite error is essential to a clear apprehension and deep feeling of its truth. But there is a commoner case than either of these; when the conflicting doctrines, instead of being one true and the other false, share the truth between them; and the nonconforming opinion is needed to supply the remainder of the truth, of which the received doctrine embodies only a part. Popular opinions, on subjects not palpable to sense, are often true, but seldom or never the whole truth. They are a part of the truth; sometimes a greater, sometimes a smaller part, but exaggerated, distorted, and disjointed from the truths by which they ought to be accompanied and limited. Heretical opinions, on the other hand, are generally some of these suppressed and neglected truths, bursting the bonds which kept them down, and either seeking reconciliation with the truth contained in the common opinion, or fronting it as enemies, and setting themselves up, with similar exclusiveness, as the whole truth. The latter case is hitherto the most frequent, as, in the human mind, one-sidedness has always been the rule, and many-sidedness the exception. Hence, even in revolutions of opinion, one part of the truth usually sets while another rises. Even progress, which ought to superadd, for the most part only substitutes, one partial and incomplete truth for another; improvement consisting chiefly in this, that the new fragment of truth is more wanted, more adapted to the needs of the time, than that which it displaces. Such being the partial character of prevailing opinions, even when resting on a true foundation, every opinion which embodies somewhat of the portion of truth which the common opinion omits, ought to be considered precious, with whatever amount of error and confusion that truth may be blended. No sober judge of human affairs will feel bound to be indignant because those who force on our notice truths which we should otherwise have overlooked, overlook some of those which we see. Rather, he will think that so long as popular truth is one-sided, it is more desirable than otherwise that unpopular truth should have one-sided assertors too; such being usually the most energetic, and the most likely to compel reluctant attention to the fragment of wisdom which they proclaim as if it were the whole.

Thus, in the eighteenth century, when nearly all the instructed, and all those of the uninstructed who were led by them, were lost in admiration of what is called civilisation, and of the marvels of modern science, literature, and philosophy, and while greatly overrating the amount of unlikeness between the men of modern and those of ancient times, indulged the belief that the whole of the difference was in their own favour; with what a salutary shock did the paradoxes of Rousseau explode like bombshells in the midst, dislocating the compact mass of one-sided opinion, and forcing its elements to recombine in a better form and with additional ingredients. Not that the current opinions were on the whole farther from the truth than Rousseau's were; on the contrary, they were nearer to it; they contained more of positive truth, and very much less of error. Nevertheless there lay in Rousseau's doctrine, and has floated down the stream of opinion along with it, a considerable amount of exactly those truths which the popular opinion wanted; and these are the deposit which was left behind when the flood subsided. The superior worth of simplicity of life, the enervating and demoralising effect of the trammels and hypocrisies of artificial society, are ideas which have never been entirely absent from cultivated minds since Rousseau wrote; and they will in time produce their due effect, though at present needing to be asserted as much as ever, and to be asserted by deeds, for words, on this subject, have nearly exhausted their power.

In politics, again, it is almost a commonplace, that a party of order or stability, and a party of progress or reform, are both necessary elements of a healthy state of political life; until the one or the other shall have so enlarged its mental grasp as to be a party equally of order and of progress, knowing and distinguishing what is fit to be preserved from what ought to be swept away. Each of these modes of thinking derives its utility from the deficiences of the other; but it is in a great measure the opposition of the other that keeps each within the limits of reason and sanity. Unless opinions favourable to democracy and to aristocracy, to property and to equality, to co-operation and to competition, to luxury and to abstinence, to sociality and individuality, to liberty and discipline, and all the other standing antagonisms of practical life, are expressed with equal freedom, and enforced and defended with equal talent and energy, there is no chance of both elements obtaining their due; one scale is sure to go up, and the other down. Truth, in the great practical concerns of life, is so much a question of the reconciling and combining of opposites, that very few have minds sufficiently capacious and impartial to make the adjustment with an approach to correctness, and it has to be made by the rough process of a struggle between combatants fighting under hostile banners. On any of the great open questions just enumerated, if either of the two opinions has a better claim than the other, not merely to be tolerated, but to be encouraged and countenanced, it is the one which happens at the particular time and place to be in a minority. That is the opinion which, for the time being, represents the neglected interests, the side of human well-being which is in danger of obtaining less than its share. I am aware that there is not, in this country, any intolerance of differences of opinion on most of these topics. They are adduced to show, by admitted and multiplied examples, the universality of the fact, that only through diversity of opinion is there, in the existing state of human intellect, a chance of fair play to all sides of the truth. When there are persons to be found who form an exception to the apparent unanimity of the world on any subject, even if the world is in the right, it is always probable that dissentients have something worth hearing to say for themselves, and that truth would lose something by their silence.

It may be objected, "But *some* received principles, especially on the highest and most vital subjects, are more than half-truths. The Christian morality, for instance, is the whole truth on that subject, and if any one teaches a morality which varies from it, he is wholly in error." As this is of all cases the most important in practice, none can be fitter to test the general maxim. But before pronouncing what Christian morality is or is not, it would be desirable to decide what is meant by Christian morality. If it means the morality of the New Testament, I wonder that any one who derives his knowledge of this from the book itself, can suppose that it was announced, or intended, as a complete doctrine of morals. The Gospel always refers to a pre-existing morality, and confines its precepts to the particulars in which that morality was to be corrected, or superseded by a wider and higher; expressing itself, moreover, in terms most general, often impossible to be interpreted literally, and posssesing rather the impressiveness of poetry or eloquence than the precision of legislation. To extract from it a body of ethical doctrine, has never been possible without eking it out from the Old Testament, that is, from a system elaborate indeed, but in many respects barbarous, and intended only for a barbarous people. St. Paul, a declared enemy to this Judaical mode of interpreting the doctrine and filling up the scheme of his Master, equally assumes a pre-existing morality, namely that of the Greeks and Romans; and his advice to Christians is in a great measure a system of accommodation to that; even to the extent of giving an apparent sanction to slavery. What is called Christian, but should rather be termed theological, morality, was not the work of Christ or the Apostles, but is of much later origin, having been gradually built up by the Catholic church of the first five centuries, and though not implicitly adopted by moderns and Protestants, has been much less modified by them than might have been expected. For the most part, indeed, they have contented themselves with cutting off the additions which had been made to it in the Middle Ages, each sect supplying the place by fresh additions, adapted to its own character and tendencies. That mankind owe a great debt to this morality, and to its early teachers, I should be the last person to deny; but I do not scruple to say of it that it is, in many important points, incomplete and one-sided, and that unless ideas and feelings, not sanctioned by it, had contributed to the formation of European life and character, human affairs would have been in a worse condition than they now are. Christian morality (so called) has all the characters of a reaction; it is, in great part, a protest against Paganism. Its ideal is negative rather than positive; passive rather than active; Innocence rather than Nobleness; Abstinence from Evil, rather than energetic Pursuit of Good; in its precepts (as has been well said) "thou shalt not" predominates unduly over "thou shalt." In its horror of sensuality, it made an idol of asceticism, which has been gradually compromised away into one of legality. It holds out the hope of heaven and the threat of hell, as the appointed and appropriate motives to a virtuous life:

in this falling far below the best of the ancients, and doing what lies in it to give to human morality an essentially selfish character, by disconnecting each man's feelings of duty from the interests of his fellow-creatures, except so far as a self-interested inducement is offered to him for consulting them. It is essentially a doctrine of passive obedience; it inculcates submission to all authorities found established; who indeed are not to be actively obeyed when they command what religion forbids, but who are not to be resisted, far less rebelled against, for any amount of wrong to ourselves. And while, in the morality of the best Pagan nations, duty to the State holds even a disproportionate place, infringing on the just liberty of the individual; in purely Christian ethics, that grand department of duty is scarcely noticed or acknowledged. It is in the Koran, not the New Testament, that we read the maxim — "A ruler who appoints any man to an office, when there is in his dominions another man better qualified for it, sins against God and against the State." What little recognition the idea of obligation to the public obtains in modern morality is derived from Greek and Roman sources, not from Christian; as, even in the morality of private life, whatever exists of magnanimity, highmindedness, personal dignity, even the sense of honour, is derived from the purely human, not the religious part of our education, and never could have grown out of a standard of ethics in which the only worth, professedly recognised, is that of obedience.

I am as far as any one from pretending that these defects are necessarily inherent in the Christian ethics in every manner in which it can be conceived, or that the many requisites of a complete moral doctrine which it does not contain do not admit of being reconciled with it. Far less would I insinuate this of the doctrines and precepts of Christ himself. I believe that the sayings of Christ are all that I can see any evidence of their having been intended to be; that they are irreconcilable with nothing which a comprehensive morality requires; that everything which is excellent in ethics may be brought within them, with no greater violence to their language than has been done to it by all who have attempted to deduce from them any practical system of conduct whatever. But it is quite consistent with this to believe that they contain, and were meant to contain, only a part of the truth; that many essential elements of the highest morality are among the things which are not provided for, nor intended to be provided for, in the recorded deliverances of the Founder of Christianity, and which have been entirely thrown aside in the system of ethics erected on the basis of those deliverances by the Christian Church. And this being so, I think it a great error to persist in attempting to find in the Christian doctrine that complete rule for our guidance which its author intended it to sanction and enforce, but only partially to provide. I believe, too, that this narrow theory is becoming a grave practical evil, detracting greatly from the moral training and instruction which so many well-meaning persons are now at length exerting themselves to promote. I much fear that by attempting to form the mind and feelings on an exclusively religious type, and discarding those secular standards (as for want of a better name they may be called) which heretofore co-existed with and supplemented the Christian ethics, receiving some of its spirit, and infusing into it some of theirs, there will result, and is even now resulting, a low, abject, servile type of character, which, submit itself as it may to what it deems the Supreme Will, is incapable of rising to or sympathising in the conception of Supreme Goodness. I believe that other ethics than any which can be evolved from exclusively Christian sources, must exist side by side with Christian ethics to produce the moral regeneration of mankind; and that the Christian system is no exception to the rule, that in an imperfect state of the human mind the interests of truth require a diversity of opinions. It is not necessary that in ceasing to ignore the moral truths not contained in Christianity men should ignore any of those which it does contain. Such prejudice, or oversight, when it occurs, is altogether an evil; but it is one from which we cannot hope to be always exempt, and must be regarded as the price paid for an inestimable good. The exclusive pretension made by a part of the truth to be the whole, must and ought to be protested against; and if a reactionary impulse should make the protestors unjust in their turn, this one-sidedness, like the other, may be lamented, but must be tolerated. If Christians would teach infidels to be just to Christianity, they should themselves be just to infidelity. It can do truth no service to blink the fact, known to all who have the most ordinary acquaintance with literary history, that a large portion of the noblest and most valuable moral teaching has been the work, not only of men who did not know, but of men who knew and rejected, the Christian faith.

I do not pretend that the most unlimited use of the freedom of enunciating all possible opinions would put an end to the evils of religious or philosophical sectarianism. Every truth which men of narrrow capacity are in earnest about, is sure to be asserted, inculcated, and in many ways even acted on, as if no other truth existed in the world, or at all events none that could limit or qualify the first. I acknowledge that the tendency of all opinions to become sectarian is not cured by the freest discussion, but is often heightened and exacerbated thereby; the truth which ought to have been, but was not, seen, being rejected all the more violently because proclaimd by persons regarded as opponents. But it is not on the impassioned partisan, it is on the calmer and more disinterested bystander, that this collision of opinions works its salutary effect. Not the violent conflict between parts of the truth, but the quiet suppression of half of it, is the formidable evil; there is always hope when people are forced to listen to both sides; it is when they attend only to one that errors harden into prejudices, and truth itself ceases to have the effect of truth, by being exaggerated into falsehood. And since there are few mental attributes more rare than that judicial faculty which can sit in intelligent judgment between two sides of a question, of which only one is represented by an advocate before it, truth has no chance but in proportion as every side of it, every opinion which embodies any fraction of the truth, not only finds advocates, but is so advocated as to be listened to.

We have now recognised the necessity to the mental well-being of mankind (on which all their other well-being depends) of freedom of opinion, and freedom of the expression of opinion, on four distinct grounds; which we will now briefly recapitulate.

First, if any opinion is compelled to silence, that opinion may, for aught we can certainly know, be true. To deny this is to assume our own infallibility.

Secondly, though the silenced opinion be an error, it may, and very commonly does, contain a portion of truth; and since the general or prevailing opinion on any subject is rarely or never the whole truth, it is only by the collision of adverse opinions that the remainder of the truth has any chance of being supplied.

Thirdly, even if the received opinion be not only true, but the whole truth; unless it is suffered to be, and actually is, vigorously and earnestly contested, it will, by most of those who receive it, be held in the manner of a prejudice, with little comprehension or feeling of its rational grounds. And not only this, but, fourthly, the meaning of the doctrine itself will be in danger of being lost, or enfeebled, and deprived of its vital effect on the character and conduct: the dogma becoming a mere formal profession, inefficacious for good, but cumbering the ground, and preventing the growth of any real and heartfelt conviction, from reason or personal experience.

Before quitting the subject of freedom of opinion, it is fit to take some notice of those who say that the free expression of all opinions should be permitted, on condition that the manner be temperate, and do not pass the bounds of fair discussion. Much might be said on the impossibility of fixing where these supposed bounds are to be placed; for if the test be offence to those whose opinions are attacked, I think experience testifies that this offence is given whenever the attack is telling and powerful, and that every opponent who pushes them hard, and whom they find it difficult to answer, appears to them, if he shows any strong feeling on the subject, an intemperate opponent. But this, though an important consideration in a practical point of view, merges in a more fundamental objection. Undoubtedly the manner of asserting an opinion, even though it be a true one, may be very objectionable, and may justly incur severe censure. But the principal offences of the kind are such as it is mostly impossible, unless by accidental self-betrayal, to bring home to conviction. The gravest of them is, to argue sophistically, to suppress facts or arguments, to misstate the elements of the case, or misrepresent the opposite opinion. But all this, even to the most aggravated degree, is so continually done in perfect good faith, by persons who are not considered, and in many other respects may not deserve to be considered, ignorant or incompetent, that it is rarely possible, on adequate grounds, conscientiously to stamp the misrepresentation as morally culpable; and still less could law presume to interfere with this kind of controversial misconduct. With regard to what is commonly meant by intemperate discussion, namely invective, sarcasm, personality, and the like, the denunciation of these weapons would deserve more sympathy if it were ever proposed to interdict them equally to both sides; but it is only desired to restrain the employment of them against the prevailing opinion: against the unprevailing they may not only be used without general disapproval, but will be likely to obtain for him who uses them the praise of honest zeal and righteous indignation. Yet whatever mischief arises from their use is greatest when they are employed against the comparatively defenceless; and whatever unfair advantage can be derived by any opinion from this mode of asserting it, accrues almost exclusively to received opinions. The worst offence of this kind which can be committed by a polemic is to stigmatise those who hold the contrary opinion as bad and immoral men. To calumny of this sort, those who hold any unpopular opinion are peculiarly exposed, because they are in general few and uninfluential, and nobody but themselves feels much interested in seeing justice done them; but this weapon is, from the nature of the case, denied to those who attack a prevailing opinion: they can neither use it with safety to themselves, nor, if they could, would it do anything but recoil on their own cause. In general, opinions contrary to those commonly received can only obtain a hearing by studied moderation of language, and the most cautious avoidance of unnecessary offence, from which they hardly ever deviate even in a slight degree without losing ground: while unmeasured vituperation employed on the side of the prevailing opinion really does deter people from professing contrary opinions, and from listening to those who profess them. For the interest, therefore, of truth and justice, it is far more important to restrain this employment of vituperative language than the other; and, for example, if it were necessary to choose, there would be much more need to discourage offensive attacks on infidelity than on religion. It is, however, obvious that law and authority have no business with restraining either, while opinion ought, in every instance, to determine its verdict by the circumstances of the individual case; condemning every one, on whichever side of the argument he places himself, in whose mode of advocacy either want of candour, or malignity, bigotry, or intolerance of feeling manifest themselves; but not inferring these vices from the side which a person takes, though it be the contrary side of the question to our own; and giving merited honour to every one, whatever opinion he may hold, who has calmness to see and honesty to state what his opponents and their opinions really are, exaggerating nothing to their discredit, keeping nothing back which tells, or can be supposed to tell, in their favour. This is the real morality of public discussion: and if often violated, I am happy to think that there are many controversialists who to a great extent observe it, and a still greater number who conscientiously strive towards it.

1801, 1786

THOMAS JEFFERSON

First Inaugural Address

The presidency of John Adams (1797–1801) was troubled. Marked by the rise of the French Directory to power and by the undeclared Naval War with France, it was even more deeply marked by fear of "subversive" activities. In an effort to free the country from French agents and simultaneously to fix upon the party of Jefferson the onus of following the Gallic "line," the Federalists passed the Alien and Sedition Laws in 1798. These permitted the arrest or deportation of the subjects of any foreign power with which the United States should be at war; permitted the President to arrest or deport any alien he considered dangerous; and made it a crime, punishable by fine and imprisonment, to print any "false, scandalous and malicious" writing against the American government or to stir up sedition or opposition to any lawful act of Congress or the President. Opposition to these infamous measures helped to bring Jefferson into power; and the need for restoring national unity and for reëstablishing good sense in the treatment of minority opinion explains the tone of his famous First Inaugural Address. Only the paragraphs pertinent to the problem of minority rights are here printed.

DURING THE CONTEST OF OPINION through which we have passed, the animation of discussion and of exertions has sometimes worn an aspect which might impose on strangers unused to think freely and to speak and to write what they think; but this being now decided by the voice of the nation, announced according to the rules of the constitution, all will, of course, arrange themselves under the will of the law, and unite in common efforts for the common good. All, too, will bear in mind this sacred principle, that though the will of the majority is in all cases to prevail, that will, to be rightful, must be reasonable; that the minority possess their equal rights, which equal laws must protect, and to violate which would be oppression. Let us, then, fellow-citizens, unite with one heart and one mind. Let us restore to social intercourse that harmony and affection without which liberty and even life itself are but dreary things. And let us reflect that having banished from our land that religious intolerance under which mankind so long bled and suffered, we have yet gained little if we countenance a political intolerance as despotic, as wicked, and capable of as bitter and bloody persecutions. During the throes and convulsions of the ancient world, during the agonizing spasms of infuriated man, seeking through blood and slaughter his long-lost liberty, it was not wonderful that the agitation of the billows should reach even this distant and peaceful shore; that this should be more felt and feared by some and less by others; that this should divide opinions as to measures of safety. But every difference of opinion is not a difference of principle. We have called by different names brethren of the same principle. We are all republicans — we are federalists. If there be any among us who would wish to dissolve this Union or to change its republican form, let them stand undisturbed as monuments of the safety with which error of opinion may be tolerated where reason is left free to combat it. I know, indeed, that some honest men fear that a republican government cannot be strong; that this government is not strong enough. But would the honest patriot, in the full tide of successful experiment, abandon a government which has so far kept us free and firm, on the theoretic and visionary fear that this government, the world's best hope, may by possibility want energy to preserve itself? I trust not. I believe this, on the contrary, the strongest government on earth. I believe it is the only one where every man, at the call of the laws, would fly to the standard of the law, and would meet invasions of the public order as his own personal concern. Sometimes it is said that man cannot be trusted with the government of himself. Can he, then, be trusted with the government of others? Or have we found angels in the forms of kings to govern him? Let history answer this question.

Let us, then, with courage pursue our own federal and republican principles, our attachment to our union and representative government. Kindly separated by nature and a wide ocean from the exterminating havoc of one quarter of the globe; too high-minded to endure the degradations of the others; possessing a chosen country, with room enough for our descendants to the hundredth and thousandth generation; entertaining a due sense of our equal right to the use of our own faculties, to the acquisitions of our industry, to honor and confidence from our fellow citizens, resulting not from birth but from our actions and their sense of them; enlightened by a benign religion, professed, indeed, and practiced in various forms, yet all of them including honesty, truth, temperance, gratitude, and the love of man; acknowledging and adoring an overruling Providence, which by all its dispensations proves that it delights in the happiness of man here and his greater happiness hereafter; with all these blessings, what more is necessary to make us a happy and prosperous people? Still one thing more, fellow-citizens — a wise and frugal government, which shall restrain men from injuring one another, which shall leave them otherwise free to regulate their own pursuits of industry and improvement, and shall not take from the mouth of labor the bread it has earned. This is the sum of good government, and this is necessary to close the circle of our felicities.

Bill for Establishing Religious Freedom

In the seventeenth-century colony, taxes were levied to support the "state church" on the theory that the church was in possession of the truth and that, though civil government might for practical reasons tolerate "dissent," the inhabitants, including dissenters, were taxable for the support of the truth. In Virginia the state church was Anglican (Episcopalian). Called upon, with Wythe, Pendleton, and others, in 1776 to revise the laws of Virginia, Jefferson and his committee modernized these statutes in a series of 126 bills, one hundred of which (at least) were passed by the legislature. Dear to Jefferson's heart were measures designed to abolish aristocratic and ecclesiastical control. His bill for disestablishing the church was offered to the legislature by John Harvie in 1779 and was passed in 1786. Jefferson asked that his tombstone should record only three achievements: that he was the author of the Declaration of Independence, the founder of the University of Virginia, and the creator of the Virginia statute for religious freedom. The statute emphatically declares that civil rights are not dependent upon ecclesiastical orthodoxy and that private opinion is not the concern of the state.

Section 1. Well aware that the opinions and belief of men depend on their own will, but follow involuntarily the evidence proposed to their minds; that Almighty God hath created the mind free, and manifested his supreme will that free it shall remain by making it altogether insusceptible of restraint; that all attempts to influence it by temporal punishments, or burthens, or by civil incapacitations, tend only to beget habits of hypocrisy and meanness, and are a departure from the plan of the holy author of our religion, who being lord both of body and mind, yet choose not to propagate it by coercions on either, as was in his Almighty power to do, but to exalt it by its influence on reason alone; that the impious presumption of legislature and ruler, civil as well as ecclesiastical, who, being themselves but fallible and uninspired men, have assumed dominion over the faith of others, setting up their own opinions and modes of thinking as the only true and infallible, and as such endeavouring to impose them on others, hath established and maintained false religions over the greatest part of the world and through all time: That to compel a man to furnish contributions of money for the propagation of opinions which he disbelieves and abhors, is sinful and tyrannical; that even the forcing him to support this or that teacher of his own religious persuasion, is depriving him of the comfortable liberty of giving his contributions to the particular pastor whose morals he would make his pattern, and whose powers he feels most persuasive to righteousness; and is withdrawing from the ministry those temporary rewards, which proceeding from an approbation of their personal conduct, are an additional incitement to earnest and unremitting labours for the instruction of mankind; that our civil rights have no dependance on our religious opinions, any more than our opinions in physics or geometry; and therefore the proscribing any citizen as unworthy the public confidence by laying upon him an incapacity of being called to offices of trust or emolument, unless he profess or renounce this or that religious opinion, is depriving him injudiciously of those privileges and advantages to which, in common with his fellow-citizens, he has a natural right; that it tends also to corrupt the principles of that very religion it is meant to encourage, by bribing with a monopoly of worldly honours and emoluments, those who will externally profess and conform to it; that though indeed these are criminals who do not withstand such temptation, yet neither are those innocent who lay the bait in their way; that the opinions of men are not the object of civil government, nor under its jurisdiction; that to suffer the civil magistrate to intrude his powers into the field of opinion and to restrain the profession or propagation of principles on supposition of their ill tendency is a dangerous fallacy, which at once destroys all religious liberty, because he being of course judge of that tendency will make his opinions the rule of judgment, and approve or condemn the sentiments of others only as they shall square with or suffer from his own; that it is time enough for the rightful purposes of civil government for its officers to interfere when principles break out into overt acts against peace and good order; and finally, that truth is great and will prevail if left to herself; that she is the proper and sufficient antagonist to error, and has nothing to fear from the conflict unless by human interposition disarmed of her natural weapons, free argument and debate; errors ceasing to be dangerous when it is permitted freely to contradict them.

Section II. We the General Assembly of Virginia do enact that no man shall be compelled to frequent or support any religious worship, place, or ministry whatsoever, nor shall be enforced, restrained, molested, or burthened in his body or goods, or shall otherwise suffer, on account of his religious opinions or belief; but that all men shall be free to profess, and by argument to maintain, their opinions in matters of religion, and that the same shall in no wise diminish, enlarge, or affect their civil capacities.

Section III. And though we well know that this Assembly, elected by the people for their ordinary purposes of legislation only, have no power to restrain the acts of succeeding Assemblies, constituted with powers equal to our own, and that therefore to declare this act to be irrevocable would be of no effect in law; yet we are free to declare, and do declare, that the rights hereby asserted are of the natural rights of mankind, and that if any act shall be hereafter passed to repeal the present or to narrow its operations, such act will be an infringement of natural right.

1644

JOHN MILTON

Areopagitica — A Speech for the Liberty of Unlicensed Printing, to the Parliament of England

On June 14, 1643, by order of Parliament censorship by government was re-instituted in the Commonwealth of England. Because of the "many false
. . . scandalous, seditious, and libellous" works being published, Parliament directed that nothing should be printed in England "unless the same be first approved of and licensed by such person or persons as both or either" of the Houses of Parliament "shall appoint for the licensing of the same," with much else, including an authorization for the Stationers' Company (the organized printers and publishers of the country) and the officers of Parliament to search out and destroy unlicensed presses, confiscate unlicensed books, and arrest all authors, printers, "and others" engaged in the nefarious business of bringing out uncensored books. In November 1644, unlicensed, appeared the noblest of Milton's prose pamphlets, known as the Areopagitica, one of the great utterances in English on the side of freedom of thought, speech, and printing. The pamphlet is in the form of a classical oration, and the title is derived from the Areopagus, the hill in Athens near the Acropolis where the "Upper Council" met to deliberate matters of state. By this device Milton sought to elevate a transient and local political squabble into a philosophical issue of timeless significance.

THEY, WHO TO STATES AND GOVERNORS OF THE COMMONWEALTH direct their speech, High Court of Parliament, or, wanting such access in a private condition, write that which they foresee may advance the public good; I suppose them, as at the beginning of no mean endeavour, not a little altered and moved inwardly in their minds: some with doubt of what will be the success, others with fear of what will be the censure; some with hope, others with confidence of what they have to speak. And me perhaps each of these dispositions, as the subject was whereon I entered, may have at other times variously affected; and likely might in these foremost expressions now also disclose which of them swayed most, but that the very attempt of this address thus made, and the thought of whom it hath recourse to, hath got the power within me to a passion, far more welcome than incidental to a preface. . .

I know not what should withhold me from presenting ye with a fit instance wherein to show both that love of truth which ye eminently profess, and that uprightness of your judgment which is not wont to be partial to yourselves; by judging over again that Order which ye have ordained to regulate Printing: — that no book, pamphlet, or paper shall be henceforth printed, unless the same be first approved and licensed by such, or at least one of such, as shall be thereto appointed. For that part which preserves justly every man's copy to himself, or provides for the poor, I touch not, only wish they be not made pretences to abuse and persecute honest and painful men, who offend not in either of these particulars. But that other clause of Licensing Books, which we thought had died with his brother quadragesimal and matrimonial when the prelates expired, I shall now attend with such a homily, as shall lay before ye, first the inventors of it to be those whom ye will be loth to own; next what is to be thought in general of reading, whatever sort the books be; and that this Order avails nothing to the suppressing of scandalous, seditious, and libellous books, which were mainly intended to be suppressed. Last, that it will be primely to the discouragement of all learning, and the stop of Truth, not only by disexercising and blunting our abilities in what we know already, but by hindering and cropping the discovery that might be yet further made both in religious and civil Wisdom.

I deny not, but that it is of greatest concernment in the Church and Commonwealth, to have a viligant eye how books demean themselves as well as men; and thereafter to confine, imprison, and do sharpest justice on them as malefactors. For books are not absolutely dead things, but do contain a potency of life in them to be as active as that soul was whose progeny they are; nay, they do preserve as in a vial the purest efficacy and extraction of that living intellect that bred them. I know they are as lively, and as vigourously productive, as those fabulous dragon's teeth; and being sown up and down, may chance to spring up armed men. And yet, on the other hand, unless wariness be used, as good almost kill a man as kill a good book. Who kills a man kills a reasonable creature, God's image; but he who destroys a good book, kills reason itself, kills the image of God, as it were in the eye. Many a man lives a burden to the earth; but a good book is the precious life-blood of a master spirit, embalmed and treasured up on purpose to a life beyond life. 'Tis true, no age can restore a life, whereof perhaps there is no great loss; and revolutions of ages do not oft recover the loss of a rejected truth, for the want of which whole nations fare the worse.

We should be wary therefore what persecution we raise against the living labours of public men, how we spill that seasoned life of man, preserved and stored up in books; since we see a kind of homicide may be thus committed, sometimes a martyrdom, and if it extend to the whole impression, a

kind of massacre; whereof the execution ends not in the slaying of an ele-
mental life, but strikes at that ethereal and fifth essence, the breath of reason
itself, slays an immortality rather than a life. But lest I should be condemned of introducing license, while I oppose licensing, I refuse not the
pains to be so much historical, as will serve to show what hath been done
by ancient and famous commonwealths against this disorder, till the very
time that this project of licensing crept out of the inquisition, was catched
up by our prelates, and hath caught some of our presbyters.

In Athens, where books and wits were ever busier than in any other part
of Greece, I find but only two sorts of writings which the magistrate cared
to take notice of; those either blasphemous and atheistical, or libellous.
Thus the books of Protagoras were by the judges of Areopagus commanded
to be burnt, and himself banished the territory for a discourse begun with
his confessing not to know "whether there were gods, or whether not."
And against defaming, it was agreed that none should be traduced by name,
as was the manner of Vetus Comœdia, whereby we may guess how they
censured libelling. And this course was quick enough, as Cicero writes, to
quell both the desperate wits of other atheists, and the open way of defaming, as the event showed. Of other sects and opinions, though tending to
voluptuousness, and the denying of Divine Providence, they took no heed.

Therefore we do not read that either Epicurus, or that libertine school of
Cyrene, or what the Cynic impudence uttered, was ever questiond by the
laws. Neither is it recorded that the writings of those old comedians were
suppressed, though the acting of them were forbid; and that Plato commended the reading of Aristophanes, the loosest of them all, to his royal
scholar Dionysius, is commonly known, and may be excused, if holy
Chrysostom, as is reported, nightly studied so much the same author and
had the art to cleanse a scurrilous vehemence into the style of a rousing
sermon. . .

The Romans also, for many ages trained up only to a military roughness
resembling most the Lacedæmonian guise, knew of learning little but what
their twelve Tables, and the Pontific College with their augurs and flamens
taught them in religion and law, so unacquainted with other learning, that
when Carneades and Critolaus, with the Stoic Diogenes coming ambassa-
dors to Rome, took thereby occasion to give the city a taste of their philosophy, they were suspected for seducers by no less a man than Cato the
Censor, who moved it in the Senate to dismiss them speedily, and to banish
all such Attic babblers out of Italy. But Scipio and others of the noblest
senators withstood him and his old Sabine austerity; honoured and admired
the men; and the censor himself at last, in his old age, fell to the study of
what whereof before he was so scrupulous. And yet at the same time,

Nævius and Plautus, the first Latin comedians, had filled the city with all the borrowed scenes of Menander and Philemon. Then began to be considered there also what was to be done to libellous books and authors; for Nævius was quickly cast into prison for his unbridled pen, and released by the tribunes upon his recantation; we read also that libels were burnt, and the makers punished by Augustus. The like severity, no doubt, was used, if aught were impiously written against their esteemed gods. Except in these two points, how the world went in books, the magistrate kept no reckoning.

And therefore Lucretius without impeachment versifies his Epicurism to Memmius, and had the honour to be set forth the second time by Cicero, so great a father of the commonwealth; although himself disputes against that opinion in his own writings. Nor was the satirical sharpness or naked plainness of Lucilius, or Catullus, or Flaccus, by any order prohibited. And for matters of state, the story of Titus Livius, though it extolled that part which Pompey held, was not therefore suppressed by Octavius Cæsar of the other faction. But that Naso was by him banished in his old age, for the wanton poems of his youth, was but a mere covert of state over some secret cause: and besides, the books were neither banished nor called in. From hence we shall meet with litle else but tyranny in the Roman empire, that we may not marvel, if not so often bad as good books were silenced. I shall therefore deem to have been large enough, in producing what among the ancients was punishable to write; save only which, all other arguments were free to treat on.

By this time the emperors were become Christians, whose discipline in this point I do not find to have been more severe than what was formerly in practice. The books of those whom they took to be grand heretics were examined, refuted, and condemned in the general Councils; and not till then were prohibited, or burnt, by authority of the emperor. As for the writings of heathen authors, unless they were plain invectives against Christianity, as those of Porphyrius and Proclus, they met with no interdict that can be cited, till about the year 400, in a Carthaginian Council, wherein bishops themselves were forbid to read the books of Gentiles, but heresies they might read: while others long before them, on the contrary, scrupled more the books of heretics than of Gentiles. And that the primitive Councils and bishops were wont only to declare what books were not commendable, passing no further, but leaving it to each one's conscience to read or to lay by, till after the year 800, is observed already by Padre Paolo, the great unmasker of the Trentine Council.

After which time the Popes of Rome, engrossing what they pleased of political rule into their own hands, extended their dominion over men's eyes, as they had before over their judgments, burning and prohibiting to be read what they fancied not; yet sparing in their censures, and the books not many which they so dealt with: till Martin V, by his bull, not only prohibited, but was the first that excommunicated the reading of heretical books; for about that time Wickliffe and Huss, growing terrible, were they who first drove the Papal Court to a stricter policy of prohibiting. Which course Leo X and his successors followed, until the Council of Trent and the Spanish Inquisition engendering together brought forth, or perfected, those Catalogues and expurging Indexes, that rake through the entrails of many an old good author, with a violation worse than any could be offered to his tomb. Nor did they stay in matters heretical, but any subject that was not to their palate, they either condemned in a Prohibition, or had it straight into the new Purgatory of an Index.

To fill up the measure of encroachment, their last invention was to ordain that no book, pamphlet, or paper should be printed (as if St. Peter had bequeathed them the keys of the press also out of Paradise) unless it were approved and licensed under the hands of two or three glutton friars . . .

Sometimes five Imprimaturs are seen together dialogue-wise in the piazza of one title-page, complimenting and ducking each to other with their shaven reverences, whether the author, who stands by in perplexity at the foot of his epistle, shall to the press or to the sponge. These are the pretty responsories, these are the dear antiphonies, that so bewitched of late our Prelates and their chaplains with the goodly echo they made; and besotted us to the gay imitation of a lordly Imprimatur, one from Lambeth House, another from the west end of Paul's; so apishly romanising, that the word of command still was set down in Latin; as if the learned grammatical pen that wrote it would cast no ink without Latin; or perhaps, as they thought, because no vulgar tongue was worthy to express the pure conceit of an Imprimatur; but rather, as I hope, for that our English, the language of men, ever famous and foremost in the achievements of liberty, will not easily find servile letters enow to spell such a dictatory presumption English.

And thus ye have the inventors and the original of book-licensing ripped up and drawn as lineally as any pedigree. We have it not, that can be heard of, from any ancient state, or polity or church; nor by any statute left us by our ancestors elder or later; nor from the modern custom of any reformed city or church abroad; but from the most anti-christian council and the most tyrannous inquisition that ever inquired. Till then books were ever as freely admitted into the world as any other birth; the issue of the brain was no more stifled than the issue of the womb: no envious Juno sat cross-legged over the nativity of any man's intellectual offspring; but if it proved a monster, who denies, but that it was justly burnt, or sunk into the sea? But that a book, in worse condition than a peccant soul, should be to stand before a jury ere it be born to the world, and undergo yet in darkness the judgment of Radamanth and his colleagues, ere it can pass the ferry backward into light, was never heard before, till that mysterious iniquity, provoked and troubled at the first entrance of Reformation, sought out new limbos and new hells wherein they might include our books also within the number of their damned. And this was the rare morsel so officiously snatched up, and so ill-favouredly imitated by our inquisiturient bishops, and the attendant minorities their chaplains. That ye like not now these most certain authors of this licensing order, and that all sinister intention was far distant from your thoughts, when ye were importuned the passing it, all men who know the integrity of your actions, and how ye honour Truth, will clear ye readily.

But some will say, What though the inventors were bad, the thing for all that may be good? It may be so; yet if that thing be no such deep invention, but obvious, and easy for any man to light on, and yet best and wisest commonwealths through all ages and occasions have forborne to use it, and falsest seducers and oppressors of men were the first who took it up, and to no other purpose but to obstruct and hinder the first approach of Reformation; I am of those who believe it will be a harder alchymy than Lullius ever knew, to sublimate any good use out of such an invention. Yet this only is what I request to gain from this reason, that it may be held a dangerous and suspicious fruit, as certainly it deserves, for the tree that bore it, until I can dissect one by one the properties it has. But I have first to finish, as was propounded, what is to be thought in general of reading books, whatever sort they be, and whether be more the benefit or the harm that thence proceeds?

Not to insist upon the examples of Moses, Daniel, and Paul, who were skilful in all the learning of the Egyptians, Chaldeans, and Greeks, which could not probably be without reading their books of all sorts; in Paul especially, who thought it no defilement to insert into Holy Scripture the sentences of three Greek poets, and one of them a tragedian; the question was notwithstanding sometimes controverted among the primitive doctors, but with great odds on that side which affirmed it both lawful and profitable; as was then evidently perceived, when Julian the Apostate and subtlest enemy to our faith made a decree forbidding Christians the study of heathen learning: for, said he, they wound us with our own weapons, and with our own arts and sciences they overcome us. And indeed the Christians were put so to their shifts by this crafty means, and so much in danger to decline into all ignorance, that the two Apollinarii were fain, as a man may say, to coin all the seven liberal sciences out of the Bible, reducing it into divers forms of orations, poems, dialogues, even to the calculating of a new Christian grammar. But, saith the historian Socrates, the providence of God provided better than the industry of Apollinarius and his son, by taking away that illiterate law with the life of him who devised it. So great an injury they then held it to be deprived of Hellenic learning; and thought it a persecution more undermining, and secretly decaying the Church, than the open cruelty of Decius or Diocletian . . .

Dionysius Alexandrinus was about the year 240 a person of great name in the Church for piety and learning, who had wont to avail himself much against heretics by being conversant in their books; until a certain presbyter laid it scrupulously to his conscience, how he durst venture himself among those defiling volumes. The worthy man, loth to give offence, fell into a new debate with himself what was to be thought; when suddenly a vision sent from God (it is his own epistle that so avers it) confirmed him in these words: Read any books whatever come to thy hands, for thou art sufficient both to judge aright, and to examine each matter. To this revelation he assented the sooner, as he confesses, because it was answerable to that of the Apostle to the Thessalonians, Prove all things, hold fast that which is good. And he might have added another remarkable saying of the same author: To the pure, all things are pure; not only meats and drinks, but all kind of knowledge whether of good or evil; the knowledge cannot defile, nor consequently the books, if the will and conscience be not defiled.

For books are as meats and viands are; some of good, some of evil substance; and yet God, in that unapocryphal vision, said without exception, Rise, Peter, kill and eat, leaving the choice to each man's discretion. Wholesome meats to a vitiated stomach differ little or nothing from unwholesome; and best books to a naughty mind are not unappliable to occasions of evil. Bad meats will scarce breed good nourishment in the healthiest concoction; but herein the difference is of bad books, that they to a discreet and judicious reader serve in many respects to discover, to confute, to forewarn, and to illustrate. Whereof what better witness can ye expect I should produce, than one of your own now sitting in Parliament, the chief of learned men reputed in this land, Mr. Selden; whose volume of natural and national laws proves, not only by great authorities brought together, but by exquisite reasons and theorems almost mathematically demonstrative, that all opinions, yea errors, known, read, and collated, are of main service and assistance toward the speedy attainment of what is truest. I conceive, therefore, that when God did enlarge the universal diet of man's body, saving ever the rules of temperance, He then also, as before, left arbitrary the dieting and repasting of our minds; as wherein every mature man might have to exercise his own leading capacity.

How great a virtue is temperance, how much of moment through the whole life of man! Yet God commits the managing so great a trust, without particular law or prescription, wholly to the demeanour of every grown man. And therefore when He Himself tabled the Jews from heaven, that omer, which was every man's daily portion of manna, is computed to have been more than might have well sufficed the heartiest feeder thrice as many meals. For those actions which enter into a man, rather than issue out of him, and therefore defile not, God uses not to captivate under a perpetual childhood of prescription, but trusts him with the gift of reason to be his own chooser; there were but little work left for preaching, if law and compulsion should grow so fast upon those things which heretofore were governed only by exhortation. Solomon informs us, that much reading is a weariness to the flesh; but neither he nor other inspired author tells us that such or such reading is unlawful: yet certainly had God thought good to limit us herein, it had been much more expedient to have told us what was unlawful than what was wearisome. As for the burning of those Ephesian books by St. Paul's converts; 'tis replied the books were magic, the Syriac so renders them. It was a private act, a voluntary act, and leaves us to a voluntary imitation: the men in remorse burnt those books which were their own; the magistrate by this example is not appointed; these men practised the books, another might perhaps have read them in some sort usefully.

Good and evil we know in the field of this world grow up together almost inseparably; and the knowledge of good is so involved and interwoven with the knowledge of evil, and in so many cunning resemblances hardly to be discerned, that those confused seeds which were imposed upon Psyche as an incessant labour to cull out, and sort asunder, were not more intermixed. It was from out the rind of one apple tasted, that the knowledge of good and evil, as two twins cleaving together, leaped forth into the world. And perhaps this is that doom which Adam fell into of knowing good and evil, that is to say of knowing good by evil. As therefore the state of man now is; what wisdom can there be to choose, what continence to forbear without the knowledge of evil? He that can apprehend and consider vice with all her baits and seeming pleasures, and yet abstain, and yet distinguish, and yet prefer that which is truly better, he is the true wayfaring * Christian.

I cannot praise a fugitive and cloistered virtue, unexercised and unbreathed, that never sallies out and sees her adversary, but slinks out of the race, where that immortal garland is to be run for, not without dust and heat. Assuredly we bring not innocence into the world, we bring impurity

---

* In three extant copies of the original edition, which probably passed through Milton's hands, "wayfaring" has been altered by pen to "warfaring."

much rather; that which purifies us is trial, and trial is by what is contrary. That virtue therefore which is but a youngling in the contemplation of evil, and knows not the utmost that vice promises to her followers, and rejects it, is but a blank virtue, not a pure; her whiteness is but an excremental whiteness. Which was the reason why our sage and serious poet Spenser, whom I dare be known to think a better teacher than Scotus or Aquinas, describing true temperance under the person of Guion, brings him in with his palmer through the cave of Mammon, and the bower of earthly bliss, that he might see and know, and yet abstain. Since therefore the knowledge and survey of vice is in this world so necessary to the constituting of human virtue, and the scanning of error to the confirmation of truth, how can we more safely, and with less danger, scout into the regions of sin and falsity than by reading all manner of tractates and hearing all manner of reason? And this is the benefit which may be had of books promiscuously read.

But of the harm that may result hence three kinds are usually reckoned. First, is feared the infection that may spread; but then all human learning and controversy in religious points must remove out of the world, yea the Bible itself; for that ofttimes relates blasphemy not nicely, it describes the carnal sense of wicked men not unelegantly, it brings in holiest men passionately murmuring against Providence through all the arguments of Epicurus: in other great disputes it answers dubiously and darkly to the common reader. And ask a Talmudist what ails the modesty of his marginal Keri, that Moses and all the prophets cannot persuade him to pronounce the textual Chetiv. For these causes we all know the Bible itself put by the Papist into the first rank of prohibited books. The ancientest fathers must be next removed, as Clement of Alexandria, and that Eusebian book of Evangelic preparation, transmitting our ears through a hoard of heathenish obscenities to receive the Gospel. Who finds not that Irenæus, Epiphanius, Jerome, and others discover more heresies than they well confute, and that oft for heresy which is the truer opinion?

Nor boots it to say for these, and all the heathen writers of greatest infection, if it must be thought so, with whom is bound up the life of human learning, that they writ in an unknown tongue, so long as we are sure those languages are known as well to the worst of men, who are both most able, and most diligent to instil the poison they suck, first into the courts of princes, acquainting them with the choicest delights and criticisms of sin. As perhaps did that Petronius whom Nero called his Arbiter, the master of his revels; and the notorious ribald of Arezzo, dreaded and yet dear to the Italian courtiers. I name not him for posterity's sake, whom Henry VIII named in merriment his Vicar of hell. By which compendious way all the contagion that foreign books can infuse will find a passage to the people far easier and shorter than an Indian voyage, though it could be sailed either by the north of Cataio eastward, or of Canada westward, while our Spanish licensing gags the English press never so severely.

But on the other side that infection which is from books of controversy in religion is more doubtful and dangerous to the learned than to the ignorant; and yet those books must be permitted untouched by the licenser. It will be hard to instance where any ignorant man hath been ever seduced by papistical book in English, unless it were commended and expounded to him by some of that clergy: and indeed all such tractates, whether false or true, are as the prophecy of Isaiah was to the eunuch, not to be understood without a guide. But of our priests and doctors how many have been corrupted by studying the comments of Jesuits and Sorbonists, and how fast they could transfuse that corruption into the people, our experience is both late and sad. It is not forgot, since the acute and distinct Arminius was perverted merely by the perusing of a nameless discourse written at Delft, which at first he took in hand to confute.

Seeing, therefore, that those books, and those in great abundance, which are likeliest to taint both life and doctrine, cannot be suppressed without the fall of learning and of all ability in disputation, and that these books of either sort are most and soonest catching to the learned, from whom to the common people whatever is heretical or dissolute may quickly be conveyed, and that evil manners are as perfectly learnt without books a thousand other ways which cannot be stopped, and evil doctrine not with books can propagate, except a teacher guide, which he might also do without writing, and so beyond prohibiting, I am not able to unfold, how this cautelous enterprise of licensing can be exempted from the number of vain and impossible attempts. And he who were pleasantly disposed could not well avoid to liken it to the exploit of that gallant man who thought to pound up the crows by shutting his park gate.

Besides another inconvenience, if learned men be the first receivers out of books and dispreaders both of vice and error, how shall the licensers themselves be confided in, unless we can confer upon them, or they assume to themselves above all others in the land, the grace of infallibility and uncorruptedness? And again, if it be true that a wise man, like a good refiner, can gather gold out of the drossiest volume, and that a fool will be a fool with the best book, yea or without book; there is no reason that we should deprive a wise man of any advantage to his wisdom, while we seek to restrain from a fool, that which being restrained will be no hindrance to his folly. For if there should be so much exactness always used to keep that from him which is unfit for his reading, we should in the judgment of Aristotle not only, but of Solomon and of our Saviour, not vouchsafe him good precepts, and by consequence not willingly admit him to good books; as being certain that a wise man will make better use of an idle pamphlet, than a fool will do of sacred Scripture.

'Tis next alleged we must not expose ourselves to temptations without necessity, and next to that, not employ our time in vain things. To both these objections one answer will serve, out of the grounds already laid, that to all men such books are not temptations, nor vanities, but useful drugs and materials wherewith to temper and compose effective and strong medicines, which man's life cannot want. The rest, as children and childish men, who have not the art to qualify and prepare these working minerals, well may be exhorted to forbear, but hindered forcibly they cannot be by all the licensing that Sainted Inquisition could ever yet contrive. Which is what I promised to deliver next, That this order of licensing conduces nothing to the end for which it was framed; and hath almost prevented me by being clear already while thus much hath been explaining. See the ingenuity of Truth, who, when she gets a free and willing hand, opens herself faster than the pace of method and discourse can overtake her.

It was the task which I began with, to show that no nation, or well-instituted state, if they valued books at all, did ever use this way of licensing; and it might be answered, that this is a piece of prudence lately discovered. To which I return, that as it was a thing slight and obvious to think on, so if it had been difficult to find out, there wanted not among them long since who suggested such a course; which they not following, leave us a pattern of their judgment that it was not the not knowing, but the not approving, which was the cause of their not using it . . .

For if they fell upon one kind of strictness, unless their care were equal to regulate all other things of like aptness to corrupt the mind, that single endeavour they knew would be but a fond labour; to shut and fortify one gate against corruption, and be necessitated to leave others round about wide upon.

If we think to regulate printing, thereby to rectify manners, we must regulate all recreations and pastimes, all that is delightful to man. No music must be heard, no song be set or sung, but what is grave and Doric. There must be licensing dancers, that no gesture, motion, or deportment be taught our youth but what by their allowance shall be thought honest; for such Plato was provided of; it will ask more than the work of twenty licensers to examine all the lutes, the violins, and the guitars in every house; they must not be suffered to prattle as they do, but must be licensed what they may say. And who shall silence all the airs and madrigals that whisper softness in chambers? The windows also, and the balconies must be thought on; there are shrewd books, with dangerous frontispieces, set to sale; who shall prohibit them, shall twenty licensers? The villages also must have their visitors to inquire what lectures the bagpipe and the rebeck reads, even to the ballatry and the gamut of every municipal fiddler, for these are the countryman's Arcadias, and his Monte Mayors.

Next, what more national corruption, for which England hears ill abroad, than household gluttony: who shall be the rectors of our daily rioting? And what shall be done to inhibit the multitudes that frequent those houses where drunkenness is sold and harboured? Our garments also should be referred to the licensing of some more sober workmasters to see them cut into a less wanton garb. Who shall regulate all the mixed conversation of our youth, male and female together, as is the fashion of this country? Who shall still appoint what shall be discoursed, what presumed, and no further? Lastly, who shall forbid and separate all idle resort, all evil company? These things will be, and must be; but how they shall be least hurtful, how least enticing, herein consists the grave and governing wisdom of a state.

To sequester out of the world into Atlantic and Utopian politics which never can be drawn into use, will not mend our condition; but to ordain wisely as in this world of evil, in the midst whereof God hath placed us unavoidably . . . Impunity and remissness, for certain, are the bane of a commonwealth; but here the great art lies, to discern in what the law is to bid restraint and punishment, and in what things persuasion only is to work.

If every action, which is good or evil in man at ripe years, were to be under pittance and prescription and compulsion, what were virtue but a name, what praise could be then due to well-doing, what gramercy to be sober, just, or continent? Many there be that complain of Divine Providence for suffering Adam to transgress; foolish tongues! When God gave him reason, He gave him freedom to choose, for reason is but choosing; he had been else a mere artificial Adam, such an Adam as he is in the motions. We ourselves esteem not of that obedience, or love, or gift, which is of force: God therefore left him free, set before him a provoking object, ever almost in his eyes; herein consisted his merit, herein the right of his reward, the praise of his abstinence. Wherefore did He create passions within us, pleasures round about us, but that these rightly tempered are the very ingredients of virtue?

They are not skilful considerers of human things, who imagine to remove sin by removing the matter of sin; for, besides that it is a huge heap increasing under the very act of diminishing, though some part of it may for a time be withdrawn from some persons, it cannot from all, in such a universal thing as books are; and when this is done, yet the sin remains entire. Though ye take from a covetous man all his treasure, he has yet one jewel left, ye cannot bereave him of his covetousness. Banish all objects of lust, shut up all youth into the severest discipline that can be exercised in any hermitage, ye cannot make them chaste, that came not thither so: such great care and wisdom is required to the right managing of this point. Suppose we could expel sin by this means; look how much we thus expel of sin, so much we expel of virtue: for the matter of them both is the same; remove that, and ye remove them both alike . . .

I lastly proceed from the no good it can do, to the manifest hurt it causes, in being first the greatest discouragement and affront that can be offered to learning, and to learned men.

It was the complaint and lamentation of prelates, upon every least breath of a motion to remove pluralities, and distribute more equally Church revenues, that then all learning would be for ever dashed and discouraged. But as for that opinion, I never found cause to think that the tenth part of learning stood or fell with the clergy: nor could I ever but hold it for a sordid and unworthy speech of any churchman who had a competency left him. If therefore ye be loth to dishearten heartily and discontent, not the mercenary crew of false pretenders to learning, but the free and ingenuous sort of such as evidently were born to study, and love learning for itself, not for lucre or any other end but the service of God and of truth, and perhaps that lasting fame and perpetuity of praise which God and good men have consented shall be the reward of those whose published labours advance the good of mankind, then know that, so far to distrust the judgment and the honesty of one who hath but a common repute in learning, and never yet offended, as not to count him fit to print his mind without a tutor and examiner, lest he should drop a schism, or something of corruption, is the greatest displeasure and indignity to a free and knowing spirit that can be put upon him.

What advantage is it to be a man over it is to be a boy at school, if we have only escaped the ferula to come under the fescue of an Imprimatur, if serious and elaborate writings, as if they were no more than the theme of a grammar-lad under his pedagogue, must not be uttered without the cursory eyes of a temporising and extemporising licenser? He who is not trusted with his own actions, his drift not being known to be evil, and standing to the hazard of law and penalty, has no great argument to think himself reputed in the Commonwealth, wherein he was born, for other than a fool or a foreigner. When a man writes to the world, he summons up all his reason and deliberation to assist him; he searches, meditates, is industrious, and likely consults and confers with his judicious friends; after all which done he takes himself to be informed in what he writes, as well as any that writ before him. If, in this the most consummate act of his fidelity and ripeness, no years, no industry, no former proof of his abilities can bring him to that state of maturity, as not to be still mistrusted and suspected, unless he carry all his considerate diligence, all his midnight watchings and expense of Palladian oil, to the hasty view of an unleisured licenser, perhaps much his younger, perhaps far his inferior in judgment, perhaps one who never knew the labour of book-writing, and if he be not repulsed or slighted, must appear in print like a puny with his guardian, and his censor's hand on the back of his title to be his bail and surety that he is no idiot or seducer, it cannot be but a dishonour and derogation to the author, to the book, to the privilege and dignity of Learning.

And what if the author shall be one so copious of fancy, as to have many things well worth the adding come into his mind after licensing, while the book is yet under the press, which not seldom happens to the best and diligentest writers; and that perhaps a dozen times in one book? The printer dares not go beyond his licensed copy; so often then must the author trudge to his leave-giver, that those his new insertions may be viewed; and many a jaunt will be made, ere that licenser, for it must be the same man, can either be found, or found at leisure; meanwhile either the press must stand still, which is no small damage, or the author lose his accuratest thoughts, and send the book forth worse than he had made it, which to a diligent writer is the greatest melancholy and vexation that can befall.

And how can a man teach with authority, which is the life of teaching, how can he be a doctor in his book as he ought to be, or else had better be silent, whenas all he teaches, all he delivers, is but under the tuition, under the correction of his patriarchal licenser to blot or alter what precisely accords not with the hidebound humour which he calls his judgment? When every acute reader, upon the first sight of a pedantic licence, will be ready with these like words to ding the book a quoit's distance from him: I hate a pupil teacher, I endure not an instructor that comes to me under the wardship of an overseeing fist. I know nothing of the licenser, but that I have his own hand here for his arrogance; who shall warrant me his judgment? The State, sir, replies the stationer, but has a quick return: The State shall be my governors, but not my critics; they may be mistaken in the choice of a licenser, as easily as this licenser may be mistaken in an author; this is some common stuff; and he might add from Sir Francis Bacon, That such authorised books are but the language of the times. For though a licenser should happen to be judicious more than ordinary, which will be a great jeopardy of the next succession, yet his very office and his commission enjoins him to let pass nothing but what is vulgarly received already.

Nay, which is more lamentable, if the work of any deceased author, though never so famous in his lifetime and even to this day, come to their hands for licence to be printed, or reprinted, if there be found in his book one sentence of a venturous edge, uttered in the height of zeal and who knows whether it might not be the dictate of a divine spirit, yet not suiting with every low decrepit humour of their own, though it were Knox himself, the Reformer of a Kingdom, that spake it, they will not pardon him their dash: the sense of that great man shall to all posterity be lost, for the fearfulness or the presumptuous rashness of a perfunctory licenser. And to what an author this violence hath been lately done, and in what book of greatest consequence to be faithfully published, I could now instance, but shall forbear till a more convenient season.

Yet if these things be not resented seriously and timely by them who have the remedy in their power, but that such iron-moulds as these shall have authority to gnaw out the choicest periods of exquisitest books, and to commit such a treacherous fraud against the orphan remainders of worthiest men after death, the more sorrow will belong to that hapless race of men, whose misfortune it is to have understanding. Henceforth let no man care to learn, or care to be more than worldly-wise; for certainly in higher matters to be ignorant and slothful, to be a common steadfast dunce, will be the only pleasant life, and only in request.

And as it is a particular disesteem of every knowing person alive, and most injurious to the written labours and monuments of the dead, so to me it seems an undervaluing and vilifying of the whole Nation. I cannot set so light by all the invention, the art, the wit, the grave and solid judgment which is in England, as that it can be comprehended in any twenty capacities how good soever, much less that it should not pass except their superintendence be over it, except it be sifted and strained with their strainers, that it should be uncurrent without their manual stamp. Truth and understanding are not such wares as to be monopolised and traded in by tickets and statutes and standards. We must not think to make a staple commodity of all the knowledge in the land, to mark and license it like our broadcloth and our woolpacks. What is it but a servitude like that imposed by the Philistines, not to be allowed the sharpening of our own axes and coulters, but we must repair from all quarters to twenty licensing forges? Had anyone written and divulged erroneous things and scandalous to honest life, misusing and forfeiting the esteem had of his reason among men, if after conviction this only censure were adjudged him that he should never henceforth write but what were first examined by an appointed officer, whose hand should be annexed to pass his credit for him that now he might be safely read; it could not be apprehended less than a disgraceful punishment. Whence to include the whole Nation, and those that never yet thus offended, under such a diffident and suspectful prohibition, may plainly be understood what a disparagement it is. So much the more, whenas debtors and delinquents may walk abroad without a keeper, but unoffensive books must not stir forth without a visible jailer in their title.

Nor is it to the common people less than a reproach; for if we be so jealous over them, as that we dare not trust them with an English pamphlet, what do we but censure them for a giddy, vicious, and ungrounded people; in such a sick and weak state of faith and discretion, as to be able to take nothing down but through the pipe of a licenser? That this is care or love of them, we cannot pretend, whenas, in those popish places where the laity are most hated and despised, the same strictness is used over them. Wisdom we cannot call it, because it stops but one breach of licence, nor that neither: whenas those corruptions, which it seeks to prevent, break in faster at other doors which cannot be shut.

And in conclusion it reflects to the disrepute of our Ministers also, of whose labours we should hope better, and of the proficiency which their flock reaps by them, than that after all this light of the Gospel which is, and is to be, and all this continual preaching, they should still be frequented with such an unprincipled, unedified and laic rabble, as that the whiff of every new pamphlet should stagger them out of their catechism, and Christian walking. This may have much reason to discourage the Ministers when such a low conceit is had of all their exhortations, and the benefiting of their hearers, as that they are not thought fit to be turned loose to three sheets of paper without a licenser; that all the sermons, all the lectures preached, printed, vented in such numbers, and such volumes, as have now well nigh made all other books unsaleable, should not be armour enough against one single Enchiridion, without the castle of St. Angelo of an Imprimatur.

And lest some should persuade ye, Lords and Commons, that these arguments of learned men's discouragement at this your Order are mere flourishes, and not real, I could recount what I have seen and heard in other countries, where this kind of inquisition tyrannises; when I have sat among their learned men, for that honour I had, and been counted happy to be born in such a place of philosophic freedom, as they supposed England was, while themselves did nothing but bemoan the servile condition into which learning amongst them was brought; that this was it which had damped the glory of Italian wits; that nothing had been there written now these many years but flattery and fustian. There it was that I found and visited the famous Galileo, grown old a prisoner to the Inquisition, for thinking in astronomy otherwise than the Franciscan and Dominican licensers thought.

And though I knew that England then was groaning loudest under the prelatical yoke, nevertheless I took it as a pledge of future happiness, that other nations were so persuaded of her liberty. Yet was it beyond my hope that those Worthies were then breathing in her air, who should be her leaders to such a deliverance, as shall never be forgotten by any revolution of time that this world hath to finish. When that was once begun, it was as little in my fear that, what words of complaint I heard among learned men of other parts uttered against the Inquisition, the same I should hear by as learned men at home uttered in time of Parliament against an order of licensing; and that so generally that, when I had disclosed myself a companion of their discontent, I might say, if without envy, that he whom an honest quæstorship had endeared to the Sicilians was not more by them importuned against Verres, than the favourable opinion which I had among many who honour ye, and are known and respected by ye, loaded me with entreaties and persuasions, that I would not despair to lay together that which just reason should bring into my mind, toward the removal of an undeserved thraldom upon learning. That this is not therefore the disburdening of a particular fancy, but the common grievance of all those who had prepared their minds and studies above the vulgar pitch to advance truth in others, and from others to entertain it, thus much may satisfy.

And in their name I shall for neither friend nor foe conceal what the general murmur is; that if it come to inquisitioning again and licensing, and that we are so timorous of ourselves, and so suspicious of all men, as to fear each book and the shaking of every leaf, before we know what the contents are; if some who but of late were little better than silenced from preaching shall come now to silence us from reading, except what they please, it cannot be guessed what is intended by some but a second tyranny over learning: and will soon put it out of controversy, that Bishops and Presbyters are the same to us, both name and thing. That those evils of Prelaty, which before from five or six and twenty sees were distributively charged upon the whole people, will now light wholly upon learning, is not obscure to us: whenas now the Pastor of a small unlearned Parish on the sudden shall be exalted Archbishop over a large diocese of books, and yet not remove, but keep his other cure too, a mystical pluralist. He who but of late cried down the sole ordination of every novice Bachelor of Art, and denied sole jurisdiction over the simplest parishioner, shall now at home in his private chair assume both these over worthiest and excellentest books and ablest authors that write them. . .

Well knows he who uses to consider, that our faith and knowledge thrives by exercise, as well as our limbs and complexion. Truth is compared in Scripture to a streaming fountain; if her waters flow not in a perpetual progression, they sicken into a muddy pool of conformity and tradition. A man may be a heretic in the truth; and if he believe things only because his Pastor says so, or the Assembly so determines, without knowing other reason, though his belief be true, yet the very truth he holds becomes his heresy.

There is not any burden that some would gladlier post off to another than the charge and care of their Religion. There be — who knows not that there be? — of Protestants and professors who live and die in as arrant an implicit faith as any lay Papist of Loretto. A wealthy man, addicted to his pleasure and to his profits, finds Religion to be a traffic so entangled, and of so many piddling accounts, that of all mysteries he cannot skill to keep a stock going upon that trade. What should he do? fain he would have the name to be religious, fain he would bear up with his neighbours in that. What does he therefore, but resolve to give over toiling, and to find himself out some factor, to whose care and credit he may commit the whole managing of his religious affairs? some Divine of note and estimation that must be. To him he adheres, resigns the whole warehouse of his religion, with all the locks and keys, into his custody; and indeed makes the very person of that man his religion; esteems his associating with him a sufficient evidence and commendatory of his own piety. So that a man may say his religion is now no more within himself, but is become a dividual movable, and goes and comes near him, according as that good man frequents the house. He entertains him, gives him gifts, feasts him, lodges him; his religion comes home at night, prays, is liberally supped, and sumptuously laid to sleep, rises, is saluted, and after the malmsey, or some well-spiced brewage, and better breakfasted than he whose morning appetite would have gladly fed on green figs between Bethany and Jerusalem, his Religion walks abroad at eight, and leaves his kind entertainer in the shop trading all day without his Religion.

Another sort there be who, when they hear that all things shall be ordered, all things regulated and settled, nothing written but what passes through the custom-house of certain Publicans that have the tonnaging and poundaging of all free-spoken truth, will straight give themselves up into your hands, make 'em and cut 'em out what religion ye please: there be delights, there be recreations and jolly pastimes that will fetch the day about from sun to sun, and rock the tedious year as in a delightful dream. What need they tourture their heads with that which others have taken so strictly and so unalterably into their own purveying? These are the fruits which a dull ease and cessation of our knowledge will bring forth among the people. How goodly and how to be wished were such an obedient unanimity as this, what a fine conformity would it starch us all into! Doubtless a staunch and solid piece of framework, as any January could freeze together. . .

Thus much we are hindered and disinured by this course of licensing, toward the true knowledge of what we seem to know. For how much it hurts and hinders the licensers themselves in the calling of their ministry, more than any secular employment, if they will discharge that office as they ought, so that of necessity they must neglect either the one duty or the other, I insist not, because it is a particular, but leave it to their own conscience, how they will decide it there.

There is yet behind of what I proposed to lay open, the incredible loss and detriment that this plot of incensing puts us to; more than if some enemy at sea should stop up all our havens and ports and creeks, it hinders and retards the importation of our richest Merchandise, Truth . . .

Truth indeed came once into the world with her Divine Master, and was a perfect shape most glorious to look on: but when He ascended, and His Apostles after Him were laid asleep, then straight arose a wicked race of deceivers, who, as that story goes of the Egyptian Typhon with his conspirators, how they dealt with the good Osiris, took the virgin Truth, hewed her lovely form into a thousand pieces, and scattered them to the four winds. From that time ever since, the sad friends of Truth, such as durst appear, imitating the careful search that Isis made for the mangled body of Osiris, went up and down gathering up limb by limb, still as they could find them. We have not yet found them all, Lords and Commons, nor ever shall do, till her Master's second coming; He shall bring together every joint and member, and shall mould them into an immortal feature of loveliness and perfection. Suffer not these licensing prohibitions to stand at every place of opportunity, forbidding and disturbing them that continue seeking, that continue to do our obsequies to the torn body of our martyred saint.

We boast our light; but if we look not wisely on the Sun itself, it smites us into darkness. Who can discern those planets that are oft combust, and those stars of brightest magnitude that rise and set with the Sun, until the opposite motion of their orbs bring them to such a place in the firmament, where they may be seen evening or morning? The light which we have gained was given us, not to be ever staring on, but by it to discover onward things more remote from our knowledge. It is not the unfrocking of a priest, the unmitring of a bishop, and the removing him from off the presbyterian shoulders, that will make us a happy Nation. No, if other things as great in the Church, and in the rule of life both economical and political, be not looked into and reformed, we have looked so long upon the blaze that Zuinglius and Calvin hath beaconed up to us, that we are stark blind. There be who perpetually complain of schisms and sects, and make it such a calamity that any man dissents from their maxims. 'Tis their own pride and ignorance which causes the disturbing, who neither will hear with meekness, nor can convince; yet all must be suppressed which is not found in their Syntagma. They are the troublers, they are the dividers of unity, who neglect and permit not others to unite those dissevered pieces which are yet wanting to the body of Truth. To be still searching what we know not by what we know, still closing up truth to truth as we find it (for all her body is homogeneal and proportional), this is the golden rule in theology as well as in arithmetic, and makes up the best harmony in a Church; not the forced and outward union of cold and neutral, and inwardly divided minds.

Lords and Commons of England, consider what Nation it is whereof ye are, and whereof ye are the governors: a Nation not slow and dull, but of a quick, ingenious and piercing spirit, acute to invent, subtle and sinewy to discourse, not beneath the reach of any point, the highest that human capacity can soar to. Therefore the studies of Learning in her deepest sciences have been so ancient and so eminent among us, that writers of good antiquity and ablest judgment have been persuaded that even the school of Pythagoras and the Persian wisdom took beginning from the old philosophy of this island. And that wise and civil Roman, Julius Agricola, who governed once here for Cæsar, preferred the natural wits of Britain before the laboured studies of the French. Nor is it for nothing that the grave and frugal Transylvanian sends out yearly from as far as the mountainous borders of Russia, and beyond the Hercynian wilderness, not their youth, but their staid men, to learn our language and our theologic arts.

Yet that which is above all this, the favour and the love of Heaven, we have great argument to think in a peculiar manner propitious and propending towards us. Why else was this Nation chosen before any other, that out of her, as out of Sion, should be proclaimed and sounded forth the first tidings and trumpet of Reformation to all Europe? And had it not been the obstinate perverseness of our prelates against the divine and admirable spirit of Wickliff, to suppress him as a schismatic and innovator, perhaps neither the Bohemian Huss and Jerome, no nor the name of Luther or of Calvin, had been ever known: the glory of reforming all our neighbours had been completely ours. But now, as our obdurate clergy have with violence demeaned the matter, we are become hitherto the latest and backwardest scholars, of whom God offered to have made us the teachers. Now once again by all concurrence of signs, and by the general instinct of holy and devout men, as they daily and solemnly express their thoughts, God is decreeing to begin some new and great period in His Church, even to the reforming of Reformation itself: what does He then but reveal Himself to His servants, and as His manner is, first to His Englishmen? I say, as His manner is, first to us, though we mark not the method of His counsels, and are unworthy.

Behold now this vast City: a city of refuge, the mansion house of liberty, encompassed and surrounded with His protection; the shop of war hath not there more anvils and hammers waking, to fashion out the plates and instruments of armed Justice in defence of beleaguered Truth, than there be pens and heads there, sitting by their studious lamps, musing, searching, revolving new notions and ideas wherewith to present, as with their homage and their fealty, the approaching Reformation: others as fast reading, trying all things, assenting to the force of reason and convincement. What could a man require more from a Nation so pliant and so prone to seek after knowledge? What wants there to such a towardly and pregnant soil, but wise and faithful labourers, to make a knowing people, a Nation of Prophets, of Sages, and of Worthies? We reckon more than five months yet to harvest; there need not be five weeks; had we but eyes to lift up, the fields are white already.

Where there is much desire to learn, there of necessity will be much arguing, much writing, many opinions; for opinion in good men is but knowledge in the making. Under these fantastic terrors of sect and schism, we wrong the earnest and zealous thirst after knowledge and understanding which God hath stirred up in this city. What some lament of, we rather should rejoice at, should rather praise this pious forwardness among men, to reassume the ill-reputed care of their Religion into their own hands again. A little generous prudence, a little forbearance of one another, and some grain of charity might win all these diligences to join, and unite in one general and brotherly search after Truth; could we but forego this prelatical tradition of crowding free consciences and Christian liberties into canons and precepts of men. I doubt not, if some great and worthy stranger should come among us, wise to discern the mould and temper of a people, and how to govern it, observing the high hopes and aims, the diligent alacrity of our extended thoughts and reasonings in the pursuance of truth and freedom, but that he would cry out as Pyrrhus did, admiring the Roman docility and courage: If such were my Epirots, I would not despair the greatest design that could be attempted, to make a Church or Kingdom happy. . .

First, when a City shall be as it were besieged and blocked about, her navigable river infested, inroads and incursions round, defiance and battle oft rumoured to be marching up even to her walls and suburb trenches, that then the people, or the greater part, more than at other times, wholly taken up with the study of highest and most important matters to be reformed, should be disputing, reasoning, reading, inventing, discoursing, even to a rarity and admiration, things not before discoursed or written of, argues first a singular goodwill, contentedness and confidence in your prudent foresight and safe government, Lords and Commons; and from thence derives itself to a gallant bravery and well-grounded contempt of their enemies, as if there were no small number of as great spirits among us, as his was, who when Rome was nigh besieged by Hannibal, being in the city, bought that piece of ground at no cheap rate, whereon Hannibal himself encamped his own regiment.

Next, it is a lively and cheerful presage of our happy success and victory. For as in a body, when the blood is fresh, the spirits pure and vigorous, not only to vital but to rational faculties, and those in the acutest and the pertest operations of wit and subtlety, it argues in what good plight and constitution the body is so when the cheerfulness of the people is so sprightly up, as that it has not only wherewith to guard well its own freedom and safety, but to spare, and to bestow upon the solidest and sublimest points of controversy and new invention, it betokens us not degenerated, nor drooping to a fatal decay, but casting off the old and wrinkled skin of corruption to outlive these pangs and wax young again, entering the glorious ways of truth and prosperous virtue, destined to become great and honourable in these latter ages. Methinks I see in my mind a noble and puissant nation rousing herself like a strong man after sleep, and shaking her invincible locks. Methinks I see her as an eagle mewing her mighty youth, and kindling her undazzled eyes at the full midday beam; purging and unscaling her long-abused sight at the fountain itself of heavenly radiance; while the whole noise of timorous and flocking birds, with those also that love the twilight, flutter about, amazed at what she means, and in their envious gabble would prognosticate a year of sects and schisms.

What would ye do then? should ye suppress all this flowery crop of knowledge and new light sprung up and yet springing daily in this city? should ye set an oligarchy of twenty engrossers over it, to bring a famine upon our minds again, when we shall know nothing but what is measured to us by their bushel? Believe it, Lords and Commons, they who counsel ye to such a suppressing do as good as bid ye suppress yourselves; and I will soon show how. If it be desired to know the immediate cause of all this free writing and free speaking, there cannot be assigned a truer than your own mild and free and humane government. It is the liberty, Lords and Commons, which your own valorous and happy counsels have purchased us, liberty which is the nurse of all great wits; this is that which hath rarefied and enlightened our spirits like the influence of heaven; this is that which hath enfranchised, enlarged and lifted up our apprehensions degrees above themselves.

Ye cannot make us now less capable, less knowing, less eagerly pursuing of the truth, unless ye first make yourselves, that made us so, less the lovers, less the founders of our true liberty. We can grow ignorant again, brutish, formal and slavish, as ye found us; but you then must first become that which ye cannot be, oppressive, arbitrary and tyrannous, as they were from whom ye have freed us. That our hearts are now more capacious, our thoughts more erected to the search and expectation of greatest and exactest things, is the issue of your own virtue propagated in us; ye cannot suppress that, unless ye reinforce an abrogated and merciless law, that fathers may despatch at will their own children. And who shall then stick closest to ye, and excite others? not he who takes up arms for coat and conduct, and his four nobles of Danegelt. Although I dispraise not the defence of just immunities, yet love my peace better, if that were all. Give me the liberty to know, to utter, and to argue freely according to conscience, above all liberties. . .

For who knows not that Truth is strong, next to the Almighty? She needs no policies, nor stratagems, nor licensings to make her victorious; those are the shifts and the defences that error uses against her power. Give her but room, and do not bind her when she sleeps, for then she speaks not true, as the old Proteus did, who spake oracles only when he was caught and bound, but then rather she turns herself into all shapes, except her own, and perhaps tunes her voice according to the time, as Micaiah before Ahab, until she be adjured into her own likeness. Yet is it not impossible that she may have more shapes than one. What else is all that rank of things indifferent, wherein Truth may be on this side or on the other, without being unlike herself? What but a vain shadow else is the abolition of those ordinances, that hand-writing nailed to the cross? What great purchase is this Christian liberty which Paul so often boasts of? His doctrine is, that he who eats or eats not, regards a day of regards it not, may do either to the Lord. How many other things might be tolerated in peace, and left to conscience, had we but charity, and were it not the chief stronghold of our hypocrisy to be ever judging one another?

I fear yet this iron yoke of outward conformity hath left a slavish print upon our necks; the ghost of a linen decency yet haunts us. We stumble and are impatient at the least dividing of one visible congregation from another, though it be not in fundamentals; and through our forwardness to suppress, and our backwardness to recover any enthralled piece of truth out of the gripe of custom, we care not to keep truth separated from truth, which is the fiercest rent and disunion of all. We do not see that, while we still affect by all means a rigid external formality, we may as soon fall again into a gross conforming stupidity, a stark and dead congealment of wood and hay and stubble, forced and frozen together, which is more to the sudden degenerating of a Church than many subdichotomies of petty schisms.

Not that I can think well of every light separation, or that all in a Church is to be expected gold and silver and precious stones: it is not possible for man to sever the wheat from the tares, the good fish from the other fry; that must be the Angels' Ministry at the end of mortal things. Yet if all cannot be of one mind — as who looks they should be? — this doubtless is more wholesome, more prudent, and more Christian that many be tolerated, rather than all compelled. I mean not tolerated popery, and open superstition, which, as it extirpates all religions and civil supremacies, so itself should be extirpate, provided first that all charitable and compassionate means be used to win and regain the weak and the misled: that also which is impious or evil absolutely either against faith or manners no law can possibly permit, that intends not to unlaw itself: but those neighbouring differences, or rather indifferences, are what I speak of, whether in some point of doctrine or of discipline, which, though they may be many, yet need not interrupt the unity of Spirit, if we could but find among us the bond of peace.

And if the men be erroneous who appear to be the leading schismatics, what withholds us but our sloth, our self-will, and distrust in the right cause, that we do not give them gentle meeting and gentle dismissions, that we debate not and examine the matter thoroughly with liberal and frequent audience; if not for their sakes, yet for our own? seeing no man who hath tasted learning, but will confess the many ways of profiting by those who, not contented with stale receipts, are able to manage and set forth new positions to the world. And were they but as the dust and cinders of our feet, so long as in that notion they may yet serve to polish and brighten the armoury of Truth, even for that respect they were not utterly to be cast away. But if they be of those whom God hath fitted for the special use of these times with eminent and ample gifts, and those perhaps neither among the Priests nor among the Pharisees, and we in the haste of a precipitant zeal shall make no distinction, but resolve to stop their mouths, because we fear they come with new and dangerous opinions, as we commonly forejudge them ere we understand them, no less than woe to us, while, thinking thus to defend the Gospel, we are found the persecutors.

There have been not a few since the beginning of this Parliament, both of the Presbytery and others, who by their unlicensed books, to the contempt of an Imprimatur, first broke that triple ice clung about our hearts, and taught the people to see day: I hope that none of those were the persuaders to renew upon us this bondage which they themselves have wrought so much by contemning. But if neither the check that Moses gave to young Joshua, nor the countermand which our Saviour gave to young John, who was so ready to prohibit those whom he thought unlicensed, be not enough to admonish our Elders how unacceptable to God their testy mood of prohibiting is, if neither their own remembrance what evil hath abounded in the Church by this let of licensing, and what good they themselves have begun by transgressing it, be not enough, but that they will persuade and execute the most Dominican part of the Inquisition over us, and are already with one foot in the stirrup so active at suppressing, it would be no unequal distribution in the first place to suppress the suppressors themselves: whom the change of their condition hath puffed up, more than their late experience of harder times hath made wise.

And as for regulating the Press, let no man think to have the honour of advising ye better than yourselves have done in that Order published next before this, "that no book be Printed, unless the Printer's and the Author's name, or at least the Printer's, be registered." Those which otherwise come forth, if they be found mischievous and libellous, the fire and the executioner will be the timeliest and the most effectual remedy that man's prevention can use. For this authentic Spanish policy of licensing books, if I have said aught, will prove the most unlicensed book itself within a short while; and was the immediate image of a Star Chamber decree to that purpose made in those very times when that Court did the rest of those her pious works, for which she is now fallen from the stars with Lucifer. Whereby ye may guess what kind of state prudence, what love of the people, what care of Religion or good manners there was at the contriving, although with singular hypocrisy it pretended to bind books to their good behaviour. And how it got the upper hand of your precedent Order so well constituted before, if we may believe those men whose profession gives them cause to enquire most, it may be doubted there was in it the fraud of some old patentees and monopolisers in the trade of bookselling; who under pretence of the poor in their Company not to be defrauded, and the just retaining of each man his several copy, which God forbid should be gainsaid, brought divers glosing colours to the House, which were indeed but colours, and serving to no end except it be to exercise a superiority over their neighbours; men who do not therefore labour in an honest profession to which learning is indebted, that they should be made other men's vassals. Another end is thought was aimed at by some of them in procuring by petition this Order, that, having power in their hands, malignant books might the easier scape abroad, as the event shows.

But of these sophisms and elenchs of merchandise I skill not. This I know, that errors in a good government and in a bad are equally almost incident; for what Magistrate may not be misinformed, and much the sooner, if Liberty of Printing be reduced into the power of a few? But to redress willingly and speedily what hath been erred, and in highest authority to esteem a plain advertisement more than others have done a sumptuous bribe, is a virtue (honoured Lords and Commons) answerable to your highest actions, and whereof none can participate but greatest and wisest men.

1605

FRANCIS BACON

The Advancement of Learning

It all began with Francis Bacon. The novelty of Bacon's theory of science has been disputed, but his "new" system, whatever else it may be, was a sturdy attempt to remove intellectual inquiry from under the shadow of academic scholasticism. His great "Instauration of the Sciences" was left incomplete when he died, but The Advancement of Learning *is a systematic outline of the Baconian approach to knowledge. The second and larger part is a critical survey of the fields of learning. In Book I, however, Bacon refutes such allegations as that scientists are per se atheists and that learned men are bad citizens. The prejudices Bacon discussed have not disappeared in the twentieth century. Accordingly, those portions of Book I are here reprinted (in modernized form) in which learning is defended against the kinds of attack it experiences today.*

. . . TO CLEAR THE WAY, and, as it were to make silence to have the true testimonies concerning the dignity of learning to be better heard, without the interruption of tacit objections — I think good to deliver it from the discredits and disgraces which it hath received, all from ignorance, but ignorance severally disguised: appearing sometimes in the zeal and jealousy of divines, sometimes in the severity and arrogancy of politics, and sometimes in the errors and imperfections of learned men themselves.

I hear the former sort say that knowledge is of those things which are to be accepted of with great limitation and caution; that the aspiring to overmuch knowledge was the original temptation and sin whereupon ensued the fall of man; that knowledge hath in it somewhat of the serpent, and therefore where it entereth into a man it makes him swell — *Scientia inflat* [knowledge puffs up]; that Solomon gives a censure, 'That there is no end of making books, and that much reading is weariness of the flesh;' and again in another place, 'That in spacious knowledge there is much contristation, and that he that increaseth knowledge increaseth anxiety;' that St. Paul gives a caveat, 'That we be not spoiled through vain philosophy;' that experience demonstrates how learned men have been arch-heretics, how learned times have been inclined to atheism, and how the contemplation of second causes doth derogate from our independence upon God, who is the First Cause.

To discover then the ignorance and error of this opinion, and the misunderstanding in the grounds thereof, it may well appear these men do not observe or consider that it was not the pure knowledge of nature and universality, a knowledge by the light whereof man did give names unto other creatures in Paradise as they were brought before him, according unto their proprieties, which gave the occasion to the fall; but it was the proud knowledge of good and evil, with an intent in man to give law unto himself and to depend no more upon God's commandments, which was the form of the temptation. Neither is it any quantity of knowledge, how great soever, that can make the mind of man to swell; for nothing can fill, much less extend, the soul of man, but God and the contemplation of God. And therefore Solomon, speaking of the two principal senses of inquisition, the eye and the ear, affirmeth that the eye is never satisfied with seeing, nor the ear with hearing; and if there be no fulness, then is the continent greater than the content. So of knowledge itself, and the mind of man, whereto the senses are but reporters, he defineth likewise in these words, placed after that calendar or ephemerides which he maketh of the diversities of times and seasons for all actions and purposes, and concludeth thus: 'God hath made all things beautiful, or decent, in the true return of their seasons: Also he hath placed the world in man's heart, yet cannot man find out the work which God worketh from the beginning to the end;' declaring not obscurely that God hath framed the mind of man as a mirror or glass capable of the image of the universal world, and joyful to receive the impression thereof, as the eye joyeth to receive light; and not only delighted in beholding the variety of things and vicissitude of times, but raised also to find out and discern the ordinances and decrees which throughout all those changes are infallibly observed. And although he doth insinuate that the supreme or summary law of nature, which he calleth 'The work which God worketh from the beginning to the end,' is not possible to be found out by man; yet that doth not derogate from the capacity of the mind, but may be referred to the impediments, as of shortness of life, ill conjunction of labors, ill tradition of knowledge over from hand to hand, and many other inconveniences whereunto the condition of man is subject. For that nothing parcel of the world is denied to man's inquiry and invention he doth in another place rule over, when he saith, 'The spirit of man is as the lamp of God, wherewith he searcheth the inwardness of all secrets.' If then such be the capacity and receipt of the mind of man, it is manifest that there is no danger at all in the proportion or quanity of knowledge, how large soever, lest it should make it swell or out-compass itself; no, but it is merely the quality of knowledge, which be it in quantity more or less, if it be taken without the true corrective thereof, hath in it some nature of venom or malignity, and some effects of that venom, which is ventosity or swelling. This corrective spice, the mixture whereof maketh knowledge so sovran, is charity, which the apostle immediately addeth to the former clause. For so saith, 'knowledge bloweth up, but charity buildeth up;' not unlike unto that which he delivereth in another place: 'If I spake,' saith he, 'with the tongues of men and angels, and had not charity, it were but as a tinkling cymbal.' Not but that it is an excellent thing to speak with the tongues of men and angels, but because, if it be severed from charity, and not referred to the good of men and mankind, it hath rather a sounding and unworthy glory than a meriting and substantial virtue. And as for that censure of Solomon concerning the excess of writing and reading books, and the anxiety of spirit which redoundeth from knowledge, and that admonition of St. Paul, 'That we be not seduced by vain philosophy;' — let those places be rightly understood, and they do indeed excellently set forth the true bonds and limitations whereby human knowledge is confined and cirmuscribed; and yet without any such contracting or coarctation but that it may comprehend all the universal nature of things. For these limitations are three. The first, that we do not so place our felicity in knowledge, as we forget our mortality. The second, the we make application of our knowledge to give ourselves repose and contentment, and not distate or repining. The third, that we do not presume by the contemplation of nature to attain to the mysteries of God. For, as touching the first of these, Solomon doth excellently expound himself in another place of the same book, where he saith: 'I saw well that knowledge recedeth as far from ignorance as light doth from darkness, and that the wise man's eyes keep watch in his head, whereas the fool roundeth about in darkness; but withal I learned that the same mortality involveth them both.' And for the second, certain it is there is no vexation or anxiety of mind which resulteth from knowledge, otherwise than merely by accident; for all knowledge and wonder (which is the seed of knowledge) is an impression of pleasure in itself. But when men fall to framing conclusions out of their knowledge, applying it to their particular, and ministering to themselves thereby weak fears or vast desires, there groweth that carefulness and trouble of mind which is spoken of; for then knowledge is no more *Lumen siccum* [a dry light], whereof Heraclitus the profound said, *Lumen siccum optima anima* [the dry light is the best soul]; but it becometh *Lumen madidum* or *maceratum* [a light heavy with moisture], being steeped and infused in the humors of the affections. And as for the third point, it deserveth to be a little stood upon, and not to be lightly passed over. For if any man shall think by view and inquiry into these sensible and material things to attain that light whereby he may reveal unto himself the nature or will of God, then indeed is he spoiled by vain philosophy; for the contemplation of God's creatures and works produceth (having regard to the works and creatures themselves) knowledge; but, having regard to God, no perfect knowledge, but wonder, which is broken knowledge. And therefore it was most aptly said by one of Plato's school, 'That the sense of man carrieth a resemblance with the sun, which, as we see, openeth and revealeth all the terrestrial globe, but then again it obscureth and concealeth the stars and celestial globe; so doth the sense discover natural things, but it darkeneth and shutteth up divine.' And hence it is true that it hath proceeded that divers great learned men have been heretical, whilst they have sought to fly up to the secrets of the Deity by the waxen wings of the senses. And as for the conceit that too much knowledge should incline a man to atheism, and that the ignorance of second causes should make a more devout dependence upon God, which is the First Cause: First, it is good to ask the question which Job asked of his friends: 'Will you lie for God, as one man will do for another, to gratify him?' For certain it is that God worketh nothing in nature but by second causes; and if they would have it otherwise believed, it is mere imposture, as it were in favor towards God, and nothing else but to offer to the Author of Truth the unclean sacrifice of a lie. But farther, it is an assured truth and a conclusion of experience, that a little or superficial knowledge or philosophy, when the second causes, which are next unto the senses, do offer themselves to the mind of man, if it dwell and stay there it may induce some oblivion of the Highest Cause; but when a man passeth on farther, and seeth the dependence of causes and the works of providence, then according to the allegory of the poets, he will easily believe that the highest link of nature's chain must needs be tied to the foot of Jupiter's chair. To conclude therefore: Let no man, upon a weak conceit of sobriety or an ill-applied moderation, think or maintain that a man can search too far or be too well studied in the book of God's Word, or in the book of God's Works — Divinity or Philosophy; — but rather let men endeavor an endless progress or proficience in both. Only let men beware that they apply both to charity, and not to swelling; to use, and not to ostentation; and again, that they do not unwisely mingle or confound these learnings together.

And as for the disgraces which learning receiveth from politics, they be of this nature: that learning doth soften men's minds, and makes them more unapt for the honor and exercise of arms; that it doth mar and pervert men's dispositions for matter of government and policy, in making them too curious and irresolute by variety of reading, or too peremptory or positive by strictness of rules and axioms, or too immoderate and overweaning by reason of the greatness of examples, or too incompatible and differing from the times by reason of the dissimilitude of examples; or at least that it doth divert men's travails from action and business, and bringeth them to a love of leisure and privateness; and that it doth bring into states a relaxation of discipline, whilst every man is more ready to argue than to obey and execute. Out of this conceit Cato, surnamed the Censor, one of the wisest men indeed that ever lived, when Carneades the philosopher came in embassage to Rome, and that the young men of Rome began to flock about him, being allured with the sweetness and majesty of his eloquence and learning, gave counsel in open senate that they should give him his dispatch with all speed, lest he should infect and enchant the minds and affections of the youth, and at unawares bring in an alteration of the manners and customs of the state. Out of the same conceit or humor did Virgil, turning his pen to the advantage of his country and the disadvantage of his own profession, make a kind of separation between policy and government and between arts and sciences, in the verses so much renowned, attributing and challenging the one to the Romans, and leaving and yielding the others to the Grecians; *Tu regere imperio populos, Romane, memento, Hae tibi erunt artes*, etc. [Yours, Roman, be the lesson to govern the nations as their ruler; yours be the arts, etc.]. So likewise we see that Anytus, the accuser of Socrates, laid it as an article of charge and accusation against him that he did, with the variety and power of his discourses and disputations, withdraw young men from due reverence to the laws and customs of their country; and that he did profess a dangerous and pernicious science, which was to make the worse matter seem the better, and to suppress truth by force of eloquence and speech.

But these and the like imputations have rather a countenance of gravity than any ground of justice; for experience doth warrant that both in persons and in times there hath been a meeting and concurrence in learning and arms, flourishing and excelling in the same men and the same ages. For as for men, there cannot be a better nor the like instance, as of that pair, Alexander the Great and Julius Cæsar the Dictator; whereof the one was Aristotle's scholar in philosophy, and the other was Cicero's rival in eloquence; — or if any man had rather call for scholars that were great generals than generals that were great scholars, let him take Epaminondas the Theban, or Xenophon the Athenian; whereof the one was the first that abated the power of Sparta, and the other was the first that made way to the overthrow of the monarchy of Persia. And this concurrence is yet more visible in times than in persons, by how much an age is a greater object than a man. For both in Egypt, Assyria, Persia, Grecia, and Rome, the same that are times most renowned for arms are likewise most admired for learning; so that the greatest authors and philosophers and the greatest captains and governors have lived in the same ages. Neither can it otherwise be: for as in man the ripeness of strength of the body and mind cometh much about an age, save that the strength of the body cometh somewhat the more early; so, in states, arms and learning, whereof the one correspondeth to the body, the other to the soul of man, have a concurrence or near sequence in times.

And for matter of policy and government, that learning should rather hurt than enable thereunto is a thing very improbable. We see it is accounted an error to commit a natural body to empiric physicians, which commonly have a few pleasing receipts whereupon they are confident and adventurous, but know neither the causes of diseases, nor the complexions of patients, nor peril of accidents, nor the true method of cures. We see it is a like error to rely upon advocates or lawyers which are only men of practice and not grounded in their books, who are many times easily surprised when matter falleth out besides their experience, to the prejudice of the causes they handle. So by like reason it cannot be but a matter of doubtful consequence if states be managed by empiric statesmen, not well mingled with men grounded in learning. But, contrariwise, it is almost without instance contradictory that ever any government was disastrous that was in the hands of learned governors. For howsoever it hath been ordinary with politic men to extenuate and disable learned men by the names of pedants, yet in the records of time it appeareth in many particulars that the governments of princes in minority (notwithstanding the infinite disadvantage of that kind of state) have nevertheless excelled the government of princes of mature age, even for that reason which they seek to traduce, which is, that by that occasion the state hath been in the hands of pedants: for so was the state of Rome for the first five years, which are so much magnified, during the minority of Nero, in the hands of Seneca, a pedant; so it was again for ten years' space or more, during the minority of Gordianus the younger, with great applause and contentation in the hands of Misitheus, a pedant; so was it before that, in the minority of Alexander Severus, in like happiness, in hands not much unlike, by reason of the rule of the women, who were aided by the teachers and preceptors. Nay, let a man look into the government of the bishops of Rome, as by name into the government of Pius Quintus and Sextus Quintus in our times, who were both at their entrance esteemed but as pedantical friars, and he shall find that such popes do greater things, and proceed upon truer principles of estate, than those which have ascended to the papacy from an education and breeding in affairs of estate and courts of princes. For although men bred in learning are perhaps to seek in points of convenience and accommodating for the present, which the Italians call *ragioni di stato* [reasons of state], whereof the same Pius Quintus could not hear spoken with patience, terming them inventions against religion and the moral virtues; yet on the other side, to recompense that, they are perfect in those same plain grounds of religion, justice, honor, and moral virtue, which if they be well and watchfully pursued, there will be seldom use of those other, no more than of physic in a sound or well-dieted body. Neither can the experience of one man's life furnish examples and precedents for the events of one man's life; for as it happeneth sometimes that the grandchild, or other descendant, resembleth the ancestor more than the son, so many times occurrences of present times may sort better with ancient examples than with those of the later or immediate times. And lastly, the wit of one man can no more countervail learning, than one man's means can hold way with a common purse.

And as for those particular seducements, or indispositions of the mind for policy and government, which learning is pretended to insinuate; if it be granted that any such thing be, it must be remembered withal that learning ministereth in every of them greater strength of medicine or remedy than it offereth cause of indisposition of infirmity. For if by a secret operation it make men perplexed and irresolute, on the other side by plain precept it teacheth them when, and upon what ground, to resolve; yea, and how to carry things in suspense without prejudice till they resolve. If it make men positive and regular, it teacheth them what things are in their nature demonstrative, and what are conjectural; and as well the use of distinctions and exceptions as the latitude of principles and rules. If it mislead by disproportion or dissimilitude of examples, it teacheth men the force of circumstances, the errors of comparisons, and all the cautions of application; so that in all these it doth rectify more effectually than it can pervert. And these medicines it conveyeth into men's minds much more forcibly by the quickness and penetration of examples. For let a man look into the errors of Clement the Seventh, so lively described by Guicciardine, who served under him, or into the errors of Cicero, painted out by his own pencil in his epistles to Atticus, and he will fly apace from being irresolute. Let him look into the errors of Phocion, and he will beware how he be obstinate or inflexible. Let him but read the fable of Ixion, and it will hold him from being vaporous or imaginative. Let him look into the errors of Cato the Second, and he will never be one of the antipodes, to tread opposite to the present world.

And for the conceit that learning should dispose men to leisure and privateness, and make men slothful, it were a strange thing if that which accustometh the mind to a perpetual motion and agitation should induce slothfulness; whereas contrariwise it may be truly affirmed that no kind of men love business for itself but those that are learned. For other persons love it for profit, as an hireling that loves the work for the wages; or for honor, as because it beareth them up in the eyes of men, and refresheth their reputation, which otherwise would wear; or because it putteth them in mind of their fortune, and giveth them occasion to pleasure and displeasure; or because it exerciseth some faculty wherein they take pride, and so entertaineth them in good humor and pleasing conceits toward themselves; or because it advanceth any other their ends. So that as it is said of untrue valors, that some men's valors are in the eyes of them that look on, so much men's industries are in the eyes of others, or at least in regard of their own designments. Only learned men love business as an action according to nature, as agreeable to health of mind as exercise is to health of body, taking pleasure in the action itself, and not in the purchase; so that of all men they are the most indefatigable, if it be towards any business which can hold or detain their mind.

And if any man be laborious in reading and study, and yet idle in business and action, it groweth from some weakness of body or softness of spirit such as Seneca speaketh of — *Quidam tam sunt umbratiles, ut putent in turbido esse quicquid in luce est* [there are some men so fond of the shade that they think whatever is in the light is in danger] — and not of learning. Well may it be that such a point of a man's nature may make him give himself to learning, but it is not learning that breedeth any such point in his nature.

And that learning should take up too much time or leisure: I answer, the most active or busy man that hath been or can be, hath, no question, many vacant times of leisure, while he expecteth the tides and returns of business (except he be either tedious and of no dispatch, or lightly and unworthily ambitious to meddle in things that may be better done by others); and then the question is but how those spaces and times of leisure shall be filled and spent, whether in pleasures or in studies; as was well answered by Demosthenes to his adversary Æschines, that was a man given to pleasure, and told him 'that his orations did smell of the lamp:' 'Indeed,' said Demosthenes, 'there is a great difference between the things that you and I do by lamp-light.' So as no man need doubt that learning will expulse business; but rather it will keep and defend the possession of the mind against idleness and pleasure, which otherwise at unawares may enter to the prejudice of both.

Again, for that other conceit that learning should undermine the reverence of laws and government, it is assuredly a mere depravation and calumny, without all shadow of truth. For to say that a blind custom of obedience should be a surer obligation than duty taught and understood, it is to affirm that a blind man may tread surer by a guide than a seeing man can by a light. And it is without all controversy that learning doth make the minds of men gentle, generous, maniable, and pliant to government, whereas ignorance makes them churlish, thwart, and mutinous; and the evidence of time doth clear this assertion, considering that the most barbarous, rude,

and unlearned times have been most subject to tumults, seditions, and
changes. . . Let this therefore serve for answer to politics, which in their
humorous severity or in their feigned gravity have presumed to throw imputations upon learning; which redargution nevertheless — save that we
know not whether our labors may extend to other ages — were not needful
for the present, in regard of the love and reverence towards learning which
the example and countenance of two so learned princes, Queen Elizabeth
and Your Majesty, being as Castor and Pollux, *lucida sidera*, stars of excellent light and most benign influence, hath wrought in all men of place and
authority in our nation.

Now therefore we come to that third sort of discredit or diminution of
credit, that groweth unto learning from learned men themselves, which
commonly cleaveth fastest. It is either from their fortune, or from their
manners, or from the nature of their studies. For the first, it is not in their
power; and the second is accidental; the third only is proper to be handled.
But because we are not in hand with true measure, but with popular estimation and conceit, it is not amiss to speak somewhat of the two former.
The derogations therefore which grow to learning from the fortune or condition of learned men, are either in respect of scarcity of means, or in respect
of privateness of life and meanness of employments.

Concerning want, and that it is the case of learned men usually to begin
with little, and not to grow rich so fast as other men by reason they convert
not their labors chiefly to lucre and increase, — it were good to leave the
common place in commendation of poverty to some friar to handle, to whom
much was attributed by Machiavel in this point, when he said 'that the
kingdom of the clergy had been long before at an end, if the reputation and
reverence towards the poverty of friars had not borne out the scandal of the
superfluities and excesses of bishops and prelates.' So a man might say that
the felicity and delicacy of princes and great persons had long since turned
to rudeness and barbarism, if the poverty of learning had not kept up civility
and honor of life. But without any such advantages, it is worth the observation what a reverent and honored thing poverty of fortune was for some
ages in the Roman state, which nevertheless was a state without paradoxes. . . To conclude this point, as it was truly said, that *Rubor est virtutis color* [a blush is virtue's coloring], though sometime it comes from
vice; so it may be fitly said, that *Paupertas est virtutis fortuna* [the fortune
of virtue is poverty], though sometime it may proceed from misgovern-
ment and accident. Surely Solomon hath pronounced it both in censure,
Qui festinat ad divitias, non erit insons [he who hurries to be rich shall not
remain innocent], and in precept, 'Buy the truth, and sell it not;' and so of
wisdom and knowledge; judging that means were to be spent upon learn-

ing, and not learning to be applied to means. And as for the privateness or obscureness (as it may be in vulgar estimation accounted) of life of contemplative men: it is a theme so common to extol a private life not taxed with sensuality and sloth, in comparison and to the disadvantage of a civil life, for safety, pleasure, and dignity, or at least freedom from indignity, as no man handleth it but handleth it well; such a consonancy it hath to men's conceits in the expressing, and to men's consents in the allowing. This only I will add, that learned men forgotten in states, and not living in the eyes of men, are like the images of Cassius and Brutus in the funeral of Junia; of which not being represented, as many others were, Tacitus saith, *Eo ipso praefulgebant, quod non visebantur* [they shone through their very absences].

And for meanness of employment, that which is most traduced to contempt is that the government of youth is commonly allotted to them; which age, because it is the age of least authority, it is transferred to the disesteeming of those employments wherein youth is conversant, and which are conversant about youth. But how unjust this traducement is — if you will reduce things from poularity of opinion to measure of reason — may appear in that we see men are more curious what they put into a new vessel than into a vessel seasoned, and what mould they lay about a young plant than about a plant corroborate; so as the weakest terms and times of all things use to have the best applications and helps. And will you hearken to the Hebrew Rabbins? 'Your young men shall see visions, and your old men shall dream dreams;' say they, youth is the worthier age, for that visions are nearer apparitions of God than dreams. And let it be noted that howsoever the conditions of life of pedants hath been scorned upon theatres, as the ape of tyranny, and that the modern looseness or negligence hath taken no due regard to the choice of schoolmasters and tutors; yet the ancient wisdom of the best times did always make a just complaint that states were too busy with their laws and too negligent in point of education. Which excellent part of ancient discipline hath been in some sort revived of late times by the colleges of the Jesuits; of whom, although in regard of their superstition I may say *Quo meliores, eo deteriores* [the better they are, the worse they are], yet in regard of this and some other points concerning human learning and moral matters, I may say as Agesilaus said to his enemy Pharnabazus, *Talis quum sis, utinam noster esses* [being what you are, I wish you were one of us]. And thus much touching the discredits drawn from the fortunes of learned men.

As touching the manners of learned men, it is a thing personal and individual, and no doubt there be amongst them, as in other professions, of all temperatures; but yet so as it is not without truth which is said, that *abeunt studia in mores,* studies have an influence and operation upon the manners of those that are conversant in them.

But upon an attentive and indifferent review, I for my part cannot find any disgrace to learning can proceed from the manners of learned men, not inherent to them as they are learned; except it be a fault — which was the supposed fault of Demosthenes, Cicero, Cato the Second, Seneca, and many more — that because the times they read of are commonly better than the times they live in, and the duties taught better than the duties practised, they contend sometimes too far to bring things to perfection, and to reduce the corruption of manners to honesty of precepts or examples of too great height. And yet hereof they have caveats enough in their own walks. For Solon, when he was asked whether he had given his citizens the best laws, answered widely, 'Yea, of such as they would receive.' . . .

Another fault likewise much of this kind hath been incident to learned men, which is, that they have esteemed the preservation, good, and honor of their countries or masters before their own fortunes or safeties. For so saith Demosthenes unto the Athenians: 'If it please you to note it, my counsels unto you are not such whereby I should grow great amongst you, and you become little amongst the Grecians; but they be of that nature as they are sometimes not good for me to give, but are always good for you to follow.' And so Seneca, after he had consecrated that 'quinquennium Neronis' to the eternal glory of learned governors, held on his honest anl loyal course of good and free counsel, after his master grew extemely corrupt in his government. Neither can this point otherwise be; for learning endueth men's minds with a true sense of the frailty of their persons, the casualty of their fortunes, and the dignity of their soul and vocation; so that it is impossible for them to esteem that any greatness of their own fortune can be a true or worthy end of their being and ordainment, and therefore are desirous to give their account to God, and so likewise to their masters under God (as kings and the states that they serve) in these words: *Ecce tibi lucrifeci* [lo, I have gained for thee], and not *Ecce mihi lucrifeci* [lo, I have gained for myself]. Whereas the corrupter sort of mere politics, that have not their thoughts established by learning in the love and apprehension of duty, nor never look abroad into universality, do refer all things to themselves, and thrust themselves into the centre of the world, as if all lines should meet in them and their fortunes; never caring in all tempest what becomes of the ship of estates, so they may save themselves in the cock boat of their own fortune; whereas men that feel the weight of duty, and know the limits of self-love, use to make good their places and duties, though with peril. And if they stand in seditious and violent alterations, it is rather the reverence which many times both adverse parts do give to honesty, than any versatile advantage of their own carriage. But for this point of tender sense and fast obligation of duty which learning doth endue the mind withal, howsoever fortune may tax it, and many in the depth of their corrupt principles may despise it, yet it will receive an open allowance, and therefore needs the less disproof or excusation. . .

There is yet another fault (with which I will conclude this part) which is often noted in learned men, that they do many times fail to observe decency and discretion in their behavior and carriage, and commit errors in small and ordinary points of actions, so as the vulgar sort of capacities do make a judgment of them in greater matters by that which they find wanting in them in smaller. But this consequence doth oft deceive men; for which I do refer them over to that which was said by Themistocles, arrogantly and uncivilly being applied to himself out of his own mouth, but being applied to the general state of this question pertinently and justly; when being invited to touch a lute, he said 'He could not fiddle, but he could make a small town a great state.' So no doubt many may be well seen in the passages of government and policy, which are to seek in little and punctual occasions. I refer them also to that which Plato said of his master Socrates, whom he compared to the gallipots of apothecaries, which on the outside had apes and owls and antiques, but contained within sovran and precious liquors and confections; acknowledging that to an external report he was not without superficial levities and deformities, but was inwardly replenished with excellent virtues and powers. And so much touching the point of manners of learned men. . .

Now I proceed to those errors and vanities which have intervened amongst the studies themselves of the learned, which is that which is principal and proper to the present argument; wherein my purpose is not to make a justification of the errors, but, by a censure and separation of the errors, to make a justification of that which is good and sound, and to deliver that from the aspersion of the other. For we see that it is the manner of men to scandalize and deprave that which retaineth the state and virtue, by taking advantage upon that which is corrupt and degenerate; as the heathens in the primitive church used to blemish and taint the Christians with the faults and corruptions of heretics. But nevertheless I have no meaning at this time to make any exact animadversion of the errors and impediments in matters of learning which are more secret and remote from vulgar opinion, but only to speak unto such as do fall under, or near unto, a popular observation.

There be therefore chiefly three vanities in studies, whereby learning hath been most traduced. For those things we do esteem vain which are either false or frivolous, those which either have no truth or no use; and those persons we esteem vain which are either credulous or curious; and curiosity is either in matter or words. So that in reason, as well as in experience, there fall out to be these three distempers, as I may term them, of learning: — the first, fantastical learning; the second, contentious learning; and the last, delicate learning; vain imaginations, vain altercations, and vain affectations; and with the last I will begin.

Martin Luther, conducted no doubt by an high providence, but in discourse of reason, finding what a province he had undertaken against the bishop of Rome and the degenerate traditions of the church, and finding his own solitude, being no ways aided by the opinions of his own time, was enforced to awake all antiquity, and to call former times to his succors to make a party against the present time. So that the ancient authors, both in divinity and in humanity, which had long time slept in libraries, began generally to be read and revolved. This by consequence did draw on a necessity of a more exquisite travail in the languages original wherein those authors did write, for the better understanding of those authors and the better advantage of pressing and applying their words. And thereof grew again a delight in their manner of style and phrase, and an admiration of that kind of writing; which was much furthered and precipitated by the enmity and opposition that the propounders of those primitive, but seeming new, opinions had against the schoolmen, who were generally of the contrary part, and whose writings were altogether in a differing style and form; taking liberty to coin and frame new terms of art to express their own sense and to avoid circuit of speech, without regard to the pureness, pleasantness, and, as I may call it, lawfulness of the phrase or word. And again, because the great labor then was with the people, of whom the Pharisees were wont to say, *Execrabilis ista turba quae non novit legem* [this people who knoweth not the law are cursed]; for the winning and persuading of them there grew of necessity in chief price and request eloquence and variety of discourse, as the fittest and forciblest access into the capacity of the vulgar sort. So that these four causes concurring — the admiration of ancient authors, the hate of the schoolmen, the exact study of languages, and the efficacy of preaching — did bring in an affectionate study of eloquence and copie of speech, which then began to flourish. This grew speedily to an excess; for men began to hunt more after words than matter, and more after the choiceness of the phrase, and the round and clean composition of the sentence, and the sweet falling of the clauses, and the varying and illustration of their works with tropes and figures, than after the weight of matter, worth of subject, soundness of argument, life of invention, or depth of judgment. . . Then grew the learning of the schoolmen to be utterly despised as barbarous. In sum, the whole inclination and bent of those times was rather towards copie than weight.

Here therefore [is] the first distemper of learning, when men study words and not matter; whereof though I have represented an example of late times, yet it hath been and will be . . . in all time. And how is it possible but this should have an operation to discredit learning, even with vulgar capacities, when they see learned men's works like the first letter of a patent or limned book; which though it hath large flourishes, yet is it but a letter. It seems to me that Pygmalion's frenzy is a good emblem or portraiture of this vanity; for words are but the images of matter, and except they have life of reason and invention, to fall in love with them is all one as to fall in love with a picture. . .

The second [distemper], which followeth, is in the nature worse than the former; for as substance of matter is better than beauty of words, so contrariwise vain matter is worse than vain words. Wherein it seemeth the reprehension of St. Paul was not only proper for those times, but prophetical for the times following, and not only respective to divinity, but extensive to all knowledge: *Devita profanas vocum notitates, et oppositiones falsi nominis scientiae* [avoid the profane novelties of words, and oppositions of science falsely so called]. For he assigneth two marks and badges of suspected and falsified science: the one, the novelty and strangeness of terms; the other, the strictness of positions, which of necessity doth induce oppositions, and so questions and altercations. Surely, like as many substances in nature which are solid do putrefy and corrupt into worms, so it is the property of good and sound knowledge to putrefy and dissolve into a number of subtle, idle, unwholesome, and, as I may term them, vermiculate questions, which have indeed a kind of quickness and life of spirit, but no soundness of matter or goodness of quality. This kind of degenerate learning did chiefly reign amongst the schoolmen, who — having sharp and strong wits, and abundance of leisure, and small variety of reading, but their wits being shut up in the cells of a few authors (chiefly Aristotle their dictator) as their persons were shut up in the cells of monasteries and colleges, and knowing little history, either of nature or time — did, out of no great quantity of matter, and infinite agitation of wit, spin out unto us those laborious webs of learning which are extant in their books. For the wit and mind of man, if it work upon matter, which is the contemplation of the creatures of God, worketh according to the stuff, and is limited thereby; but if it work upon itself, as the spider worketh his web, then it is endless, and brings forth indeed cobwebs of learning, admirable for the fineness of thread and work, but of no substance or profit.

This same unprofitable subtility or curiosity is of two sorts: either in the subject itself that they handle, when it is a fruitless speculation or controversy (whereof there are no small number both in divinity and philosophy) or in the manner or method of handling of a knowledge, which amongst them was this: upon every particular position or assertion to frame objections, and to those objections, solutions, — which solutions were for the most part not confutations, but distinctions; — whereas indeed the strength of all sciences is, as the strength of the old man's faggot, in the bond. For the harmony of a science, supporting each part the other, is and ought to be the true and brief confutation and suppression of all the smaller sorts of objections. . .

Notwithstanding, certain it is that if those schoolmen to their great thirst of truth and unwearied travail of wit had joined variety and universality of reading and contemplation, they had proved excellent lights, to the great advancement of all learning and knowledge. But as they are, they are great undertakers indeed, and fierce with dark keeping; but as in the inquiry of the divine truth their pride inclined to leave the oracle of God's word and to vanish in the mixture of their own inventions, so in the inquisition of nature they ever left the oracle of God's works, and adored the deceiving and deformed images which the unequal mirror of their own minds, or a few received authors or principles, did represent unto them. And thus much for the second diseases of learning.

For the third vice or disease of learning, which concerneth deceit or untruth, it is of all the rest the foulest as that which doth destroy the essential form of knowledge, which is nothing but a representation of truth; for the truth of being and the truth of knowing are one, differing no more than the direct beam and the beam reflected. This vice therefore brancheth itself into two sorts: delight in deceiving, and aptness to be deceived, — imposture and credulity. Which, although they appear to be of a diverse nature, the one seeming to proceed of cunning, and the other of simplicity, yet certainly they do for the most part concur; for as the verse noteth, *Percontatorem fugito, nam garrulus idem ist,* an inquisitive man is a prattler, so upon the like reason a credulous man is a deceiver. As we see it in fame, that he that will easily believe rumors will as easily augment rumors and add somewhat to them of his own; which Tacitus wisely noteth when he saith, *Fingunt simul creduntque* they believe one tale and at once make another; so great an affinity hath fiction and belief.

This facility of credit, and accepting or admitting things weakly authorized or warranted, is of two kinds, according to the subject: for it is either a belief of history (or, as the lawyers speak, matter of fact), or else of matter of art and opinion. As to the former, we see the experience and inconvenience of this error in ecclesiastical history, which hath too easily received and registered reports and narrations of miracles wrought by martyrs, hermits, or monks of the desert, and other holy men, and their relics, shrines, chapels, and images; which though they had a passage for a time, by the ignorance of the people, the superstitious simplicity of some, and the politic toleration of others, holding them but as divine poesies; yet after a period of time, when the mist began to clear up, they grew to be esteemed but as old wives' fables, impostures of the clergy, illusions of spirits, and badges of Antichrist, to the great scandal and detriment of religion.

So in natural history we see there hath not been that choice and judgment used as ought to have been, as may appear in the writings of Plinius, Cardanus, Albertus, and divers of the Arabians, being fraught with much fabulous matter, a great part not only untried but notoriously untrue, to the great derogation of the credit of natural philosophy with the grave and sober kind of wits. Wherein the wisdom and integrity of Aristotle is worthy to be observed, that, having made so diligent and exquisite a history of living creatures, hath mingled it sparingly with any sin or feigned matter; and yet on the other side hath cast all prodigious narrations which he thought worthy the recording into one book; excellently discerning that matter of manifest truth, such whereupon observation and rule was to be built, was not to be mingled or weakened with matter of doubtful credit; and yet again that rarities and reports that seem incredible are not to be suppressed or denied to the memory of men.

And as for the facility of credit which is yielded to arts and opinions, it is likewise of two kinds: either when too much belief is attributed to the arts themselves, or to certain authors in any art. The sciences themselves, or to certain authors in any art. The sciences themselves which have had better intelligence and confederacy with the imagination of man than with his reason, are three in number: Astrology, Natural Magic, and Alchemy; of which sciences nevertheless the ends or pretenses are noble. For Astrology pretendeth to discover that correspondence or concatenation which is between the superior globe and the inferior. Natural Magic pretendeth to call and reduce natural philosophy from variety of speculations to the magnitude of works. And Alchemy pretendeth to make separation of all the unlike parts of bodies which in mixtures of nature are incorporate. But the derivations and prosecutions to these ends, both in the theories and in the practices, are full of error and vanity, which the great professors themselves have sought to veil over and conceal by enigmatical writings, and referring themselves to auricular traditions and such other devices, so save the credit of impostures. And yet surely to Alchemy this right is due, that it may be compared to the husbandman whereof Æsop makes the fable, that when he died told his sons that he had left unto them gold buried under ground in his vineyard; and they digged over all the ground, and gold they found none, but by reason of their stirring and digging the mould about the roots of their vines, they had a great vintage the year following; so assuredly the search and stir to make gold hath brought to light a great number of good and fruitful inventions and experiments, as well for the disclosing of nature as for the use of man's life.

And as for the overmuch credit that hath been given unto authors in sciences, in making them dictators, that their words should stand, and not consuls to give advice; the damage is infinite that sciences have received thereby, as the principal cause that hath kept them low, at a stay, without growth or advancement. For hence it hath come that in arts mechanical the first deviser comes shortest, and time addeth and perfecteth, but in sciences the first author goeth furthest, and time leeseth and corrupteth. So we see, artillery, sailing, printing, and the like, were grossly managed at the first, and by time accommodated and refined; but contrariwise the philosophies and sciences of Aristotle, Plato, Democritus, Hippocrates, Euclides, Archimedes, of most vigor at the first, and by time degenerated and embased. Whereof the reason is no other but that in the former many wits and industries have contributed in one, and in the latter many wits and industries have been spent about the wit of some one, whom many times they have rather depraved than illustrated. For as water will not ascent higher than the level of the first spring-head from whence it descendeth, so knowledge derived from Aristotle, and exempted from liberty of examination, will not rise again higher than the knowledge of Aristotle . . . for disciples do owe unto masters only a temporary belief, and a suspension of their own judgment till they be fully instructed, and not an absolute resignation or perpetual captivity. And therefore to conclude this point, I will say no more but: So let great authors have their due, as time, which is the author of authors, be not deprived of his due, which is, further and further to discover truth.

Thus have I gone over these three diseases of learning; besides the which there are some other, rather peccant humors than formed diseases, which nevertheless are not so secret and intrinsic but that they fall under a popular observation and traducement, and therefore are not to be passed over.

The first of these is the extreme affecting of two extremities, — the one antiquity, the other novelty; wherein it seemeth the childrn of time do take after the nature and malice of their father. For as he devoureth his children, so one of them seeketh to devour and suppress the other, while antiquity envieth there should be new additions, and novelty cannot be content to add, but it must deface. . . Antiquity deserveth that reverence, that men should make a stand thereupon and discover what is the best way; but when the discovery is well taken, then to make progression. And to speak truly, *Antiquitas saeculi juventus mundi* [antiquity in time is the youth of the world]. These times are the ancient times, when the world is ancient, and not those which we account ancient, *Ordine retrogrado*, by a computation backward from ourselves.

Another error, induced by the former, is a distrust that anything should be now to be found out, which the world should have missed and passed over so long time; as if the same objection were to be made to time that Lucian maketh to Jupiter and other the heathen gods, of which he wondereth that they begot so many children in old time and begot none in his time, and asketh whether they were become septuagenary, or whether the law Papia, made against old men's marriages, had restrained them. So it seemeth men doubt lest time is become past children and generation; wherein contrariwise we see commonly the levity and unconstancy of men's judgments, which, till a matter be done, wonder that it can be done, and as soon as it is done wonder again that it was no sooner done; as we see in the expedition of Alexander into Asia, which at first was prejudged as a vast and impossible enterprise, and yet afterwards it pleaseth Livy to make no more of it than this, *Nil aliud quam bene ausus vana contemnere* [it was no more than taking courage to despise vain apprehensions]. And the same happened to Columbus in the western navigation. But in intellectual matters it is much more common; as may be seen in most of the propositions of Euclid, which till they be demonstrate, they seem strange to our assent; but being demonstrate, our mind accepteth of them by a kind of relation, as the lawyers speak, as if we had known them before.

Another error that hath also some affinity with the former, is a conceit that of former opinions or sects, after variety and examination, the best hath still prevailed and suppressed the rest; so as, if a man should begin the labor of a new search, he were but like to light upon somewhat formerly rejected, and by rejection brought into oblivion; as if the multiude, or the wisest for the multitude's sake, were not ready to give passage rather to that which is popular and superficial than to that which is substantial and profound; for the truth is that time seemeth to be of the nature of a river or stream, which carrieth down to us that which is light and blown up, and sinketh and drowneth that which is weighty and solid.

Another error, of a diverse nature from all the former, is the over-early and peremptory reduction of knowledge into arts and methods; from which time, commonly, sciences receive small or no augmentation. But as young men, when they knit and shape perfectly, do seldom grow to a further stature, so knowledge, while it is in aphorisms and observations, it is in growth; but when it once is comprehended in exact methods, it may perchance be further polished and illustrate, and accommodated for use and practice, but it increaseth no more in bulk and substance.

Another error, which doth succeed that which we last mentioned, is that after the distribution of particular arts and sciences, men have abandoned universality, *philosophia prima*, which cannot but cease and stop all progression. For no perfect discovery can be made upon a flat or a level; neither is it possible to discover the more remote and deeper parts of any science, if you stand but upon the level of the same science, and ascent not to a higher science.

Another error hath proceeded from too great a reverence, and a kind of adoration, of the mind and understanding of man; by means whereof men have withdrawn themselves too much from the contemplation of nature and the observations of experience, and have tumbled up and down in their own reason and conceits. Upon these intellectualists, which are nothwithstanding commonly taken for the most sublime and divine philosophers, Heraclitus gave a just censure, saying, 'Men sought truth in their own little worlds, and not in the great and common world;' for they disdain to spell, and so by degrees to read, in the volume of God's works; and contrariwise by continual meditation and agitation of wit do urge and as it were invocate their own spirits to divine, and give oracles unto them, whereby they are deservedly deluded.

Another error that hath some connexion with this latter is that men have used to infect their meditations, opinions, and doctrines, with some conceits which they have most admired, or some sciences which they have most applied; and given all things else a tincture according to them, utterly untrue and unproper. . . .

Another error is an impatience of doubt, and haste to assertion without due and mature suspension of judgment. For the two ways of contemplation are not unlike the two ways of action commonly spoken of by the ancients: the one plain and smooth in the beginning, and in the end impassable, the other rough and troublesom in the entrance, but after a while fair and even. So it is in contemplation; if a man will begin with certainties, he shall end in doubts, but if he will be content to begin with doubts, he shall end in certainties.

Another error is in the manner of the tradition and delivery of knowledge, which is for the most part magistral and peremptory, and not ingenuous and faithful; in a sort as may be soonest believed, and not earliest examined. It is true that in compendious treatises for practice that form is not to be disallowed. But in the true handling of knowledge, men ought . . . to propound things sincerely, with more or less asseveration, as they stand in a man's own judgment proved more or less.

Other errors there are in the scope that men propound to themselves, whereunto they bend their endeavors; for whereas the more constant and devote kind of professors of any science ought to propound to themselves to make some additions to their science, they convert their labors to aspire to certain second prizes, as to be a profound interpreter or commenter, to be a sharp champion or defender, to be a methodical compounder or abridger; and so the patrimony of knowledge cometh to be sometimes improved, but seldow augmented.

But the greatest error of all the rest is the mistaking or misplacing of the last or furthest end of knowledge. For men have entered into a desire of learning and knowledge, sometimes upon a natural curiosity and inquisitive appetite; sometimes to entertain their mind with variety and delight; sometimes for ornament and reputation; and sometimes to enable them to victory of wit and contradiction; and most times for lucre and profession; and seldom sincerely to give a true account of their gift of reason, to the benefit and use of men. As if there were sought in knowledge a couch, whereupon to rest a searching and restless spirit; or a terrace, for a wandering and variable mind to walk up and down with a fair prospect; or a tower of state, for a proud mind to raise itself upon; or a fort or commanding ground, for strife and contention; or a shop, for profit or sale; and not a rich storehouse, for the glory of the Creator and the relief of man's estate. But this is that which will indeed dignify and exalt knowledge, if contemplation and action may be more nearly and straitly conjoined and united together than they have been; a conjunction like unto that of the two highest planets, Saturn the planet of rest and contemplation, and Jupiter the planet of civil society and action. Howbeit, I do not mean, when I speak of use and action, that end before-mentioned of the applying of knowledge to lucre and profession, for I am not ignorant how much that diverteth and interrupteth the prosecution and advancement of knowledge; like unto the golden ball thrown before Atalanta, which while she goeth aside and stoopeth to take up, the race is hindered: —

Declinat cursus, aurumque volubile tollit.
[She leaves her course, and lifts the rolling gold.]

Neither is my meaning, as was spoken of Socrates, to call philosophy down from heaven to converse upon the earth: that is, to leave natural philosophy aside, and to apply knowledge only to manners and policy. But as both heaven and earth do conspire and contribute to the use and benefit of man, so the end ought to be, from both philosophies to separate and reject vain speculations and whatsoever is empty and void, and to preserve and augment whatsoever is solid and fruitful; that knowledge may not be as a courtesan, for pleasure and vanity only, or as a bond-woman, to acquire and gain to her master's use, but as a spouse, for generation, fruit, and comfort.